MARK MY WORDS

Joseph O'Hanlon

MARK MY WORDS

ST PAULS

Cover design by MaryLou Winters

ST PAULS
Middlegreen, Slough SL3 6BT, United Kingdom
Moyglare Road, Maynooth, Co. Kildare, Ireland

© Joseph O'Hanlon 1994

ISBN 085439 472 9

Printed by The Guernsey Press Co. Ltd, Guernsey, C.I.

ST PAULS is an activity of the priests and brothers of the Society of St Paul who proclaim the Gospel through the media of social communication

Contents

Preface

Mark my words is an attempt to present an understanding of one of Christianity's earliest documents and its first Gospel, the little pamphlet with an unpretentious title, *The Gospel according to Mark*. Because *the Gospel according to Matthew* contains all but a few lines of Mark, it came to be called and, indeed, to be the catechism of the Church. Mark lay virtually neglected until the last century but since then has been at the storm-centre of Gospel study. Much work has been done to attempt to establish what Mark thought he was writing, the circumstances which impelled him to write and the audience he sought for his efforts. This commentary seeks to unearth how this little pamphlet came to be, what issues it sought to address and how it met the needs of its first readers. Admittedly, most readers today will seek to discover a meaning in Mark for their own lives. They will look to him to be a nourisher of their faith. But we must first attend to the concerns of Mark for his own day, to seek to understand what he wished to say to the Christians of his time and his place before we can translate his vision of the Lord Jesus to our time and to our place. This is not to ignore the present relevance of Mark's story. It is to affirm that contemporary relevance must be rooted in what Mark wished to convey nearly nineteen hundred years ago. Most chapters of this book will end with a call to prayer. It is here that Mark's story will be brought to bear on present-day concerns.

Francis of Assisi was not a man given to abstract speculation. His language is that of one in touch with the feel of things. He speaks, not of the Incarnation but of *when Jesus received the flesh of humanity.* He never speaks of the Eucharist, rather, of *the Body and Blood of Our Lord Jesus Christ.* He does not speak of Sacred Scripture but of *His most holy written words.* This commentary seeks the same direct and concrete language. It strives to say in the plainest language of today what the plainest language of Mark attempted to convey to his first readers. While the most difficult and often infuriating problems which surface in any attempt to read an ancient text will not be avoided, every effort will be made to express complexity as simply as possible.

There are many who deserve thanks for anything of worth in these pages. Teachers, colleagues and students, too numerous to name, over many years have enriched my journey through *his most holy written words*. I must, however, thank Dr Elizabeth Taylor and Tracy Hansen for their advice, encouragement and not least for relieving me of much of the burden of proof-reading. The *Catholic Gazette* has so often opened its pages to me that I must record my thanks to its editors, staff and readers.

Finally, I would like to dedicate this book to my sisters, to Mary, Johanna, Fidelma, Eithne and Breda. Francis cautions us to listen to Sister Moon.

Introduction

In July, 64 C.E.,* about thirty years after the death of Jesus, a tremendous fire, lasting for more than six days, reduced the greater part of the city of Rome to ashes. Emperor Nero (54-68 C.E.) quickly began to rebuild the ruined city on a most ambitious scale. The very speed with which he undertook his elaborate reconstruction aroused the suspicions of the people. Perhaps the plans had been drawn up before the fire? And so a rumour spread that the fire had been malicious, that it had been a deliberate act of high authority. Indeed, the people were beginning to believe that the emperor himself had instigated the burning of the city. The citizens were certainly right in their suspicions. But Nero could ill afford to have his guilty secret exposed. In order to root out suspicions, Nero needed a scapegoat. He picked on the Christians.

Christians were an odd lot. They kept to themselves and revealed their prayers and rituals only to tried and tested members of their close-knit communities. Such secrecy gave rise to malicious gossip and many believed Christians got up to all sorts of unspeakable practices. Furthermore, the reluctance of Christians to participate in pagan festivals and idol worship caused considerable resentment. In the circumstances, it was easy for Nero to pin the blame for the fire on the hapless parish of Roman Christians.

Christians were declared to be "enemies of the human race". A few were rounded up and, sadly, these named others and soon a great number were in custody. It is true that nothing was found which implicated them in the fire. Nevertheless, they were sentenced to death but not by simple execution. Some were sewn up

---

*   I prefer to use the terms C.E. (Common Era) for the more usual A.D., and B.C.E. (Before the Common Era) to denote the years before Christ (B.C.). I do this out of respect for our Jewish brothers and sisters, who use these terms, and from whom our heritage of Scripture comes.

in bags of animal skins and mauled by vicious dogs; some were crucified; some were wrapped in cloths dipped in pitch, hung up on trees and used as human torches to light up the imperial gardens on the Janiculum hill. Everyone was invited to the spectacle.

A Roman historian, Tacitus (56-118 C.E.), is our main source of information on this horrendous crime. Here is some of his report:

> Nero fastened the guilt (for the fire) and inflicted the most refined torture on a class of people hated for their abominations, called Christians by the people. The author of this name was Christ, who, during the reign of Tiberius, had been executed by Pontius Pilate, the procurator. Momentarily checked, the deadly superstition broke out again, not only in Judea, the source of this evil, but also in the city of Rome, where all outrageous and shameful practices from every part of the world converge and are fervently proclaimed. Accordingly, an arrest was made of all who pleaded guilty ... then an immense multitude was convicted, not so much for the crime of setting fire to the city, as of hatred against humankind. Mockery of every sort was added to their deaths. Covered with skins of beasts, they were torn by dogs and perished, or were nailed to crosses, or were burnt to serve as nightly illuminations when daylight had expired. Nero offered his gardens for the spectacle. ... Hence, even for criminals who deserve extreme and exemplary punishment, there arose a feeling of compassion; for it was not, as it seemed, for the public good, but to satisfy one man's cruelty, that they were destroyed (*Annals of Rome*, 15.44).

Two of the victims are known to us. It is highly probable that St Peter was crucified and that St Paul, a Roman citizen, was put to the sword in this grim holocaust.

Imagine the pain and desolation of a community of Christians so bereft. Not only the tragic loss of upwards of two thousand of its people in such brutal circumstances weighed on its heart. There was also the knowledge that most of their friends went to their deaths betrayed by their brothers and sisters. One can hear the forlorn cry of this frightened people, "My God, my God, why have you forsaken us?"

One man set out to resuscitate the faith of this terrified people.

What he attempted was to explain why the tragedy had occurred and what could be learned from it about the risks, and, indeed, the rewards of Christian discipleship. To accomplish the mammoth task, this man, whose nickname was "Stumpyfingers", did an altogether incredible thing: he wrote a pamphlet. We know the name of this man: Mark. And we know the name of his pamphlet: *The Gospel according to Mark*.

The extraordinary thing is that it worked. This little pamphlet saved the faith of Rome and has gone on creating and nurturing Christian faith ever since. Mark's little work occupies twenty pages in my Bible. How could so little achieve so much? Who is Mark? What did he say?

MARK: THE GOSPEL EXPERIENCE

We know Mark but not very well. We do not know where he was born, where he was brought up, what kind of education, if any, he may have had. What little we know of him relates to the Gospel he wrote. The name Mark occurs eight times in the New Testament. Look up Acts of the Apostles 12:12, 25; 15:37, 39; Colossians 4:10; 2 Timothy 4:11; Philemon 24; 1 Peter 5:13. If we put together all the information to be gleaned from these verses, we find that Mark's first name was John, that his mother, called Mary, was a prominent member of the church in Jerusalem, that their house was a centre of Christian activity, that St Peter went to their house when he was delivered from prison, that he was at one time a companion of Paul and Barnabas (Mark's first cousin), that Peter held him in such affection that he called him "my son".

The difficulty about this composite portrait is that it assumes that every time the New Testament refers to Mark it is pointing to the same person. But the name Mark was as common in the Roman world as Smith is in Britain. Which Smith is Smith? It is difficult to believe that the Mark who wrote the Gospel ever lived in Jerusalem or even in Palestine. As we make our journey through the pages of Mark's pamphlet, we shall have to notice how inaccurate is his knowledge of the geography of the Holy Land. Certainly, a native would be presumed to be better informed than Mark appears to have been.

Mark wrote his Gospel in Greek which was the *lingua franca* of the Mediterranean world. Ordinary people, even in Rome, spoke Greek. St Paul wrote to the Christians of Rome in Greek, not Latin. But Mark's Greek is weak. His grasp of grammar is quite poor, his style is clumsy and his vocabulary limited. Our translations polish Mark's style. Here is what he sounds like, if we translate him warts and all:

> And immediately coming out, out of the synagogue, they went into the house of Simon and of Andrew with Jacob and John. But the mother-in-law of Simon was laid up being feverish and immediately they were saying to him concerning her and approaching, he raised her, taking the hand, and the fever left her and she was serving him (Mark 1:29-31).

On the six occasions he uses Aramaic (the language Jesus spoke), he is careful to provide his readers with a translation. Look up 5:41; 7:11, 34; 14:36; 15:22. 34. Aramaic may well have been Mark's native tongue.

Another feature of Mark's style is his use of Latin words dressed up in Greek letters. He uses *praetorium* (an official residence), *legio* (a Roman legion), *denarius* (a coin), *centurio* (a centurion), *speculator* (a soldier of the guard), *quadrans* (a coin), *sextarius* (a pitcher). Now while we can be sure that many Latin words found their way into the other languages of the Roman Empire, it is surprising to find so many in Mark (there are none in Luke's Gospel and only one in Matthew's).

Mark is familiar with Jewish laws and customs, which he takes pains to explain to his readers who, one must conclude, were not. He explains the ritual washing of hands, cups and pitchers. He knows about scribes and Pharisees and other groups within Jewish society.

A detective might conclude from these clues that Mark was a Jew (since he was a poor Greek writer but knew Aramaic), that he came from a Jewish community outside Palestine (since he knew Jewish customs but had a poor knowledge of the geography of Palestine), that he wrote for a community which was mainly, but not exclusively, Gentile (since he translated Aramaic words and explained Jewish customs). We might even conclude that he wrote in or around Rome (one would not be surprised if the Greek spoken in the capital city was peppered with more Latin words than in the provinces).

Early christian writers have much to say about Mark and his Gospel, though many modern scholars are inclined to take what they have to say with a large pinch of salt (for serious reasons, let it be said). Nonetheless, I am inclined to believe at least the gist of what they have to say. Here are some of the earliest references to Mark:

Matthew composed his Gospel among the Hebrews in their own language, while Peter and Paul proclaimed the gospel in Rome and founded the community. After their death, Mark, the disciple and interpreter of Peter, transmitted his preaching to us in written form (St Irenaeus [130-200 C.E.], *Against Heresies*).

Mark's Gospel originated as follows: When, at Rome, Peter had openly preached the word and the spirit had proclaimed the gospel, the large audience urged Mark, who had followed him for a long time and remembered what had been said, to write it all down. This he did, making his Gospel available to all who wanted it. When Peter heard about this, he made no objection and gave no special encouragement (Clement of Alexandria [150-215 C.E.], *Hypotyposeis*).

...Mark declared, who is called "Stumpyfingers" because he ad short fingers in comparison with the size of the rest of his body. He was Peter's interpreter. After the death of Peter himself, he wrote down this same Gospel in the regions of Italy (*The Anti-Marcionite Prologue* [200 C.E.]).

Mark, who had been Peter's interpreter, wrote down carefully, but not in order, all that he remembered of the Lord's sayings and doings. For he had not heard of the Lord or been one of his followers, but later, as I said, one of Peter's [followers]. Peter used to adapt his teaching to the occasion, without making a systematic arrangement of the Lord's sayings, so that Mark was quite justified in writing down some things just as he remembered them. For he had one purpose only – to leave out nothing that he had heard, and to make no misstatement about it (Eusebius [263-339 C.E.], *The Ecclesiastical History*).

The last quotation is from Eusebius, the "Father of Church History". He was born in Palestine and educated in the town of Caesarea on the Mediterranean coast, a town of which he became bishop. Eusebius was himself quoting from a work called *Sayings of the Lord*, written by a man called Papias who was born in 60 C.E. and died in 135 C.E. He, in turn, claimed to have heard this story about Mark and Peter from somebody called John the Elder. Though this would push the story back to the days of Mark himself, caution is necessary. No copy of Papias' book has survived and we don't know how careful he was in checking his sources or how reliable his sources were in the first place. For all we know, he might have made the whole thing up in order to bolster the authority of Mark's Gospel by associating it with St Peter. However, while I would not go to the stake to defend the fact or otherwise of Mark's association with Peter (though I think it is plausible), I am convinced that he wrote his Gospel in Rome and in the circumstances which followed on the persecution of the Christians there by Emperor Nero

A PLAN OF MARK'S GOSPEL

Mark does not provide us with a plan and the reader of his Gospel has to work out a plan from the text itself. Different readers have come up with different plans, some very complicated, others over-simplified. It has been suggested that Mark's plan was based on geography: the first part of his Gospel takes place in Galilee and the second part in Judea and its chief city, Jerusalem. But this plan omits to take account of the fact that the Gospel opens emphatically in the wilderness and that three of its most important episodes take place "in the country of the Gerasenes" (5:1), in "the region of Tyre and Sidon" (7:24), and in "the villages of Caesarea Philippi" (8:27), all of which were outside both Galilee and Judea.

Mark's Gospel was, of course, written in Greek. It contains about 11,050 words. Almost in the exact middle of Mark, we find the story of the Transfiguration with the dramatic pronouncement, "This is my beloved Son; listen to him!" (9:7). There are 5,393 words before the Transfiguration account and 5,447 after it. Noticing this, some scholars have suggested that Mark planned his Gospel around the Transfiguration with its momentous revelation of the divine sonship of Jesus. Everything moves toward the heavenly proclamation and moves away from it in an orderly pattern. Mark opens his Gospel with a heavenly messenger (John the Baptist) and closes it with one (the young man at the tomb). His story begins in the wilderness, a place believed to be infested with demons, and therefore with terror and death. It closes at a tomb, another place associated with demons and death (see 5:2-5). At the beginning, Jesus is declared to be God's Son (1:1) and so he is at the close (15:39). In other words, there is a complicated symmetry between all that leads up to the Transfiguration and all that follows from it.

There is much to be said for this and there can be no doubt that for Mark the most important issue in his Gospel is that Jesus is the Son of God. Attractive as this understanding of Mark is, we shall proceed by means of a plan (outlined below) which will enable us to do justice to Mark's assertion that Jesus is the Son of God and, at the same time, keep matters relatively simple, yet faithful to the text of Mark's Gospel.

Mark's opening sentence declares that Jesus is at once the Christ and the Son of God. Nearly half-way through the Gospel, Peter, a Jew, speaking outside the land of Israel, declares that Jesus is the Christ (8:29). Near the end, a Gentile, a pagan soldier, speaking in Jerusalem, declares that Jesus is the Son of God (15:39). So the Gospel divides neatly into two acts: the first culminating in the declaration of Peter that Jesus is the Christ, the second in the declaration by the centurion at the foot of the cross that Jesus is the Son of God. Each act may be divided into three scenes and there is a prologue and an epilogue. Such a plan will help to provide a clear path through the story, ensuring that we do not miss the wood for the trees. I do not claim that it is Mark's plan (the endless theories would suggest that we do not know what that was) but it helps to make sense of what Mark wrote.

A PLAN OF MARK'S GOSPEL

THE PROLOGUE
MARK 1:1-15: AN ASSEMBLY OF WITNESSES

Act one

A QUESTION OF IDENTITY
MARK 1:16-8:30: WHO IS JESUS?

SCENE 1: The mission of Jesus provokes a plot to kill him: 1:16-3:6
SCENE 2: A New Family is created but the Baptist is killed: 3:7-6:29
SCENE 3: The Disciples proclaim that Jesus is the Christ: 6:30-8:30

Act two

A QUESTION OF DESTINY:
MARK 8:31-15:39: DEATH ON A CROSS

SCENE 1: The Way of the Cross for Jesus and Disciples: 8:31-10:52
SCENE 2: The Fate of Jesus, Disciples and Jerusalem: 11:1-13:37
SCENE 3: The Passion reveals Jesus to be Son of God: 14:1-15:39

THE EPILOGUE
MARK 15:40-16:8: WITNESSES AT A TOMB

Prologue
Mark 1:1-15

Mark begins his Gospel with as assembly of witnesses. Each witness will be called to provide evidence as to the identity of Jesus and the nature of his mission. The first witness is, of course, Mark himself. His whole book is a witness to Jesus. His opening verse may be taken as a caption which summarises all that he wants to teach. Mark calls his story a "gospel", a word which means "good news", specifically good news of a victory in battle. At the very outset, we are assured of a victory, though much in Mark's little book will seem like defeat. The good news is all that Mark is going to record about Jesus, the words and work of Jesus and Mark's understanding of them. If the frightened community for which he wrote can grasp that Jesus is the Christ, the Son of God, if they can listen to Mark's understanding of his life and teaching, then this good news will renew their faith and restore their hope.

Jesus the Messiah

Mark does not explain the meaning of the name Jesus. The name is a Greek form of the Hebrew name Joshua, which means "Lord, help". It was quite a common name.

Jesus is given two titles. First, Mark names him Messiah or Christ. The word "messiah" means "anointed one". In the Old Testament it occurs thirty-nine times, mainly in reference to kings who were anointed with precious oils at their coronation (see 1 Kings 1:38-40 for the coronation of Solomon). Occasionally, it was used of the High Priest and once of Abraham, Isaac and Jacob who are called "my anointed ones" because they were regarded as prophets (Psalm 105:15; 1 Chronicles 16:22). Anointing was clearly a ceremonial way of indicating that one was undertaking a new role on behalf of the people. The word "Christian" is based on the word "Christ". Christians claim to be messiahs, anointed at baptism for a special role in God's care for all peoples.

When the kingship died out in Israel (due to the frequency with which the little country was conquered), people began to look forward to a time when God would assert himself on behalf of his people. Some looked forward to a restored monarchy. Others, not trusting in the idea of kingship, looked for another ruler who would restore the fortunes of Israel. Such a one was sometimes called "the anointed one", the Messiah. But the term was not common and was always used with a future connotation, as if the Messiah was always expected but never arrived. Revolutionaries around the time of Jesus who sought to overthrow the hated Roman occupation regularly had themselves declared king but not Messiah. It was, therefore, a daring step for followers of Jesus to name him Messiah, to foster belief that in Jesus God had finally decided to act on behalf of all his people. Every book in the New Testament, with the exception of the tiny Third Letter of John, calls Jesus the Messiah.

Jesus Son of God

The title "Son of God" has a long history. The ancient Pharaohs were called "sons of God" because the sun-god Re was regarded as their father. Emperors were regularly called "sons of God". Famous people, such as Plato and Pythagorus, were called "son of God". In the Old Testament, angels were called "sons of God" (Genesis 6:2; Job 1:6). The title was given to the whole people of Israel, in recognition of their status as God's chosen people: *Thus says the Lord, Israel is my first-born son* (Exodus 4:22). Again, *When Israel was a child, I loved him, and out of Egypt I called my son* (Hosea 11:1). The king was called "son of God" (2 Samuel 7:14). Indeed, in a psalm which was probably used in the coronation service, the poet has God say to the king, *You are my son* (Psalm 2:7). The title could be used of any upright Jew noted for his piety. Ecclesiasticus (or *The Wisdom of Jesus the son of Sirach*) advises us to take care of widows and orphans *for you will then be like a son of the Most High* (4:10). However, as we make our way through Mark, we will discover that the writer has an altogether more profound meaning for the title when he applies it to Jesus.

Thus Mark lays out his stall in his opening verse. He wants his readers (more likely, his hearers, for most would have heard the

Gospel read to them) to believe that recognition of Jesus as the Messiah and Son of God is gospel, good news. Throughout the rest of his narrative he will demonstrate what it means to believe that Jesus is Messiah, Son of God.

THE SECOND WITNESS (1:2-3)

The witness of Scripture is essential to Mark's design, for if God is about to undertake a new initiative on behalf of humanity, then there must be some hint in the Bible. It was widely believed that the prophet Elijah, who was taken up to heaven in a chariot of fire (2 Kings 2:1-12), would return to witness God's initiative. Mark seizes on Old Testament passages which witness to this belief. He offers a quotation from Isaiah but close examination shows that Mark has amalgamated several texts.

The first is taken from Malachi 3:1: *Behold, I send my messenger to prepare the way before me.* Malachi identifies this messenger (the Greek word is *angelos*, angel) as Elijah: *Behold, I will send you Elijah the prophet before the great and terrible day of the Lord* (4:5). Malachi understood that the Lord's messenger would appear in the Temple in Jerusalem but Mark is hostile to that institution. Instead, he sees the desert as the place of preparation. After the Exodus from Egypt the people of Israel spent forty years in the desert learning about the God who had saved them from slavery and who was about to lead them into *a land flowing with milk and honey* (Exodus 3:8). Whenever the prophets wished to promote religious fervour, they call for an imaginary return to the desert to renew the desert spirit. The desert is the place to meet God, in their estimation. Isaiah looked to a time when there would be, as it were, a road across the desert on which would march a renewed people:

A voice cries:
in the wilderness prepare the way of the Lord,
make straight in the desert a highway for our God
(Isaiah 40:3).

A messenger, then, is to appear in the desert to prepare the way for the coming of the Lord. But the one being prepared for is Jesus. Is Jesus the Lord? What is Mark hinting at here?

THE THIRD WITNESS (1:4-6)

John the Baptist appeared in the wilderness, near the river Jordan. The location was entirely unsuitable for mass baptisms and the assembly of large numbers of people. The Jordan flows in a deep crevasse with unstable marl clay banks which are lined with trees and tall reeds. We know that John baptised *at Aenon near Salim* (John 3:22-24), in Samaria. Mark refers to an initial mission of the Baptist in the Jordan because of that region's association with Elijah. John appears exactly where Elijah had disappeared (2 Kings 2:4-11). For Mark, John the Baptist is Elijah. Here is a powerful witness, indeed.

John called on the people to repent, that is, to turn from ungodly ways, to adopt a God's eye view of the world. His washing in the river was a sign that one had determined to leave the old ways and set out on a new path, *the way of the Lord*. Mark will have much to say about the new way.

Mark is given to exaggeration. We can hardly believe that all the people of Judea and all the population of Jerusalem flocked to the Jordan, particularly as it is a very inaccessible place. But his exaggeration affirms the success of the Baptist's efforts.

John's dress sense and eating habits are not recorded for curiosity's sake. The Second Book of Kings relates that Elijah *wore a garment of haircloth, with a girdle about his loins* (1:8). The Baptist has taken on the mantle of Elijah.

THE FOURTH WITNESS (1:7-8)

The location of his ministry, the act of preparing the people, the dress, the diet, all witness to the credentials of John the Baptist. He is Elijah returned. Now the voice of this man, crying out in desert places, points to the one to come. Such is the greatness of Jesus that the Baptist is not worthy to perform even a slave's task on his behalf. John's baptism was a sign of repentance, a symbol of readiness. But the coming one will cause the outpouring of God's spirit and the creation of a new people (see Ezekiel 36:25-29).

As a matter of fact, Jesus is the one who is baptised and receives the Spirit. There is no account of Jesus baptising anyone in Mark's Gospel. But the careful reader will note that Jesus must undergo another baptism, namely, his death (10:39) and will understand that the Spirit given to Jesus will, after his death, be given to his followers to strengthen them in their trials (13:11).

THE FIFTH WITNESS (1:9-11)

It may well be that Jesus came to John on his way to or from a pilgrimage visit to Jerusalem. They were related (Luke 1:36) and it is not impossible that Jesus became John's assistant for a time. After all, Elijah had his Elisha (1 Kings 19:16-21). We might speculate that, after John withdrew from the Jordan to Samaria (John 3:23), Jesus continued a baptising ministry in the region of the Jordan as part of a coordinated campaign by Jesus and John to win both Jews and Samaritans to their cause.

Initially, Jesus came from Nazareth, an insignificant village in the centre of the northern province of Palestine, Galilee. Most translations omit Mark's opening phrase in verse 9: *And it came to pass in those days*. The phrase occurs very frequently in the Bible and carries the suggestion that what has happened is God's doing. Things happen because God wants them to happen. Thus the coming of Jesus to the Jordan is part of the divine purpose. We will not be surprised that momentous events are afoot.

Jesus the Messiah comes to John the Preparer. The mission of Jesus will grow out of the seed sown by John. As Jesus comes up from the water (as the ancient people came out of the waters of the Sea of Reeds), he saw the heavens opened. We must not be too prurient here. The language used to describe Jesus' experience is conventional. Ezekiel 1:1 records that *the heavens opened and I saw visions of God*. Such language is in keeping with the mysterious nature of these experiences and we have no way of knowing "what actually happened".

The Spirit descended like a dove. Just as the Spirit hovered over the waters at Creation (Genesis 1:2), so now, at this new beginning (The beginning of the gospel of Jesu ... 1:1), the Spirit is poured out. Jewish belief was that the Spirit had ceased to be given when the last of the prophets had died and that it would not be given again until the days of the Messiah:

And in the last days it shall be, God declares,
that I will pour out my Spirit upon all flesh,

21

and your sons and your daughters shall prophesy,
and your old men shall dream dreams;
and your young men shall see visions.
Even upon the menservants and on my maidservants
in those days, I will pour out my Spirit (Joel 2:28-29).

It is Mark's belief that the day of the baptism of Jesus marks the day of the Spirit's new outpouring, the day of the coming of the Messiah.

The voice from heaven is, of course, God's voice. Again, we must be cautious not to seek to know too much. Mark is telling the reader, in the conventional language available to him, that God is witness to the identity of Jesus. We have God's word on it, so that, as we read the rest of the Gospel, no matter what crises arise, we know that Jesus is the beloved Son. The word for "beloved" can be translated as "only", as in "an only son". In Genesis 22:2, God calls Abraham to *Take your son, your only son Isaac, whom you love, and go the the land of Moriah.* Abraham's beloved son is saved from death by God's intervention. What will happen to God's beloved, only Son?

THE SIXTH WITNESS (1:12-13)

And immediately! This little phrase occurs some forty-seven times in Mark's Gospel, giving a heady rush of excitement to his story. As Israel came out of the waters in the Exodus story and was led into the desert for testing and maturing, so, too, with Jesus. Thus Jesus remains in the wilderness for forty days, as the people of Israel remained there for forty years. To say that Jesus was tempted by Satan is not to imply that he was tested as we are. Rather, the wilderness is the battle-ground between the power of evil and the power of Jesus the Messiah, the beloved Son. Throughout the Gospel we shall see Jesus casting out (that is, overcoming) Satan's demons.

The wild beasts symbolise the terrors of the desert. The desert is, indeed, the place to meet with God but it is a dangerous place. Life may be threatened there. Yet the angels minister to him, that is to say, the powers of God provide a protective shield. God's Messiah is not left alone in his fight with Satan. The incident in the wilderness witnesses that Jesus' destiny is to engage in a life-

and-death struggle with the power of evil and the presence of the angels enables us to be confident of its outcome.

THE SEVENTH WITNESS (1:14-15)

And the last witness in Mark's prologue is, of course, Jesus himself. The opening sentence was *The beginning of the gospel of Jesus* ... but now from Jesus we hear that it is, in fact, *the gospel of God*. There is no confusion. What one can say of God, one can, to Mark's way of thinking, say of Jesus. This is his most profound insight. The work of Jesus is the work of God. The word of Jesus is the word of God.

At last the time has come. All the prophetic yearnings are fulfilled. The kingdom of God is about to be established amongst his people. We need to look no further than the Lord's Prayer to understand what Jesus means by the kingdom of God. We pray,

Thy kingdom come,
Thy will be done
on earth,
as it is in heaven.

The second line means exactly the same as the first. God's kingdom is not a place. Rather, it is a state; wherever God's will is done, we find signs of his rule, his authority. Jesus is saying that with his coming God is asserting his authority in the world. His will will be done on earth as it is in heaven. Our task is to adjust (for that is what to repent means) to that reality and to realise that God's authority is not a threat. It is, in fact, gospel, good news.

But there are ominous signs. Jesus begins to preach in Galilee after John has been handed over into the power of Herod Antipas, the political ruler (under the Romans) of Galilee and Perea. We shall soon discover that John is put to death. Thus the ministry of Jesus begins under the shadow of imprisonment and death. How will it end?

PRAYER

Mark's prologue begins with the word "gospel" and it ends with the same word. Jesus is good news for humanity. He comes

23

from God, not bearing threats but promises. As readers we have been told who Jesus is, where he comes from, what power he has, who his enemies are and what his fate will be. As we read through the story, unlike the characters in the drama, we are on the high ground. Even in the deepest crisis, even at the foot of the cross, we know that God's angels will minister to him.

John the Baptist called people to repentance, to a change of heart. A good prayer to set readers off on a journey through Mark's Gospel is the great prayer of repentance, Psalm 51: *Have mercy on me, O God, according to thy steadfast love ...*

ACT ONE

A QUESTION OF IDENTITY:
MARK 1:16-8:30: WHO IS JESUS?

SCENE 1: The mission of Jesus provokes a plot to kill him: 1:16-3:6
SCENE 2: A New Family is created but the Baptist is killed: 3:7-6:29
SCENE 3: The Disciples proclaim that Jesus is the Christ: 6:30-8:30

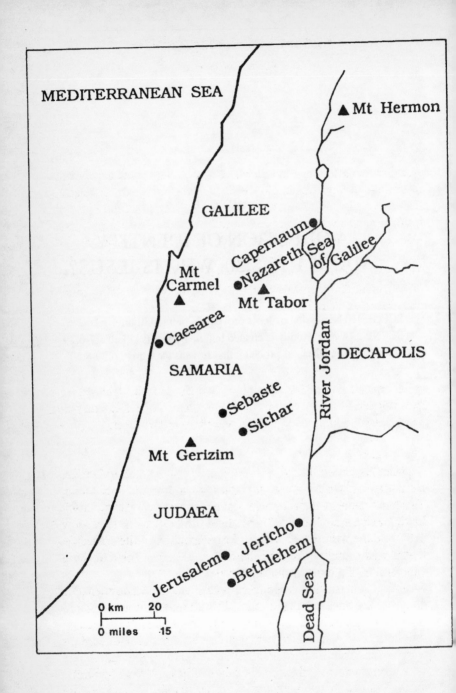

MEDITERRANEAN SEA

▲ Mt Hermon

GALILEE

Capernaum ●
● Nazareth
Sea of Galilee

Mt Carmel ●
▲ Mt Tabor

● Caesarea

DECAPOLIS

River Jordan

SAMARIA

● Sebaste
● Sichar

▲ Mt Gerizim

JUDAEA

Jerusalem ● Jericho ●
● Bethlehem

Dead Sea

0 km   20
0 miles   15

The call to discepleship
Mark 1:16-45

Actions speak louder than words. Clearly, Mark was a believer in the old saying for his Gospel is, for the most part, a breathless succession of events. To be sure, there are moments of reflection on the teaching of Jesus, there are discussions with his disciples and with Jewish authorities but the preponderant atmosphere of the Gospel is a heady rush of exciting activity. Thus, it is mainly in the flow of events that the crucial question of the identity of Jesus is posed. Who is this in whom such powers are at work?

READING THROUGH

There are a number of matters which must be cleared up before proceeding. A number of these occur quite frequently in Mark's story and demand careful attention at the outset.

Sea of Galilee

Mark describes Jesus *as passing along by the Sea of Galilee*. He is the first writer (as far as we know) so to refer to the lake. The local name at the time was Lake Gennesar. St Luke calls it Lake Gennesaret (Luke 5:1). Matthew follows Mark (Matthew 4:18) and the writer(s) of John's Gospel explains, quite correctly, that it was sometimes called the Sea of Tiberias, for that town was (and is) the most important on its shores.

Lake Gennesar is a large fresh-water lake in the northeast of the province of Galilee (see map). It is about ten miles long and stretches to six miles at its widest point. It is exquisitely beautiful and full of fish. Locally, nowadays, it is called Kinnereth, a word which means a harp and that is the shape of the lake.

By conferring on the lake the status of a sea, Mark highlights its importance in the ministry of Jesus. By the Sea of Galilee Jesus calls his first disciples. There he teaches the crowds and

heals those who come to him. There are six dramatic sea cross-
ings in the course of which the disciples are given the opportunity to learn who Jesus is, to understand the nature and source of
his power. We shall see that Mark's Sea of Galilee has much to
do with several rich strands of Old Testament sea-imagery. It has
much to do, too, with Mark's fertile imagination.

Capernaum

Capernaum was a busy fishing village on the northeastern
shore of the Sea of Galilee. It would appear to have been Jesus'
headquarters during his ministry in Galilee (see 2:1, where it is
called his home). It is on the water's edge, on the lake itself, and
in the adjoining countryside that the mystery of the identity of
Jesus will begin to unfold.

The Sabbath

The institution of the Sabbath as a day of rest is variously
explained. In some passages of Scripture, the Sabbath is seen as a
reminder of deliverance from slavery in Egypt (Deuteronomy
5:15); in others, it is seen as an occasion for reflection so that the
devout *may come to know that I am the Lord your God* (Ezekiel
20:20) who gives holiness to his people (Ezekiel 20:12). Other
passages, such as Genesis 2:3, point out that the Sabbath rest is
observed in imitation of God's rest after creation. God himself,
we are told, was obliged to observe the Sabbath rest and it was
said that there were but two works allowed to the Lord on the
holy day: He could cause a baby to be born and receive the dead
into paradise. Jesus' activity on the Sabbath soon becomes a
focus of suspicion and hostility.

Synagogues

Synagogues existed in every large town and substantial village in Israel. Originally, the word referred to the whole of the
assembly of the people of Israel; later on, it was used for any
assembly of people but especially a religious assembly. By the
time of Jesus, the word regularly refers to the building in which
people met for prayer and the reading and exposition of Scripture.

Teaching was the chief purpose of the synagogue service.
After the readings, any competent person was invited by the
authorities to preach. An excellent account of part of a typical

28

synagogue service is to be found in Luke 4:16-31. In the earliest days, Christian preachers first took the message of Jesus to the synagogues of the Jewish people (see, for example, Acts of the Apostles 13:5).

Scribes

The scribes were authorities on the holy Law of Jewish faith, the Torah or Teaching, as it was called. Their business was to interpret the Law's demands and to expound the traditions handed down to them by venerable scholars of old. Their authority came from learning, not from the divine gift of the prophetical spirit which the people sensed in the words of Jesus. The profession of a scribe tended to be a lay profession.

Demons

Disciples, crowds, the halt and the lame, religious authorities, civil and political leaders, tax men, parents and children, people in many ways like ourselves, inhabit the world of Mark's story. But there are other characters with whom we are not familiar. Demons, evil spirits, stalk his pages.

Have you ever been awe-struck? Have you ever been panic-stricken? Have you ever been struck by an illness? If so, you are fair set to understand the world of demons. We know that our feelings and emotions, our moods and impulses, come from within us. We know, too, that diseases come from organic disorder. But the ancient world attributed such things to outside agencies, to spirits. Should you fall in love, you have been struck by Cupid's arrow. Sickness indicated one had been struck down by an evil demon. Everyone eventually was struck down by death. The century in which Jesus lived was obsessed by spirits, good and bad. Good fortune was the work of good spirits and misfortune the work of evil spirits.

Evil spirits were seen to be the enemies of God and his creation. They were unclean, that is to say, unacceptable to God, opposed to everything holy in human affairs. They were said to delight in harming God's creatures by taking possession of them and causing them physical damage and leading them into sin. From before the time of Jesus, Jewish teaching considered them to be fallen angels, implacably opposed to God. Their leader was called Satan (1:13) or Beelzebul, the prince of demons (3:22).

Leprosy

Leprosy is a dreaded disease. No less than their neighbours, the people of Israel evolved rules and regulations to prevent the spread of such a chronic infection. All of chapters 13 and 14 of the Book of Leviticus is devoted to legislation designed to contain its spread, for leprosy was not merely a matter of personal tragedy. In the perspective of many ancient peoples, illness inevitably affects others: the family, the neigbourhood, the village. All sickness was perceived as divine retribution for sin. Illness was not simply a matter of health; it was a loss of holiness. The sick were unclean, unacceptable to God.

The leper was cast out from his home, his family, his town or village. He was required to cover his mouth with his hand and shout, "Unclean! Unclean!", at the approach of other people. The sentence of the Book of Leviticus (13:45-46) is no harsher than that of other ancient codes: *he shall dwell alone in a habitation outside the camp*.

READING THROUGH AGAIN

Before Jesus can begin his mission, he must gather disciples, for the task is not a matter for Jesus alone; it is not something done without disciples. Followers are essential, if the work is to begin and to prosper. We will do well to note the presence of the disciples in the events which unfold the first scene of Mark's drama.

Fishers of men (1:16-20)

We might enquire whether it is likely that prosperous fishermen would leave their boats and nets instantly to follow an itinerant preacher. Is it not more likely that Simon and Andrew, James and John, had met Jesus over some considerable time, that they had come to know him, were inspired by his teaching, and gradually became convinced that they should throw in their lot with the man from Nazareth? Perhaps so. But Mark is not concerned with historical speculation. He is not writing a history or biography of Jesus. He is writing to convince the frightened Christians of Rome that, as a matter of urgency, they must again take up the cross and follow Jesus. So he begins with the call to discipleship in order to invite his readers to begin again their discipleship. Mark is inviting his readers to set out anew on that voyage of discovery which first led them to Jesus. He is asking them to compare their own discipleship with that of Simon and Andrew and the sons of Zebedee as they make their journey from Galilee to Jerusalem and beyond.

Jesus invites the fishermen to become fishers of men. Despite our Christian instinct to interpret the invitation as referring to the "saving of souls", Mark's meaning is otherwise. As ever, his eye is on the Old Testament:

> Behold, I am sending for many fishermen,
> says the Lord,
> and they will catch them (Jeremiah 16:16).

The fishermen of Jeremiah's imagination are God's agents who will catch them, that is, bring to book the rich and the powerful who oppress the poor and the needy. The same image is to be found in the prophet Amos, where rich women (the cows of Bashan) who incite their husbands to provide for their whims by further oppressing the weak and poor are warned:

> Hear this word, you cows of Bashan,
> who are in the mountains of Samaria,
> who oppress the poor, who crush the needy,
> who say to their husbands,
> "Bring, that we may drink!"
> The Lord God has sworn by his holiness,
> that, behold, the days are coming upon you,
> when they shall take you away with hooks,
> even the last of you with fish-hooks (Amos 2:1-2).

The "hooking of fish" is a symbol of God exercising his judgement on the powerful and privileged (see Ezekiel 29:2-5; 38:1-6; Habakkuk 1:14-17). Jesus is calling disciples, not to "save souls", but to join with him in his struggle to overthrow the status quo of the rich and uncaring and to facilitate the appearance of a new order, an order which Jesus has already called the kingdom of God.

Another Old Testament vein mined by Mark is Elijah's call to Elisha to take on the mantle of a prophet in Israel (1 Kings 19:19-21). Elijah passes by (as Jesus passes by) and calls Elisha by the dramatic gesture of throwing his cloak upon him. Not stopping to leave his parents, Elisha burns the yoke of oxen with which he

31

had been ploughing as a sign of renunciation of his former life, just as Simon and the others (all, presumably, married men) leave their boats and families to engage in the adventure of discipleship (see 1 Corinthians 9:5).

A summary section (1:21-22)

At first sight, verses 21 and 22 would appear to be an introduction to the miracle story which follows (1:23-27). But that is not the case. These verses are a summary, one of about twenty such passages throughout Mark. These summary statements show a preference for the Greek imperfect tense, a verbal form expressing continuous, repeated action or customary action in the past. Mark uses his summaries to suggest a wider canvas that that which he presents. He implies that the ministry of Jesus was much more extensive than we might gauge from a superficial reading of his narrative. The generalised descriptions of the ministry of Jesus are intended to expand the story beyond the horizons of the few typical incidents narrated in the Gospel. Like the other gospel-makers, Mark is concerned, not with the biography of Jesus, but with his identity. He selects from his store of Jesus stories in order to present his particular answer to the question, "Who is this man?"

The Holy One of God (1:23-28)

Jesus contended with Satan in the wilderness for forty days. Now we are to see evidence of the outcome of that contest. The power of Satan was broken in the wilderness campaign and now Jesus puts his troops to rout. But the evil spirits (note the plural "us"), precisely because they belong to the supernatural world, know who Jesus is and thus they can reveal his true identity. He is the Holy One of God, who has, indeed, come to destroy them.

Jesus *rebukes* the unclean spirit, a word used in the Bible to denote the opposite of God's creative word. Just as God's creative word is instantly effective (*Let there be light! And there was light!* – Genesis 1:3), so his rebuking word destroys that against which it is uttered. The question, *Have you come to destroy us?*, is better taken as a statement of fact: that is precisely why Jesus has come. The unclean spirit is immediately silenced and driven out (that is, destroyed). What is of extreme importance is that the very words Scripture uses to describe the action and power of God are now on the lips of Jesus. Who then is Jesus?

The reaction of the people in the synagogue has the effect of a summary statement: all the actions of Jesus give rise to amazement and awe. Notice that it is the activity of Jesus which is described as teaching. In Mark, it is the activity of Jesus, for the most part, which promotes those who witness it to ask who he is.

A woman healed (1:29-31)

Jesus moves from the synagogue to a private house, just as early Christians moved from synagogues to homes for worship. He takes Simon's mother-in-law by the hand, an act contrary to decorum and likely to give rise to suspicions of evil desire. It also makes Jesus unclean. But Jesus breaks through social and religious conventions to reach out to the sick.

Jesus *lifted her up*; we might say that he raised her and, indeed, the verb is used of his resurrection. The woman, once raised from her infirmity, serves Jesus and his disciples. The word used for served is the Greek word which lies behind the word "deacon". The woman in the house "deacons" for them. According to some authorities, women were not permitted to serve men at table. All the more strange that the woman offers such service on the Sabbath. If we think of the role of women in the house-churches of early christian times, we will see in the woman's service of Jesus and his disciples a role now sadly often denied to her sisters in the Church.

The day ends with all the sick and possessed gathered with their friends at the door of the house and all are healed. The demons are forbidden to speak for they know the true identity of Jesus. Humans are not to know the full truth until they take their stand at the foot of the cross (15:39). On the following day, Jesus retreats to the wilderness to pray. Simon and the others seek him out and Mark provides another of his summary statements about the character and breadth of the ministry of Jesus.

Touching a leper (1:40-45)

We have been told that the fame of Jesus spread throughout the whole region of Galilee (1:28). Even the lepers heard of it. Yet it is startling, given the cruel (but understandable) conventions of the time, that a leper comes to Jesus, calling on him and kneeling before him. Laws of hygiene, of public health and religious tradition, on the one hand, natural dread and fear, on the other, are swept away in a moment of loving intimacy: *Moved with pity, he stretched out his hand and touched him.* As with the creative word of God, so with Jesus. It is enough to speak: *I will; be clean.*

Presently, Jesus will engage in sharp and acrimonious disputes concerning deep matters of Jewish Law. Such conflicts run like a festering sore through Mark's story. At the outset, Mark cautions that Jesus did not ignore the Law. He commanded the leper to carry out its demands (see Leviticus 13:49 and 14:2-32). The matter of Jesus' attitude to the Law is of some complexity and will further engage our attention. But let one thing be clear from the beginning: Jesus was not put to death because of legal disputes.

That Jesus *sternly charged* (*speaking harshly* might be a better translation) the healed leper would suggest some anger on the part of Jesus. It may be that Mark is anxious to show that Jesus was not an out-an-out opponent of the Torah. That Jesus commanded the man to silence, as he had done the demons, is part of Mark's plan. The people in his story are not to know of the true identity of Jesus until they are confronted with his suffering and death. But the man spreads the word and the fame of Jesus grows so that he is forced out of the towns and villages. But still the people come.

PRAYER

The prayer of Raguel in the Book of Tobit (8:15-17) beautifully responds to God's goodness. With little adaptation, it may be prayed in joyous thanks for what the people beheld on the first day of the ministry of Jesus of Nazareth:

Blessed art thou, O God,
with every pure and holy blessing.
Let thy saints and all thy creatures bless thee;
let all thy angels and thy chosen people
bless thee for ever.
Blessed art thou
because thou hast made us glad.
It has not happened to us as we expected;
but thou hast treated us
according to thy great mercy.
Blessed art thou
because thou hast compassion on thy children.

Stories of conflict
Mark 2:1–3:6

Mark now presents five conflict stories. The initial mission of preaching and healing had won the hearts of the crowd. But the voice of officialdom has to be heard and, sadly, it will prove to be an acrimonious voice. The outcome of the controversies is a resolve to destroy Jesus.

The conflict stories are not linked chronologically. Mark assembles them together for theological purposes: his intention is to show that the person and power of Jesus inflamed the ire of some religious and political groups within Judaism. As ever, the question of the identity of Jesus is the root cause of the conflict.

READING THROUGH

Blasphemy
The Greek words from which we get the English word "blasphemy" mean "an injurious or harmful saying". In the Old Testament blasphemy generally refers to contemptuous or disrespectful speech or actions against God or against his people. The blasphemer might deny God's power (2 Kings 19:4), oppress God's people (Isaiah 52:5), even kill them (Tobit 1:18). To speak insultingly of God, or of the Temple where God dwelt, was a blasphemy. To curse God was to invite death: *Whoever curses his God shall bear his sin. One who blasphemes the name of the Lord shall be put to death; all the congregation shall stone him* (Leviticus 24:15-16). The Jewish historian, Josephus, says "Let him that blasphemeth God be stoned, then hung for a day, and buried ignominiously and in obscurity." It is not certain that, at the time of Jesus, only a blasphemy which involved cursing God's holy name was punishable by death. A lesser blasphemy was punished by excommunication from the synagogue.

Son of man

In the Old Testament and in the languages of the Jewish people, to say of someone, "he is a son of man", was no more than to say "he is a human being". A "son of man" simply meant a member of the human race, male or female. When people are in distress and find help in the Lord, then,

Let them thank the Lord for his steadfast love,
for his wonderful works to the sons of men! (Psalm 107:21).

In one Old Testament text, the term is used of a heavenly figure who will be endowed with divine power and who will come to earth to overcome all that is opposed to God:

I saw in the night visions,
and, behold, with the clouds of heaven
there came one like a son of man,
and he came to the Ancient of Days [God]
and was presented before him.
And to him was given dominion
and glory and kingdom,
that all peoples, nations and languages
should serve him;
his dominion is an everlasting dominion,
which shall not pass away,
and his kingdom one that shall not be destroyed
(Daniel 7:13-14).

The prophet Daniel is recounting a dream which is subsequently interpreted for him as meaning that the enemies of God's people will be overcome and that the people will live in everlasting peace. We must not take all these poetic images at their face value; it is difficult to see how anyone could travel on a cloud! But the meaning is clear enough: the cruel empires of the world which terrify God's family will not have the last say. It is the power of God, exercised by the mysterious *one like a son of man*, which will win out in the end.

With one exception (Act of the Apostles 7:56), in the New Testament only Jesus refers to himself as the Son of man. There are three kinds of situations in which he so describes himself: (i) to refer to his God-given authority on earth; (ii) to refer to his suffering, death and resurrection; (iii) to refer to his role in the judgement of creation at the end of time. We can see that Jesus uses the phrase to assert, not only his humanity (as one who will suffer and die), but also, in the face of opposition, to the divine source of his authority and to his destiny in the divine scheme of things.

Tax collectors

The Gospels lump tax collectors and sinners together as a pair (Matthew 9:10-11; Luke 5:29-30) and, indeed, Matthew puts them in the same bracket as prostitutes (Matthew 21:31). Tax collectors were classed with sinners because they were Jewish people who collected taxes for the brutal Roman imperial power or its representatives (in Levi's case, for Herod Antipas, who ruled Galilee and Perea as Rome's agent). Not only were tax collectors invariably cheats and extortionists, they were traitors to their own people and collaborators with the enemy. But much more than that, they were guilty of sacrilege.

The whole Bible speaks of Israel as God's holy land. The pious Jew regarded the land as God's precious and inalienable gift to his people. God dwelt in the land of Israel as nowhere else: Israel was God's little acre. When a Jewish traveller returned to the Holy Land (we still call Israel/Palestine by that name), he would take off his sandals and slap the soles together over the side of the ship in order *to shake off the dust of his feet* (6:11). In this way, he made sure that the holy ground of Israel was not contaminated by the dust and dirt of pagan lands. The tax collector took the produce of God's acre and gave it to pagans. He took the holy gift of God's harvest and handed it over to heathens. He took what was holy and gave it to heathen dogs.

Sinners

The *sinners* of 2:15 are not to be confused with people who committed sin. For such people (everyone), the rituals and prayers of everyday life assured God's forgiveness. Rather, the term is a technical one, referring to people, generally peasants, who did not observe the Law with the full rigour of a Pharisee. These impoverished "people of the land", as they were contemptuously called, were unable to undertake all the ritual washings of themselves, to provide the wide range of cooking and eating utensils (see 7:1-19) required by religious traditions which were possible for the more wealthy and leisured classes in Jerusalem. To regard such people as sinners was as much a prejudice of social class as of religious elitism.

Pharisees

Judaism at the time of Jesus was a rich tapestry of many different religious tendencies. The Pharisees were but one of many contending religious strands within Judaism. Though the origins of the Pharisee movement are obscure, they seem to have emerged in the turmoil of the Maccabean period (the Maccabee revolt started in 167 B.C.E.). They sought to live a life of scrupulous exactness to the observance of God's laws and promoted a host of traditions which they regarded as defining correct behaviour and provided the best interpretation of the ancient Torah (Law or Teaching) found in the first five books of the Bible. The name "Pharisee" is often traced to a Hebrew word meaning "separatist", indicating that Pharisees were exclusive and kept to themselves, particularly in refusing to eat with others not of their ilk less the food and its preparation were not up to their exacting religious standards. Another possible origin of the name is in a word stressing exactness and highlighting the Pharisees' belief that they, and they alone, had the correct understanding of the divine requirements enshrined in the Law and interpreted by their own scholarly scribes.

The Pharisees were, for the most part, a party of lay people. They were not priests and it should be noted that lay groups within Judaism (such as scribes, Pharisees), while they had fierce arguments with Jesus (himself a layman), played no part in his death.

Herodians

The Herodians would appear to be supporters of Herod Antipas who was the political ruler, under the Romans, of Galilee. It is strange to find the devout Pharisees in league with the friends of the man who was responsible for the death of John the Baptist and who had been living in sin with his sister-in-law for many a year. We find the Herodians on the scene again at 12:13 and, again, in the company of Pharisees and pressing a very political question on Jesus. Since the Pharisees despised Roman rule, it is odd to see them hand-in-hand with those who supported it.

READING THROUGH AGAIN

Though the issues in the conflict stories vary from eating with tax collectors to healing on the sabbath, the one constant matter throughout is the authority of Jesus and the source of that authority.

Who can forgive sins? (2:1-12)

The issue at stake is the power to forgive sins. The scribes are perfectly correct: only God can do so. Their silent protest echoes the words of Isaiah: *I, I am he who blots out your transgressions for my own sake, and I will not remember your sins* (Isaiah 43:25). For a mere human to claim to forgive sin is, indeed, to blaspheme. It is to presume on God's prerogative. Clearly, the man had been brought by friends to Jesus for healing and their strenuous efforts speak of their glowing faith in the ability of Jesus to grant their wish. But Jesus does not immediately do so. Rather, he declares that the man's sins are forgiven. Since it was commonly believed that sin and sickness were linked as cause to effect (John 5:14; 9:2; Psalm 103:3), the removal of the cause will overcome the effect. This story makes a fundamental statement about the nature of Jesus' healing ministry. Healing the sick and forgiving the sinner represents two sides of the same coin. Jesus is destroying the power of Satan everywhere in evidence in the ravages of sin and sickness. Thus, in healing the cripple, Jesus is demonstrating his authority over the powers which crippled him in the first place, the powers of Satan. The splendid spectacle of the man walking out before the assembled people is clear proof *that the Son of man has authority on earth to forgive sin*. The careful reader will notice that the people give thanks to God for what the Son of man has done and will note, too, that the charge of blasphemy will come up again (14:64).

Eating with sinners (2:13-17)

The summary note of 2:13 again broadens the scope of Jesus' ministry without the necessity of narrating every detail. *As he passed by* associates the call of Levi with that of Simon and Andrew (1:16) and further links such calls with the Elijah/Elisha narratives. The invitation of Levi to accept discipleship gives Mark the opportunity to define more closely Jesus' attitudes to sinners. Not only does he forgive sin, sinners become his table companions.

The *scribes of the Pharisees* are the complainants on this occasion. These legal experts (who favoured the Pharisees' understanding of the Law) would, as we have seen, be particularly offended by Jesus eating with sinners (both in the sense explained above and in the ordinary sense). Jesus will have none of this. It is as natural for Jesus to be with the sinful outcast (such as Levi) and the despised poor (the sinners) as it is for a doctor to be found among the sick. And there may be deeper matters here. Jeremiah asserts that God alone is the Physician: *I will heal your faithlessness* (Jeremiah 3:22). It is to the Lord that one must turn for true healing (Jeremiah 17:14; 30:17; Hosea 14:4). The fact that Jesus refers to himself as the physician is a declaration that he has come to dispense God's healing. Again, who is this man?

A time to fast (2:18-22)

The only fast day enjoined by the Law was that of the Day of Atonement (Yom Kippur), a day on which the whole nation looked for forgiveness of its sins (Leviticus 16:29). There may have been other occasions when fasting was deemed appropriate (Zechariah 8:19; Esther 9:31; Nehemiah 9:1). Fasting by individuals was an expression of mourning (2 Samuel 12:21), of penance (1 Kings 21:27) or of supplication (Daniel 9:3). The Pharisees fasted twice a week (Luke 5:33; 18:12) and on other days of historical significance. The point at issue in this conflict is, however, not about the merits of fasting but about its suitability in the new state of affairs ushered in by the coming of Jesus. The Pharisees fast from religious conviction. The Baptist's disciples fast because their master had been imprisoned. But Jesus the Bridegroom is with his disciples and fasting is inappropriate at a wedding. But when the bridegroom is taken away (when Jesus is done to death), then his disciples will fast. Mark is saying that the grim days between the death of Jesus and his coming again will provide ample scope for fasting.

There may be deeper matters here, too. In the Old Testament God is sometimes presented as the Bridegroom of his people (Isaiah 54:5-6; Jeremiah 2:2; and see Ezekiel 16). If Jesus deems it appropriate to describe his relationship with his disciples in terms otherwise used of God and his people, who is this *Son of man* claiming to be?

The homely images of the proper patch and the new wineskins point to the newness of the enterprise of Jesus. The kingdom cannot be constrained by old categories. Christians must not cling too tenaciously to the old lest they fail to appreciate the radical nature of the new.

Lord of the Sabbath (2:23-28)

This story requires close reading. At first, it would appear to be a straightforward clash between the Pharisees who wish to maintain a strict Sabbath observance and Jesus who takes a more liberal view. Read on this level, the matter is simple enough. The disciples of Jesus are plucking corn, albeit just a few ears, thus technically harvesting on the holy day.

Yet the story bristles with oddities (not least the fact that Jesus names the wrong high priest – see 1 Samuel 21:1-6). Why were Jesus and his disciples making a journey on the Sabbath? While it was permissible for a traveller to pick an ear of corn or two on a weekday (Deuteronomy 23:24), why did the disciples so needlessly disregard the Sabbath rule? And how did the Pharisees (all of them?) manage to pop up in the middle of the same field precisely on cue to make their complaint? Were they walking on the Sabbath? And what relevance is the story about David to the matter, since David did not demand the bread on the Sabbath? And if what David did was not right, how does that make right what the disciples did?

These matters are easily resolved if we bear in mind that the story is not about the niceties of the Law. It concerns the person and authority of Jesus. Jesus is claiming the same authority over the Law as the great King David. As he goes on to point out, the Sabbath was ordained for the benefit of humanity, not as a burden to satisfy some religious whim. More tellingly, Jesus claims that his authority extends over the God-given institutions of the Law. Yet again, what manner of man dare make such a claim?

Sabbath healing (3:1-6)

Five conflict stories. Five illustrations of the power and authority of the Son of man. Five stories which are deadly portents of things to come. The conflict over the healing on the Sabbath brings matters to a head and we find enemies waiting to make accusations and powerful allies plotting destruction.

Jesus is now under the official eye, a suspect against whom plots must be laid. One feels the hostility in the story: *they watched him ... so that might accuse him.* Even Jesus is mightily angry.

The common view was that relief might be given on the Sabbath if life itself were in danger. Since that is not the case here, will Jesus act unlawfully? Jesus, however, turns the tables by altering the basis for the discussion. Forget about whether it is lawful or not. Ask, rather, is it good? If the Sabbath is made for humanity's benefit, then surely it is a day for doing good. To refuse the good is to court evil. The answer is clear: *Stretch out your hand*.

PRAYER

The first episodes in the tragedy of Jesus of Nazareth are full of delight. Joyful, expectant crowds, relishing a profound renewal of their faith in God, disciples leaving all to follow, demons driven out, fevers, diseases, even leprosy and sin, are driven out, overcome by the authority of the Son of man on earth. But terror is lurking at every turn. John the Baptist is shut up in prison; religious and political leaders have begun to take counsel. The first scene of Mark's drama ends on a warning note: plots are being hatched. An appropriate prayer, when danger is at every turn, is Psalm 22, a prayer Jesus will pray himself one day (15:34).

A new family
Mark 3:7-35

We have seen and heard many strange things. We have watched John the Baptist, in the garb of Elijah, baptising all the peoples of Jerusalem and the countryside around. We have listened to his witness to the one who is to come. We have seen Jesus baptised and been privy to a heavenly voice claiming him for a son. Unlike the people in Mark's story, we have been allowed to hear the demons identify the Holy One of God. We have seen the possessed reclaimed for God's good world; we have seen leprosy disappear and rejoiced with the crowds that the crippled are sent away without crutches and without sin.

Yet all this gospel, all this good news, comes in deep shadow. John the Baptist has been handed over into prison, the expert scribes speak of blasphemy, the Pharisees object to fellowship with the sinner-outcast and the poor. An unholy alliance of Pharisees and the time-serving Herodians is formed to seek to destroy Jesus. As we make our way through the second scene of the first act of Mark's drama, we shall see more ominous signs. As the plot thickens, so does the sense of impending doom.

READING THROUGH

The Twelve

Jesus appoints the Twelve to be with him, to be sent out to preach and to have power over demons. It may seem contradictory that the Twelve are sent out, yet are to be with Jesus. Mark intends that they are to be with Jesus until they are sent out. Only later, when they have been sent out on a temporary trial mission and successfully completed it, are they called "apostles", a word which means "one who is sent out". The word occurs once in Mark (6:30), once in Matthew (10:2), once in John (13:16), though not in reference to a named individual, and six times in Luke. But the word occurs 28 times in the Acts of the Apostles and 34 times in the writings of Paul. Clearly, the term "apostle" was a significant word in the life of the early churches, though apparently not so much, if at all, during the lifetime of Jesus. The word makes more sense after the resurrection when people are sent out (that is, made apostles) with authority to carry out their mission in the name of the risen Jesus.

The names of the Twelve are to be found in Matthew (10:2-4), in Luke (6:14-16), here in Mark, and there is a list of eleven in Acts of the Apostles 1:13. The lists do not agree perfectly but they all begin with Simon on whom Jesus placed the name Peter. It is important to realise that no such name existed (in Greek) before Jesus coined it as a kind of nickname for the fisherman from Capernaum. The word in the language of Jesus is "kepha" and means a stone or rock (and this may have existed as a pet name). From this point on, Simon is always called Peter, with one exception. It is poignant to note that in Gethsemane, just as Peter is about to run away and, indeed, to deny all knowledge of the Lord, Jesus calls him Simon (14:37) and, on another ominous occasion, calls him Satan (8:33).

James and John may have been called *Boanerges* because they were twins. Mark tells us that the new name means *sons of thunder,* though it is not clear how this may be explained in Greek. Nicknames are not always self-explanatory. The second Simon is called *the Cananaean*, a name which suggests that he belonged to a fiercely nationalistic tendency which, later, would form the Zealot party, much given to terrorist activity against the Romans. Judas is called *Iscariot*, a name which remains unexplained. Some suggest that it means "the man from Kerioth" but this is not certain (see Joshua 15:25; Jeremiah 48:24). Others suggest that it comes from *ish sakariot*, the man in charge of payment, that is, the treasurer. John's Gospel adds some weight to this view. Of Judas it says *he had the money-box and he used to take whatever was put into it* (John 12:6). But perhaps the best guess is that it means "reddish-brown" or "ruddy". So Judas was named Judas the Red. Did he have red hair? Judas is always named last in the lists for the sad reason that it was he who handed him over.

Satan

Mark does not use the term "devil". Yet his Gospel, particularly its first act, is full of demons (mentioned thirteen times) and unclean spirits (mentioned eleven times). The leader of these forces is called Satan on six occasions and Beelzebul at 3:22. The name Beelzebul is based on Baalzebub, the god of Ekron mentioned in 2 Kings 1:2. Obviously, the Bible has little but scorn for false gods and it will come as no surprise to learn that Baalzebub which means "Lord Prince" or "Lord of the divine abode" was popularly knows as "Lord of the Flies". By way of mockery, Jewish people gave the name to the prince of demons, otherwise known as Satan. In the Old Testament the name "Satan" does not refer to the chief devil but to a functionary of God's court who has the task of accusing human beings before God's throne and, after investigation, God then acquits or condemns the defendant (see Job 1:6-8; 1 Chronicles 21:1; Zechariah 3:1-3). The word might be translated "adversary" or "accuser". But time gradually altered the role of Satan and the people who left *The Dead Sea Scrolls* had a far from heavenly view of his role:

> Cursed be Satan for his sinful purpose and may he be execrated for his wicked rule! Cursed be all the spirits of his company for their ungodly purpose and may they be execrated for all their service of uncleanness! Truly they are the company of Darkness, but the company of God is one of [eternal] Light (1QM 13:4).

In the Gospel Satan is portrayed as the adversary of Jesus (1:13), the enemy of his work (3:23-27). The name Satan will be given to Peter, insofar as he is not on God's side in his estimation of a suffering Messiah (8:33). Satan is depicted as destroying God's work by taking away the word planted in people (4:15). The minions of Satan possess people, cause people to convulse and cry out (1:26) and even provoke people to destroy themselves (9:22). The first public act of Jesus is an exorcism, an attack on the power of Satan.

READING THROUGH AGAIN

A summary section (3:7-12)
   This is the fifth of Mark's summary statements which he uses to extend the ministry of Jesus beyond the relatively few details recorded in his pages. Of particular note here is that not only are we told that people flocked to Jesus from all corners of the land

of Israel, from Galilee in the north, Judea and its capital city, Jerusalem, in the south, and Idumea on the west bank of the Dead Sea, but also from pagan lands. The phrase *beyond the Jordan* is probably intended to refer to Perea, a region under the jurisdiction of Herod Antipas. But Mark may also wish to include the region known as the Decapolis, to the south of the Sea of Galilee. We shall have more to say about this region when we come to chapter five. Tyre and Sidon are two ports in what is now Lebanon and we shall meet them again. At this point, it is important to note that Mark has extended the mission of Jesus to Gentiles, to pagans. Nobody is to be excluded from the mission and concern of the Son of man.

The sea to which Jesus withdraws is, of course, Lake Kinnereth, the scene of so much of his activity. Just as the desert has a symbolic significance, so, too, does the sea. It is a place to which Jesus retreats to engage in his war with demonic powers. The battle which was enjoined in the wilderness (1:13) is continued on the sea. Traditionally, both the desert and the sea were considered to be inhabited by evil forces hostile to God. In Mark's Gospel, the sea is the battleground to which the Holy One of God repairs in order to destroy the evil ones (3:11) by the force of his power and the authority of his word.

The boat which the disciples are instructed to make ready will play a significant role presently, both as a place from which Jesus teaches and in which he demonstrates his power over the demons of the deep (4:1; 4:35-41).

All who had diseases pressed upon him to touch him. Touching is important to Mark. Jesus takes people by the hand and, as here, people seek to touch him (1:31; 1:41; 5:28-31; 5:41; 6:56; 7:33; 8:23; 10:13). People who were sick or suffered some deformity were regarded as unclean, that is, unacceptable to God. Whole sections of the Book of Leviticus are devoted to spelling out the circumstances in which people become unclean. Particularly unpleasant are the rules regarding menstruation, conception and child-bearing (see Leviticus 12). To touch an unclean person was to become unclean oneself. When Jesus touches the sick and is touched by them, he is, in effect, abolishing such inhuman legislation and stating that no one is unclean, no one is unacceptable to God. No one is beyond his concern or outside his care.

46

He appointed Twelve (3:13-19)

Some English translations state that Jesus went up *into the hills* but the Greek text is clear: Jesus went up *the mountain*. Notice *the* mountain, not *a* mountain. For, as with the desert and the sea, the mountain has a special significance. It is not only the remote place which serves as a place of retreat from the pressing crowds (6:46). The mountain is a place of revelation and covenant. In the Book of Exodus God reveals his intentions to Moses and declares his unilateral, unconditional love of his people (= covenant) on Mount Sinai (Exodus 19-24). This mountain thus came to occupy a special place in the religious imagination of the Jewish people. Whenever the prophets wished to call the people back to religious fervour, they would invite them to journey to the desert of Sinai and its holy mountain to hear again the word of God and to renew the covenant. We shall see that Mark's account of the Transfiguration (9:2-8) takes place on a mountain and an important message for the future is given on the Mount of Olives (13:3-37).

Just as Moses called the people to Mount Sinai to meet with their God and to be formed into his holy people, so Jesus calls those whom he desired in order to create the nucleus of his movement. It is better to say that Jesus created or made the Twelve, rather than *appointed* them. For Mark has in mind such Old Testament lines as,

> But now thus says the Lord,
> he who created you, O Jacob
> (= the people of Israel),
> he who formed you, O Israel:
> "Fear not, for I have redeemed you;
> I have called you by name,
> you are mine" (Isaiah 43:1).

and

> But now hear, O Jacob my servant,
> Israel whom I have chosen!
> Thus says the Lord who made you,
> who formed you from the womb
> and will help you (Isaiah 44:1-2).

Just as God created the people of Israel from all the world's peoples to be bearers of his Law, so Jesus creates his own people

47

to be his standard-bearers (and see also Exodus 18:25). The activity of Jesus parallels the activity of God, raising yet again the question of the identity of the Son of man.

The fact that Jesus creates twelve confirms the fact that he is founding a new community. God formed the people of Israel on the twelve sons of Jacob (also called Israel, Genesis 32:28) who became the fathers of the so-called Twelve Tribes. Likewise, the Twelve are the nucleus of the movement Jesus initiates. His authority will be extended in the activities of the Twelve.

A Marcan sandwich (3:20-35)

Mark likes sandwiches, at least, the kind made with words. Some would have it that the whole of his Gospel is a sandwich, with the Transfiguration providing the meat and what goes before is the top slice and what follows is the bottom slice. We are on more certain ground in smaller sections. For example, look how he treats Peter's denial of Jesus (14:53-72). First we are told that Peter made his way into the courtyard and takes his place at the fire to observe the trial (top slice). Then we are given part of the trial, where Jesus insists that *I am* and bravely defends himself (the meat). Finally, we have the denial (I am not ...) when Peter denies all knowledge of Jesus (the bottom slice). You will appreciate that the three layers interact, creating suspense and enriching the story. The section we are about to examine is a Marcan sandwich: a family story, a conflict story, and another family story. We shall see how the layers interact to startling effect.

A family story (3:20-21)

Mark 3:20-21, the top layer of our sandwich, has caused endless problems and various translations try to get around the awkward fact that the family of Jesus thought he was mad. But there is no point in trying to soften the story out of embarrassment. Mark, after all, shows no such reticence.

Jesus went home, that is, to Capernaum (see 2:1), and the crowds flocked to him. But his family came to seize him because they thought he was mad. The verb translated as se*ized* is the same used in 6:17 of the arrest of John the Baptist and of the arrest of Jesus (12:12; 14:1, 44, 46, 49, 51). But it is also used of Jesus taking people by the hand (1:31; 5:41) so that Mark may not mean that any violence occurred.

48

Two points need to be borne in mind. First, we may so dilute the message of Jesus that we miss its radical nature. We may so water down his demands that we fail to be shocked by what we read in the Gospels. It is all quite harmless stuff. But Jesus challenged the social, religious and political forces of the land in which he lived. He was a dangerous man, if you happened to belong to the establishment. Its not difficult to imagine that his family considered him to be mad and wished to save him from worse excesses (as they saw it) of the mission he had undertaken. It is surely significant that Mark tells us that the crowds flocked to Jesus so that he hardly had time to eat. You don't attract that kind of attention by mouthing pious platitudes.

Secondly, Mark is not the only one to have embarrassing stories about Jesus. In John 7:5 we are told that even *his brothers did not believe him.* This may not appear as shocking as Mark's account, but in John's Gospel refusing to believe is the most heinous of crimes because it is a rejection of God himself. If both Mark and John remember that Jesus had trouble with his family, there must be something in the story.

A *conflict story* (3:22-30)

The middle of our sandwich is a conflict story concerning the source of Jesus' power over Satan. The experts in Jewish religious law, the biblical experts of their day, from Jerusalem, the capital of the religious establishment, come (sounding like an official delegation) to declare much the same thing but more forcefully: *he is possessed by Beelzebul, the prince of demons.*

The reply of Jesus to the charge is typically vigorous. If the house of Satan is divided, as a kingdom might be divided in a civil war, what power has it? If a devil is casting out a devil, then the kingdom of devils is coming to an end. To be sure, Satan is a strong man but a stronger man (Jesus himself) has broken into his house, tied up the devil and *plundered his possessions,* that is, cast out demons possessing people. Jesus points to his work of exorcism as a sure sign that Satan's power over people is being broken.

The work of Jesus is the work of God's Holy Spirit, given to Jesus at his baptism (1:10). To deny that, to maintain that the work of God is Satan's work, is to place oneself outside forgiveness. Forgiveness is God's prerogative (2:7). To suggest that this is Satan's work is to place oneself where forgiveness cannot reach.

49

Another family story (3:31-35)

The third part of Mark's sandwich is the most difficult for the Christian to contemplate. The vague "family" of verse 21 is now clearly identified as *his mother and brothers*. The first difficulty concerns the fact that Mark speaks of the brothers of Jesus. A little later (6:3), he will give their names, James, Joses, Judas and Simon, and refer to the sisters of Jesus. The obvious meaning is that Jesus did have brothers and sisters. But some early Christians believed, not only that Mary conceived Jesus miraculously without human intervention, but that Mary remained a virgin all her life. One writer, Epiphanius (c. 382 C.E.), believed that the brothers and sisters were the children of Joseph by a previous marriage. Unfortunately, there is no evidence for this. St Jerome (c. 383 C.E.) proposed that they were cousins of Jesus, the children of Mary, the wife of Clopas, who was Mary's sister (John 19:25). Jerome argued that the words for brother and sister in Greek could refer to cousins. Greek outside the New Testament does use the word for brother (*adelphos*) to signify various relationships of blood and law. For example, "brother" is applied to one's husband, sometimes in an incestuous relationship, or by a father writing to his son. But there is a perfectly ordinary Greek word for cousin (to be found in Colossians 4:10) and it is difficult to understand why Mark does not use it if that is what he meant.

Perhaps Mark had scant knowledge of the family of Jesus and used what little he had to indicate that the real family of Jesus is not to be found in Nazareth. When Mary and the brothers came they remained on the outside and had to shout to attract attention. The crowd around Jesus pointed out that his family were outside (notice the emphasis on *outside*). Jesus turned to those around him (the inner circle, as it were) and declared that they and not the outsiders were his true mother, brother and sister, explaining that those who do God's will are his true family. The implication (and this is the force of the sandwich) is that neither the family which came to seize him, nor those among his religious family (some of the scribes) who insist that Jesus is doing the devil's work, will ever find their way into the intimacy of those who sit around Jesus and listen to his voice.

PRAYER

We have seen and heard strange matters. We have seen crowds flocking to Jesus but not all become disciples; we have seen the Twelve chosen for onerous tasks. But we have seen, too, that in the creation of a new family there is rejection by the old. Psalm 86 seems a suitable response to the perplexities we have encountered: *Teach me thy way, O Lord.*

Teaching in parables
Mark 4:1-34

Mark's favourite title for Jesus is "Teacher". Given that his is the shortest Gospel, he uses it more than the other three gospel-makers. Yet Mark does not give us much of the actual teaching of Jesus. His concern is more with what Jesus did. Nonetheless he presents some of the teaching and we may assume that the little he does pass on is of particular importance to him. Mark says that Jesus taught in parables, even that *he did not speak to them without a parable* (4:34). We need to know what a parable is.

READING THROUGH

Parables

A parable is a short story which illustrates a point by making a comparison. Here is an example from the Book of Ecclesiastes:

> There was a little city with a few men in it; and a great king came against it and besieged it, building great siegeworks against it. But there was found in it a poor wise man, and he by his wisdom delivered the city (Ecclesiastes 9:14-15).

The writer is defending the merits of wisdom as against might by means of a story. We might say, "The pen is mightier than the sword" and it is true that a parable is very often capable of being reduced to a proverb or simple saying. But a story is more memorable and more effective because human beings love stories. There is also an element of surprise which engages attention. The teacher who tells good stories will hold his pupils.

Another feature of the parables is that they subvert and challenge the views of the listener. Parables are meant to hurt, to force one to examine one's position and change it. Consider the case of King David. After his adultery with Bathsheba and the murder of her husband, the prophet Nathan was sent to impress on the king the horrendous nature of his crimes. Did Nathan rush in and read David a lecture? Certainly not. He told a parable:

> There were two men in a certain city, the one rich and the other poor. The rich man had very many flocks and herds; but the poor man had nothing but one little ewe, which he had bought. And he brought it up, and it grew up with him and his children; it used to eat of his morsel, and drink from his cup, and lie down in his bosom, and it was like a daughter to him. Now there came a traveller to the rich man, and he was unwilling to take one of his own flock or herd to prepare for the wayfarer who had come to him, but he took the poor man's lamb, and prepared it for the man who had come to him (2 Samuel 12:1-4).

David flew into a rage and pronounced that the rich man deserved death *because he did this thing and because he had no pity*. Then Nathan said to David, *You are the man*. You can see how the parable forced the king to realise the full horror of what he had done and to demand that he change his life. Parables have a way of getting under your skin.

There are many parables in the Old Testament (2 Samuel 14:4-7; Isaiah 5:1-7; Ezekiel 17:1-10; 24:2-5) and in Jewish writing generally. We must not think that only Jesus taught in parables. Peoples all over the world tell stories in order to teach.

Organisation and Language (4:1-34)

We need to take note of how Mark organises his material in this section. His plan would appear to be as follows:

a. Introduction – verses 1-2
b. Parable of the Sower – verses 3-9
c. First explanation of the Sower Parable – verses 10-12
d. Second explanation of the Sower Parable – verses 13-20
e. Various sayings – verses 21-25
f. Further parables about the Kingdom of God – verses 26-32
g. Summary Statement – verses 33-34

We shall follow this plan which will enable us to see the trees without losing sight of the wood.

Mark's language also demands attention. We are constantly told to hear, to listen, to take heed, to behold, to understand. The repetition is clearly intended by Mark to plead with his readers to pay the closest attention to what he has to say in his parable section.

READING THROUGH AGAIN

Introduction (4:1-2)

The sea, Lake Kinnereth, is going to play a very important role, an increasingly important role, in Mark's story. We have seen its symbolic value for Mark and presently we shall see the power of Jesus over the demons of the deep. In 3:9 Jesus asks his disciples to get a boat ready for him because of the press of the crowd and now it is called into service. Mark carefully sets the impressive scene. Jesus sits in the boat a little distance from the land. A very large crowd is assembled on the shore. It is as if Jesus were in a pulpit overlooking a multitude seated below. Clearly, Mark wants to impress upon his readers the solemnity of the occasion. He wants, too, to emphasise what Jesus is doing here: he is teaching. Notice, *he began to teach, and he taught them, and in his teaching*. Every item of Mark's setting of the scene points to the fact that he wishes to impress upon his readers the importance of what is to follow.

Parable of the sower (4:3-9)

The basic idea of all the parables and sayings in chapter four seems to be a contrast between beginnings and endings. What are apparently not very hopeful beginnings turn out (surprisingly) to be very successful in the end.

The sower is beset by birds, rocky ground, scorching sun and thorns. But there is good ground and there the seeds thrive, producing a harvest of great abundance. In order to emphasise that the Lord was with Isaac, we are told that he sowed and *reaped in the same year a hundredfold* (Genesis 26:11). Similarly, the apparently blighted crop of the sower, against all the odds, yields a generous harvest.

First explanation of the sower parable (4:10-12)

The parable is offered to anyone with ears to hear but its meaning is to be perceived only by disciples (*those about him with the twelve*). Mark's readers are, of course, let in on the secret so we will find in his explanation much to encourage the frightened and dispirited Christians in Rome.

The presence of those about him with the twelve does not contradict the statement that Jesus is alone (see 9:2, 8). The rather odd way of putting the matter emphasises that the people now with Jesus are to be distinguished from those outside (see 3:32-33), those who do not hear the word of God and do not keep it. The people around Jesus with the Twelve are his new family. Of the very large crowd who came (4:1) some, obviously, did not hear with sufficient attention to become disciples.

The disciples ask Jesus *concerning the parables*. Notice the plural. Note, too, that they ask what the parables mean, not why Jesus teaches in parables. What the disciples want is a key to all the parables and Jesus will go on to say that an understanding of the parable of the sower is the key (4:13).

Jesus explains that the disciples have been given *the mystery of the kingdom of God*. By "mystery" Mark does not mean some fact or idea which we cannot understand. He means that the disciples are let in on a secret. They are recipients of a revelation, a disclosure. What could the secret, the disclosure be? What have the disciples been given. They have been given Jesus! They have been called by him, they have listened to him, they have accepted him and followed him. They see (or will come to see) in Jesus the one in whose words and deeds God himself is at work. Those who do not see this point, those who attribute his words and deeds to a demon (3:30), for example, miss the whole point and they remain "outside", that is, they do not follow Jesus. The parables, to such people, remain just unintelligible riddles. They fail to grasp their essential meaning. To them can be applied the words of Isaiah 6:9-10 (verse 12 is a quotation):

Hear and hear, but do not understand;
see and see, but do not perceive.
Make the heart of this people fat,
and their eyes heavy
and shut their eyes,
lest they see with their eyes
and hear with their ears,
and understand with their hearts
and turn and be healed.

Those who reject Jesus are like those who in the past rejected the prophets when they called people to repentance. The prophets were listened to by some people but rejected by most and those who rejected the advice of the prophets were not able to repent, to return from God. It is not for nothing that the material in 3:20-35 is all about people who misunderstand Jesus completely. They are condemned to be outsiders.

Thus the first explanation would be that God is the sower, the seed is Jesus who is, as it were, sown in the world and the world (the ground) reacts to him in one of two ways. Either they reject him or they accept him. Those who accept him may not amount to much but, in the final analysis, there will be a mighty harvest (see 10:28-31).

Second explanation of the sower (4:13-20)

Jesus points to the Parable of the Sower as the key to all other parables because it teaches that he is the mystery of the kingdom of God, that is, he is the one in whose person the kingdom comes. He is the one who inaugurates the reign of God. In his life and work we see the will of God being done on earth as it is in heaven. This parable is the key to all parables because it is the key to the career of Jesus himself. But this second explanation extends the sowing to those who, in Jesus' name, preach the word. The mystery of the kingdom is, from one point of view, Jesus himself, yet, from another point of view, may be said to be the gospel, the word about Jesus. At 10:29 Jesus outlines the destiny of those who leave house or brothers or sister, even mother and father, children and lands *for my sake and for the gospel*. The same interrelation of Jesus and the gospel of Jesus would seem to be understood here.

Mark gives a detailed account of the enemies who destroy the word in the hearts of the many who hear it but do not keep it. As ever in Mark's story, the chiefest enemy is Satan who is implacably opposed to the word. Mark's persecuted and despairing Roman Christians will see themselves in those who *when tribulation or persecution arises on account of the word, immediately fall away*. The cares of the world, the delight in riches, the desire for all sorts of things, choke the human spirit and quench the thirst for the good news. But the frightened Christians will have been encouraged that not all fall away. The First Letter of Peter counsels the reader to *cast all your anxie-*

ties on [God], for he cares for you (5:7). Those who do so make up the good soil which embraces the seed and puts forth a mighty harvest.

Various sayings (4:21-25)

An important clue as to how Mark wants us to understand the material in this chapter may be found in verse 21. So startling is this verse that many translations conceal rather than reveal its implications. Properly translated, the verse reads, *And he was saying to them, Surely the lamp does not come to be placed under a measuring bowl, or under a bed, and not on a lamp stand?* What kind of lamp comes in as if it were alive? There is no such walking lamp! Mark is clearly using the idea of a lamp to stand for something else. Who comes as a light? Whose person and teaching enlightens, though, for the time being, that light is hidden? Who has an obscure beginning but will have a glorious outcome when he comes again (look carefully at 13:26)? It is, of course, Jesus. The preceding two chapters in Mark are a record of Jesus being misunderstood by religious authorities (2:7,16,18,24; 3:2,6,22) and even by his own family (3:21). The significance of this Jesus, in whom God's kingdom dawns, remains hidden. It is not at all clear that the appearance of Jesus on the scene indicates a decisive manifestation of God's authority. The crowds recognise the authority of Jesus (1:27) but authorities question it (2:7) and even point to Satan as its source (3:22). Yet the source and significance of Jesus' authority, the meaning of his coming, will not remain hidden for ever. He may be misunderstood and rejected by the authorities both during his life and at the end of it (*and be rejected by the elders and the chief priests and the scribes*; 8:31). But what has begun obscurely, in apparent failure, will, by the power of God, result in such a magnificent harvest that the angels themselves must reap it from the four corners of the earth (13:27).

The three sayings continue the contrast between beginnings and endings. Things that are hidden eventually come to light. A secret will not remain a secret for ever. At this point Mark adds another caution to hear, to realise the seriousness of the matter, for the extent to which one responds to the offer made by God in Jesus, to that extent will the divine offer be made. Mark concludes the paragraph with two further sayings which make much the same point: the more you respond to God's offer, the more you will receive; the less you offer, the less you end up with.

Further parables of the kingdom (4:26-32)

The remaining two parables deal with humble beginnings and surprising endings. The kingdom of God (we shall explore this phrase presently) is like a farmer who does no more than scatter seeds. After that, he continues his daily routine and the earth must do the rest. The kingdom cannot be forced; it will come to fruition in God's good time.

The mustard seed is not, as it happens, the smallest of all the seeds on earth but it was proverbially regarded as such in Israel. Contrast, says Mark, the tiny seed with the huge shrub. The insignificant and apparently hopeless ministry of Jesus may not seem to be the sort of endeavour which will usher in the kingdom of God. But look at the mustard seed. Consider not its size; consider its potential.

Conclusion (4:33-34)

Mark does not give all the parables of Jesus. But the samples he provides are tailored to his purpose. By presenting the ministry of Jesus as only marginally successful, punctured by rejection, betrayal and ultimately death, he is asking his frightened Roman Christian brothers and sisters to look at themselves. They, too, have suffered rejection, death and betrayal but, says Mark, as in the case of Jesus, their day will come.

PRAYER

The Christian Church is a mighty institution. It has, indeed, grown from a tiny seed to a great shrub. But we must not confuse the Church with the Kingdom. The will of God is borne by the Spirit and the Spirit blows where it wills. There is need for humility when we contemplate the misery we human beings cause on this planet which was doing quite nicely for 4,600 million years before we turned up. We need humility to see our place in creation and a deeper humility still to recognise God's place. The prayer of the Lamb of God in Revelation 15:3-4 is the kind of prayer that has the right perspective.

The coming of the kingdom
Mark 4:35-41

A large number of parables in the Gospels begin with the phrase, *The kingdom of God is like...* Because he has a particular reverence for the word of God, Matthew speaks of the kingdom of heaven. The proclamation of the kingdom of God is a dominant theme in the message of Jesus. Indeed, Mark provides a summary of that message in one sentence:

> The time is fulfilled, amd the kingdom of God is at hand! Repent and believe in the gospel! (1:15).

We have considered this verse and made a preliminary excursion into the meaning of the kingdom of God. The phrase occurs fourteen times in Mark, indicating its importance in the teaching of Jesus and we must now make a deeper exploration.

The kingdom of God

There is no clear-cut formal definition of the kingdom of God. Instead we are presented with a poet's rich profusion of similes and metaphors. What the kingdom is like and the evidence of its presence is conveyed in parables, short vivid sentences and sometimes in enigmatic sayings. But those who first heard Jesus speak of the kingdom of God would not have found it an unfamiliar idea. The expectation that God's kingdom would come was a familiar part of Jewish faith. We may be misled by the word "kingdom". It suggests an area, a country such as the United Kingdom or the Kingdom of Norway. It implies a body of citizens, the subjects of a royal person. But the kingdom of God does not refer to a place or a people. What the Jews longed for and confidently expected was the absolute exercise of God's authority throughout creation.

To be sure, it was a commonplace of Jewish thinking that *there is no authority except from God* (Romans 13:1) and that the powers that be have been established by God:

By me kings reign,
and rulers decree what is just;
by me princes rule,
and nobles govern the earth (Proverbs 8:15-16).

For your dominion was given you from the Lord,
and your sovereignty from the Most High (Wisdom of
Solomon 6:3).

But such authority over people must be exercised in line with
its God-given nature. Those who rule, rule in God's name and
abuse of power will be met by divine retribution:

Because as servants of his kingdom
you did not rule rightly,
nor keep the law,
nor walk according to the purpose of God,
he will come upon you terribly and swiftly,
because severe judgement falls on those in high places.
For the lowliest man may be pardoned in mercy,
but mighty men will be mightily tested.
For the Lord of all will not stand in awe of any one,
nor show deference to greatness;
because he himself made both small and great,
and he takes thought for all alike.
But a strict inquiry is in store for the mighty.
To you then, O monarchs,
my words are directed,
that you may learn wisdom and not transgress
(Wisdom of Solomon 6:4-9).

The corruption of human authority, the injustices committed
in its name, were seen as signs of demon powers at work in the
world. God could not forever tolerate the usurpation of his sovereignty. The time must surely come when God would reassert his
authority. God's people, the Jews, who knew this unalterable
truth, expressed it in the phrase "the coming of the kingdom of
God". Theirs was the task to wait, and waiting, to be obedient to
the will of God as expressed in their holy Law. But they knew
that the time would come for God to take the decisive action to
destroy corrupt human power and to restore all creation in accord
with his intention. Of course, the struggle against Satan and his
cohorts would not be easy and the battle between God and his

enemies would be bitter. But those who remained faithful to the vision of the future would be vindicated.

How startling then was the proclamation with which Jesus began his preaching: *the kingdom of God is at hand!* (1:15). Prophets and righteous people had desired to see the triumph of God's purposes but did not see it (Matthew 13:17). What Jesus announced to the crowds in Galilee was "you're seeing it now". The announcement that the kingdom was at hand caused great excitement and, to those who believed it, it brought joyful expectancy. The kingdom was coming in the person and teaching of Jesus. The power which Jesus exercised was turned against Satan, the prince of demons, and his minions. The effects of Satan's rule, everywhere visible in sickness and deformity, were under attack. Not only did Jesus cast out demons but he restored the sick to health. What the people were invited to accept was that the power of Jesus to cast out and to heal was nothing less than the power of God. The kingdom had come.

The difficulty, of course, was to accept that the kingdom, God's rule, was coming in the work of the carpenter from Nazareth. To be sure, Jesus spoke with authority, he healed the sick and overcame demons but so did great people before, prophets like Elijah and Elisha, leaders like the prophetess Deborah. Not all were convinced that the signs of God's reign were evident in the works of Jesus. From the beginning, there was hostility. In the end, there would be crucifixion. Lest Mark's readers, in their dark days, begin to doubt the source of Jesus' power and authority, he will now tell four stories which will establish beyond all doubt that God's rule, his power, is to be found at work in the doings of Jesus. The kingdom is coming in the life and times of the man from Nazareth.

READING THROUGH

Mark is about to relate four mighty works of power. The power of a great storm is reduced to a great calm. An unfortunate, whom no one could bind even with a chain and who is possessed by a legion of demons, is found, sitting down, clothed and in his right mind. A woman whose fortune has been devoured by useless physicians is healed at a secret touch. And the last enemy, death, is destroyed as it seeks to claim a little girl.

A distinction is sometimes made between nature miracles and healing miracles, that is, between those miracles in which Jesus overcomes the forces of nature and those in which he overcomes sickness and disease. The distinction, however, does not help us to understand Mark. Such a distinction would mean little in his world. What all the miracles show is that the power of God is revealed in the work of Jesus. Mark's questions are not necessarily ours. He is concerned to show what these awesome deeds tell about Jesus. What will the effect be on his disciples, on the crowds, on the authorities? And what of Mark's readers? Will these stories speak to their situation?

READING THROUGH AGAIN

Stilling the Storm (4:35-41)

The boat which made its first appearance at 3:9 and which turned into a pulpit at 4:1 will play an important role in Mark's story down to 8:21. We have explored the significance of the sea in Mark's narrative and we will bear that in mind.

At the end of the teaching beside the sea, Jesus proposes to go across to the other side. What is of great moment here is that Jesus proposes to go into Gentile territory, to leave the holy land of Israel and set foot on unholy, pagan soil. What will happen on the way? And what awaits him on the other side of the sea?

Though Jesus had instigated the journey across the lake, Mark says that *they took him with them, just as he was, in the boat.* The verse may mean no more than that the disciples cast off and Jesus continued to sit in the stern of the boat from where he had lately been preaching. But there may well be more to it than that. Mark may be hinting that the disciples took Jesus with them to a pagan land, just as later they would take the gospel of Jesus to the whole world after the resurrection. The Teacher the disciples took to the country of the Gerasenes is the teacher they will one day take to the whole world.

Why Mark discloses that *other boats were with him* is not clear for these boats and the people in them play no part in the story. However, recall that in 4:10 we read of *those who were about him with the twelve.* It may be that *those others* are now the people in the other boats. But the *they* of verse 36 refers, not to the twelve, but to the other disciples of verse 34. Notice, too, that

Mark says that the other boats were *with him*, not *with them*, as we might expect. It has been suggested that the writer may be hinting that the disciples in the other boats were not terrified in the storm because they were *with him*, that is to say, they had faith in him, the disciples did not. However, Mark does not highlight the people in the other boats; such a fierce storm must surely threaten all on the lake and deliverance comes to all through the act of Jesus alone. The story does not point to the faith of others as motivating Jesus (see 2:5); it is the power of Jesus that is in question here.

Great storms are fairly common on the Sea of Galilee. But it is to the Old Testament that we must turn if we are to discover the meaning of Mark's storm. The Jewish people, as many ancient peoples, believed that in the beginning the whole earth was submerged under water. In order to overcome chaos, God had to put the waters in their place and rule them so that they did not threaten the earth:

> And God said, "Let the waters under the heavens be gathered together in one place, and let dry land appear" (Genesis 1:9).

The Book of Job speaks of God as the one who created the sea and keeps it within allotted confines:

> Or who shut in the sea with doors,
> when it burst forth from the womb;
> when I made clouds its garment,
> and thick darkness its swaddling band,
> and prescribed bounds for it,
> and set bars and doors,
> and said, "Thus far shall you come,
> and no farther,
> and here shall your proud waves be stayed" (Job 38:8-11).

The same notion will be found in the third verse of the beautiful but apocryphal Prayer of Manasseh.

But the sea, while it remains under God's rule (*I fear the Lord, the God of heaven, who made the sea and the dry land* – Jonah 1:9), has the power to return the world to primeval chaos. God must be vigilant and control the sea, if he is to exercise proper stewardship over creation. The psalmist prays anxiously to the Lord:

63

The floods have lifted up, O Lord,
the floods have lifted up their voice,
the floods lift up their roaring (Psalm 93:3).

But creation is safe in God's hands:
Mightier than the thunder of many waters,
mightier than the waves of the sea.,
the Lord on high is mighty! (Psalm 93:4).

So dangerous is the sea that the prophet Daniel sees it as the source of those evil powers (in this section of Daniel the winged lion represents the Babylonians, the bear the Medes, the four-headed winged leopard the Persians, the dragon-like beast the Greeks, whose ten horns represent the ten rulers who succeded Alexander the Great) which will enslave the world before they make way for the kingdom of God: *And four great beasts came out up out of the sea, different from one another* (Daniel 7:4).

The agents of evil who dwell in the deep were sometimes given names such as Leviathan and Rahab and a few Old Testament writers loved to sing of the ease with which God controls such powerful adversaries. At the end of the Book of Job, the fertile imagination of the poet imagines God pointing out to Job that the human mind cannot probe the mystery of God. In a rather mocking tone, God points out that he can play with the demon of the deep as if they were little fish: *Can you draw out Leviathan with the fish-hook, or press down his tongue with a cord* (Job 41:1). Isaiah imagines the great escape from Egypt being brought about by God slaying the dragon of the deep:

Was it not thou that didst cut Rahab in pieces,
that didst pierce the dragon?
Was it not thou that didst dry up the sea,
the waters of the great deep;
that didst make the depths of the sea a way
for the redeemed to pass over? (Isaiah 51:9-10).

The same idea is found in the Psalms:

Thou dost rule the raging of the sea;
when its waves rise thou stillest them.
Thou didst crush Rahab like a carcass,
thou didst scatter thy enemies with thy mighty arm
(Psalm 89:8-10).

It is against this background that Mark constructs his telling of the Storm at Sea. For him the storm is as much a challenge to the power and authority of Jesus as that waged by Satan and his minions or the religious powers who ascribe the source of his power to Beelzebul.

Peaceful and untroubled sleep is a sign of confident trust in God's protective care:

I lie down and sleep;
I wake again,
for the Lord sustains me (Psalm 3:5).
In peace I will lie down and sleep;
for thou, O Lord, makest me dwell in safety (Psalm 4:8).

If the sleeping Jesus radiates confidence and trust in God, the same cannot be said for his disciples. The poets of Israel often spoke of the care God expends on those who go down to the sea in ships:

When you pass through the waters
I will be with you;
and through the rivers,
they shall not overwhelm you (Isaiah 43:2).

But there were times in the history of Israel when God was felt to be far distant and it seemed that he had abandoned his people. At such perilous moments, the religious imagination of the people pictured God as having fallen asleep and, in urgent prayers, they begged him to bestir himself on their behalf:

Awake, awake, put on strength,
O arm of the Lord;
awake, as in the days of old,
the generations long ago (Isaiah 51:9).

God is is invited to wake up, to shake off the pins and needles in his arms and come to the rescue as he did generations ago in the days of the Exodus from Egypt. When the psalm-writer contemplates the destruction visited on his people by the Babylonians in 587 B.C.E., he cries out,

Rise thyself!
Why sleepest thou, O Lord?
Awake!

Do not cast us off forever!
Why dost thou hide thy face?
Why dost thou forget our affliction and our oppression?
for our soul is bowed to the dust;
our body cleaves to the ground.
Rise up, come to our help! (Psalm 44:23-26).

Thus the religious tradition of the frightened disciples every-where encourages them to turn, as Jonah did, to *the Lord, the God of heaven, who made the sea and the dry land* (Jonah 1:9) But they do not do so. They turn to their teacher: *Teacher, do you not care if we perish?* Who is this teacher, this carpenter (6:3), whose help may be sought to save from the dangers of *a great storm of wind*? The question of the power of Jesus is the linchpin of the story.

As if in answer to the ancient cry of the psalm-writer, Jesus awoke and rebuked the wind, and said to the sea, *Peace! Be still. And the wind ceased, and there was a great calm.* The tale is nearly done. By his language, his choice of words, Mark directs our steps to the great storehouse of Israel's words so that we may find the key to what he is about. Consider carefully,

Some went down to the sea in ships,
doing business on the great waters;
they saw the deeds of the Lord,
his wondrous works in the deep.
For he commanded, and raised the stormy wind,
which lifted up the waves of the sea.
They mounted up to heaven,
they went down to the depths;
their courage melted away in their evil plight;
they reeled and staggered like drunken men,
and were at their wits end.
Then they cried to the LORD in their trouble,
and he delivered them from their distress;
he made the storm still,
and the waves of the sea were hushed (Psalm 107:23-29).

Clearly, Mark tells his story of the Stilling of the Storm in the style and even the very words of Psalm 107. But whereas the deliverer in the Psalm is the LORD, the deliverer in the Gospel is Jesus of Nazareth. Note, too, that Jesus does not pray to God for the storm to end. He creates the great calm by the authority of his own word. Who is this man?

And, notice, too, that Jesus *rebuked the wind*, just as he rebukes the demons (1:25; 9:25) and will rebuke Peter whose thoughts come from Satan and not from God (8:33). God's power over forces opposed to his rule of the world is revealed in the authoritative word of Jesus.

The mighty works which engage Mark's attention in this section are startling. But there is a dark side to their telling: *Why are you afraid? Have you no faith?* The disciples had seen the healing of the halt and the lame, they had seen demons cast out. Had they faith, the great storm of wind would hold no terrors for them for they were with Jesus (3:14). Throughout his Gospel, Mark highlights the constant failure of the disciples to understand Jesus and to put their trust in him, without hesitation and without conditions. Mark's picture of the disciples is deliberately dark for he wishes to encourage his bewildered Roman readers. The disciples have no faith but the disciples are saved. In the face of the storm of persecution and the betrayal and denial it provoked amongst frightened Christians, ought they not to take courage from the fact that faithless disciples are not abandoned? They are rescued.

And they feared with a great fear (a more accurate translation than *And they were filled with awe*). Fear of God in the Old Testament is a recognition of his power. It is an admission that God is God and we are not. Fear of the Lord is the beginning of wisdom (Proverbs 9:10) for it is a recognition that the author and sustainer of the world is God and his authority will not be gainsaid. Fear of the Lord is a recognition of the right order of things.

Acknowledgement of the power of Jesus raised the inevitable question, *Who then is this, that even the wind and the sea obey him?* This is not a question; it is *the* question. For the identity of the Jesus is the secret the Gospels seek to reveal. Of every Gospel story we must ask,"What does this story tell me about who Jesus is?" Notice how persuasive a teacher Mark is. Of course, he tells us directly the identity of Jesus (1:1), he allows the demons to reveal that identity and the centurion will make an unequivocal identification (15:39). But often he allows his stories to tell their own tale. We might call his little pamphlet a Gospel of Holy Nudges. He provides his readers with the material out of which

67

they may arrive at their own answer. He goes a long way with his readers but he asks them to go the extra mile.

Finally, if we perceive the power of God present in the activity of Jesus, does this not mean that the kingdom is coming in the works of the carpenter of Nazareth?

PRAYER

Psalm 118 is a mighty prayer of trust in God, of faith (so conspicuously lacking in the boat). In 14:26 we are told that Jesus and his disciples sang a hymn as they were about to set out for the Mount of Olives. Almost certainly they sang Psalm 118. What a song on the lips of the man from Galilee as he marches out to Gethsemane and to death!

The wild man of Gerasa
Mark 5:1-20

Jesus lived in dangerous times. His country and, indeed, most of the known world, was under the jackboot of Roman imperialism. There is a tendency to romanticise the Roman empire, to speak of Roman law as if it were an instrument of protection for the poor and the weak rather than a cynical manipulation of power for the benefit of the rich. We forget that the long straight roads led to Rome to facilitate the transport of slaves and plunder to sate the appetite of its indolent inhabitants. We pass over the sexual exploitation of slaves, particularly of children, especially trained to pander to the whims of degraded men and women.

Gnaeus Julius Agricola (40-93 C.E), Roman governor of Britain, on his way north to advance Roman rule to the Firth of Forth, was confronted in the northeast, by a local leader, Calgacus by name, who decided to make a stand. His speech to his men, before his inevitable defeat, is given to us by Tacitus, the son-in-law of Agricola but an honest historian. Here, in part, is the voice of the victim:

> Children and kin are by the law of nature each man's dearest possessions; they are swept away from us by conscription to be slaves in other lands; our wives, our sisters, even when they escape a soldier's lust, are debauched by self-styled friends and guests. Our goods and chattels go for tribute; our lands and harvest in requisition of grain....To plunder, butcher, steal, these things they misname empire; they create a desert and call it peace (Tacitus, *Agricola*, 30:3-31:2).

A voice from Gaul (France) weeps for his land, "crushed between the axes in everlasting slavery" (Julius Caesar, *Bellum Gallicum*, VII, 77). *The Fourth Book of Esdras,* a Jewish book, written shortly after the time of Jesus, likewise condemns the Roman oppressor and encourages the faithful to look to a future deliverance by God. The indictment against Rome is clear:

You have judged the earth but not with truth; for you have afflicted the meek and injured the peaceable; you have hated those who tell the truth, and have loved liars; you have destroyed the dwellings of those who brought forth fruit, and have laid low the walls of those who did you no harm (IV Esdras 11:37-46).

It is against this background of universal suffering and imperial aggression, that we must read the strange story of the Gerasene Demonic.

READING THROUGH

Gerasa/Decapolis
When the generals of Alexander the Great (d.323 B.C.E.) sought to carve up his empire, they built cities throughout the Near East to act as bastions of Greek culture and to provide fortified enclaves from which they could defend their conquered territories. Some of these were founded on more ancient cities (Scythopolis on Beth Shean, for example); some were new foundations. Not only did these cities provide oases of Greek culture in the East, they attracted Greek-speaking people whose loyalties were not to the ancient ways of the Orient but to the West.

When the Romans came, led by Pompey (106-48 B.C.E.), they realised that these cities, who welcomed the new conquerors, could provide a stabilising factor in the turbulent world of the East. On the one hand, they could provide ready-to-hand fortresses for defence against the indigenous peoples who resented foreign domination. On the other, they could continue to foster Greek and Roman ways and, in a word, "europeanise" the restless natives.

Such a region was the Decapolis. The word means 'ten cities'. Pompey recognised the independence of these cities, situated (with the exception of Scythopolis) to the east of the Jordan. While nominally under the control of the Roman governor of Syria, the cities enjoyed considerable independence, as long as their loyalty to Rome was absolute, they paid their taxes and undertook military service. It was customary for such cities (we might think of them as outposts of the empire) to band together for mutual defence and trade.

Mark mentions the region of the Decapolis twice (4:20; 7:31), seeming to indicate that it was, for the most part, on the eastern side of the Sea of Galilee. The problem arises with the city of Gerasa, which lay some thirty miles southeast of the lake in the mountainous region of Gilead. Early readers of Mark felt that this was rather far for the swine *to rush down the steep bank into the sea* and some manuscripts changed Mark's text to read Gadara, a mere six miles from the water's edge. But, perhaps, Mark meant no more than that Jesus went into a pagan region, beyond the Jordan, without the precision we might demand from a trained geographer. What is of concern is that Jesus met a man whose name was Legion.

Legion

A legion of the Roman army consisted of 6,000 foot soldiers, 120 horsemen and support units. The Latin word entered the languages of the Mediterranean world to describe a great number. Whether the word in Mark's text has it colloquial or technical meaning will concern us presently.

Swine

The Books of Leviticus (11:7) and Deuteronomy (14:8) forbid the people of Israel to eat pork. It is not at all clear why this should be so. The pig was the most common animal of sacrifice with many peoples of the East and it may very well be that ancient rules forbidding the consumption of swine's flesh may be an attempt to keep people away from the worship of false gods. The animals were regarded as unclean. When Luke wants to emphasise the total degradation to which the Prodigal Son has fallen, he presents him as a swineherd (Luke 15:15). That there was a herd of swine in the region indicates that it was, in the eyes of the writer, a godless place.

READING THROUGH AGAIN

The storm-tossed boat, saved by the power of Jesus, comes to the country of the Gerasenes. Mark is careful to note that only Jesus disembarks for the work to be done here is for him alone. If this gentile territory is to be rid of its demons, then the stronger one must enter into the house of the strong and bind him (3:27).

71

A man possessed emerges from a graveyard, to the ancient mind a place where malign spirits lurked. The insane man dwelt among the tombs and had defied all efforts to restrain him. He is presented to us as a madman beyond control, inflicting terror, we may be sure, for no one had the strength to bind him securely as he wandered naked among the places of the dead. Such was the depths of agony and despair to which the demons had brought this unfortunate man that he sought to inflict even more wounds by bruising himself with stones.

The man sees Jesus and, surprisingly, kneels before him. Though many had tried to bind this madman and failed, in the presence of Jesus he falls on his knees in worship. The question of the identity of Jesus is never far from the surface in Mark's story.

That demons have knowledge of the divine origins of Jesus we know from 1:24. The demons know, too, that the approach of Jesus bodes ill for satanic forces and they cry aloud to ward off what they know to be a hostile power. The phrase, *What have you to do with me?* occurs a number of times in the Old Testament and in the New (Joshua 22:24; Judges 11:12; 2 Samuel 16:10; 1 Kings 17:18; Mark 1:24; particularly interesting is John 2:4, where Jesus is addressing his mother). It may mean that there is no common ground, no common interest, between the two parties. It can also mean, "What have you against me?" and that would appear to be its meaning here. The demon addresses Jesus as *Son of the Most High,* that is to say, Son of God (look up Genesis 14:18; Numbers 24:16; Isaiah 14:14). The reader knows that the Son of God had come to destroy the forces of evil, that the stronger one is about to bind Satan and to plunder his goods. He cries out in vain for in the battle against evil no quarter is given, no prisoners taken. The frantic demon invokes God's protection: *I adjure you by God, do not torment me.* The irony is that it is the Son of God who stands in opposition to the minions of Satan: *Come out of the man, you unclean spirit.*

It is at this point that the story takes on a dimension which can only be appreciated by those sensitive to the fact that, as we have seen, in the Jewish religious imagination, after creation the world fell under the powers of evil. Consequently, human authorities, such as the brutal Roman empire which inflicted itself on Palestine, were but the pawns of demonic forces which sought to keep the whole of creation in bondage. Jesus asks the demon his name and the reply ought to startle: *my name is Legion; for we are many*. What are we to make of the fact that this demon gives as his name, the name of the basic unit of the oppressive Roman army? Is Mark suggesting that the power sustained by its legions is nothing more than a demonic force which is worthy only to live in filthy swine and to be destroyed in the sea? Could Mark's first readers come to this story and hear of an evil force named Legion who terrorises all who come near, and who cannot be restrained by any human effort, and who is ultimately overcome by the power Jesus possesses, leaving its victim clothed and in his right mind, and not think of the imperial power which had so recently caused so many of their number to die in the most horrendous circumstances? Did not many throughout the empire, from Calgacus in Britain to the Jewish voice of Esdras, wish that Romans and their brutal legions would be driven into the sea?

The ancient belief that if one knew a demon's name one had power over it lies behind Jesus' request. The demon acknowledges this by asking to be allowed to stay in the region. Again, according to popular belief, demons were thought to inhabit a particular locality and to be unwilling to move from there (certainly, the Roman legions were rather reluctant to move!). Recognising a superior power, the demons (now plural) are pleading for terms. But there will be no reprieve.

That the demons wish to go into the pigs is evidence of their base nature. But the unclean animals are not to be a haven for the demons but a means of returning them to the deep, returning them to divine control. Once again, they are placed in God's custody.

Much ink has been spilled on the fate of the pigs. The loss of two thousand swine is seen by some as an unnecessary waste of livestock. But Mark's point is that every creature which comes under the control of demons is bound to be destroyed, unless God has other plans. The emphasis in the story is on what happens to possessed humanity when Jesus comes on the scene. The people flock to the place when the herdsmen report the matter. There they see the effect of the ministry of Jesus. The wild man is sitting quietly; the naked madman is clothed; the possessed lunatic is in his right mind. The effect on the pagan crowd is fear in the presence of such power and they ask Jesus to leave. This he will do but not before he appoints for them an apostle of the gospel. The healed man requests that he be allowed to remain with Jesus (compare the definition of discipleship at 3:14 - to be with him and to be sent out to preach). The man is sent to his own people (not just his family) to tell them what the Lord has done for him. The disciple is empowered by the Master to undertake the preaching of good news.

Have you noticed the gentle nudge that Mark has given? Jesus tells the man to go and tell what the Lord has done. The Lord is, of course, God. But the man goes to his countrymen with a report of how much Jesus had done for him. On one level, it is God who is acting, on another, it is Jesus. Who, then, is Jesus?

Another tiny detail. Notice that the people first feared (verse 150 and then marvelled (verse 20). Fear and amazement are concomitants of discipleship in Mark. We have seen the element of fear in the story of the Storm at Sea and of amazement at 1:27 and 2:12. We shall meet them again and we shall wonder why the Gospel of Mark ends with women running from the tomb in fear and amazement (16:8).

PRAYER

There is a delightful prayer in 1 Chronicles 16:8-36. King David had commanded the Ark of the Covenant (the tabernacle where God was most intimately with his people) to be brought to Jerusalem. He instructs Asaph and his brothers to sing songs of thanksgiving. The prayer opens thus:

O give thanks to the Lord, call on his name, make known his deeds among the peoples! Sing to him, sing praises to him, tell of all his wonderful works.

This is a good prayer for the former wild man of Gerasa. It is a good prayer for any one who seeks to tell what the Lord has done.

A man and a woman of faith
Mark 5:21-43

Four astounding miracles are clustered together, not haphazardly but, rather, to highlight Mark's understanding of who Jesus is and to explain the nature of his task. First, the power of God, at work in Jesus, is called to overcome the demons of the storm as they endeavour to destroy the little community of Jesus: *Teacher! do you not care if we perish?* (4:38). The demons are condemned to the deep and *there was a great calm* (4:39). Can such serene calm come to the world of the Gentiles, for it, too, is infested with satanic forces of evil and instruments of demonic power (the Roman legions, for example)? God's gift of himself in Jesus is not to be limited to the needs of one people. As Alice said, everyone wins, everyone gets a prize: *And they came to Jesus, and saw the demoniac sitting there, clothed and in his right mind, the man who had had the legion* (5:15).

The two demon miracles dramatically illustrate God's intention to free the world from what is evil. As a consequence, the chiefest of human ills, sickness and death, will be robbed of their sting. That is what Mark implies by his strategic arrangement of these four astonishing stories: if demons are impounded, if their power is overcome, then, to be sure, their capacity to wreak havoc on humanity is being brought to an end by the stronger one who has entered the strong man's house and bound him (3:27). The woman with the flow of blood and the daughter of Jairus point to God's intention. Sickness, even death, shall not have the last say concerning human destiny.

READING THROUGH

Ruler of the synagogue

Jairus belonged to a class sufficiently respected to be entrusted with the upkeep of the local synagogue, the religious meeting-house of the community. As leader, he would have had responsibility for the fabric of the building and for the arrangement of the services. Sometimes an honorary title of synagogue ruler was conferred on such a local dignitary. The meaning of the man's name, "he who enlightens", does not appear to have any bearing on the story

A flow of blood

Leviticus 12:7 commands that a woman offer a sacrifice after bearing a child; only then *shall she be clean from the flow of her blood*. While we have no specific information on what this unfortunate woman had been suffering, it would appear to have been a severe case of (intermittent?) haemorrhaging, whether from the womb or elsewhere, it is impossible to say. But we can say that the woman's plight was doubly unfortunate. Not only had she suffered many things but she was in a constant state of uncleanness, that is, to the ancient's way of thinking, unacceptable to God. The words of Leviticus are as clear as they are callous:

> If a woman has a discharge of blood for many days, not at the time of her impurity, or if she has a discharge beyond the time of her impurity, all the days of the discharge she shall continue in uncleanness; as in the days of her impurity, she shall be unclean. Every bed on which she lies ... everything on which she sits shall be unclean ... And whoever touches these things shall be unclean... (Leviticus 15:25-27).

Not only was the woman a victim of useless doctors, she would have been shunned by friends and neighbours since even the slightest touch would render them unclean. Touching is going to play a role in this story.

READING THROUGH AGAIN

The two stories provide us with an excellent example of a Marcan sandwich. First, we have the approach of Jairus, then the healing of the woman and, finally, the raising of the girl. As we shall see, the arrangement of the stories of the healing of the woman and the restoration of life to the girl, present Jesus not only as the giver of life but as the giver of eternal life.

Jairus' request

For the second time Jesus crosses the lake and comes to then western side. In a summary sentence, Mark suggests that the gathering of the crowds about him was typical of the reception accorded him. We must assume Jesus rejoined his disciples.

Jairus' approach to Jesus is reverent and, indeed, prayerful. Mark's readers will not have missed the point that, though the great ones were often opposed to Jesus, when no other hope remained, at least one of them turned to Jesus and publicly knelt before him to make a request.

The man reveals that his daughter is on the point of death and he begs that Jesus come and lay hands upon her. There are other references to laying on of hands in Mark: 6:5; 7:32; 8:23; 8:25. The Old Testament has no example of the laying on of hands for purposes of healing and, with one exception, Jewish literature is also silent in this regard. But one text from the Qumran documents envisages the Pharaoh begging Abraham "to pray for the king (that is, himself) and to lay hands upon him that he might live". What would appear to have been the usual practice of Jesus became and remains the practice of the Church (in this regard, see 6:13 and James 5:14).

The man's request will have rung bells in the minds of Mark's readers. He begs that Jesus lay hands on his child in order that she might be *made well and live*. While no one can quibble with the translation of the Greek words used here by Mark, the reader should be aware that, elsewhere in his Gospel, he uses these same words to mean "to be saved" and "to have (eternal) life". Some examples:

> Peter began to say to him, "Then who can be saved?" (10:26).
> But he who endures to the end will be saved (13:13).
> And if the Lord had not shortened, no human being would be saved (13:20).
> He is not God of the dead, but of the living (12:27).

The fact of the matter is that early Christians used these two verbs (*to make well* and *to live*) in their ordinary sense of getting well and being alive. But they also used them to suggest being saved in the religious sense and possessing eternal life. Gospel-makers made use of this double sense to indicate that, when Jesus made someone well, he was offering the gift of salvation and eternal well-being. We shall return to this matter.

Jesus responds instantly and, with a great crowd, sets off for Jairus' house. The jostling throng sets the scene for the account of the woman who touches Jesus in order that she might be made well.

A woman's touch

The full span of life of the daughter of Jairus was twelve years and for all those years the woman had a chronic haemorrhaging which ruined her life and condemned her as unclean. That this is a hopeless case can be deduced from the extended description which Mark gives of her plight. She had attended many physicians, had spent all her money on them and was the worse for their endeavours (compare Luke 8:43 – is Luke the physician being easy on his own profession?). What we have is a dreadful case of chronic illness, beyond the wit of medical care. What we have is a woman whose illness puts her beyond the pale of God's concern. Or does it? The woman has no hesitation. She had heard the things concerning Jesus and, in the press of the crowd, she touched his clothes, for she said, *"If I touch even his garments, I shall be made well"*. We might just as correctly read, "I shall be saved". Mark delights in such instructive puns.

Touching is an amazingly common feature of Mark's Gospel. Sometimes Jesus stretches out to touch people; on other occasions, he takes them by the hand. Here is a list well worth the trouble of looking up: 1:31; 1:41; 3:10; 5:27; 5:28; 5:30; 5:31; 6:5; 6:56; 7:32; 7:33; 8:22; 8:23; 9:27; 10:13; 10:16. What is amazing is that by touching the sick Jesus is taking on their status, that is, he becomes unclean. Or, rather, he abolishes the whole demeaning business of human uncleanness. He refuses to accept that human misery and the human processes of begetting and child-bearing, of being ill and dying, put one outside God's concern. Of course, we understand that ancient taboos concerning what was or was not clean sprang from fear and from a genuine concern to behave as the gods appeared to demand. What Jesus is saying so eloquently in his hands outstretched to touch and caress is that humanity's ailments do not incur divine anger; rather they incite divine pity.

It is, perhaps, supremely ironic that this desolate woman should reach out to touch Jesus. She stands in contrast to the mob at Gethsemane who likewise touched Jesus: *they laid their hands on him and seized him* (14:46).

When Jesus touched the leper (1:41), *immediately the leprosy left him, and he was made clean.* So with the woman: *And immediately the haemorrhage ceased; and she felt in her body that she was healed of her disease.* It is not the humility of the woman that excites admiration. It is her audacity. Here is an unclean woman in the midst of a crowd. What gives her courage is that she had heard the things concerning Jesus and that is enough to create an unflinching faith: *If I touch ... I shall be made well.* What she had heard enables her to reach beyond the system of legal purity and its restrictive, dehumanising and demoralising social code. It is this sublime faith that Jairus is going to need if he is to have his heart's desire. It is clear why Mark has sandwiched the stories of this man and woman together. Both are stories of faith.

The power which had gone forth from Jesus is the power everywhere evidenced in Mark's story (see 6:2; 6:14; 9:1; 13:26). It is none other than that power spoken of in 12:24 and identified in 14:62. It is the power of God, manifest in the life and work of Jesus of Nazareth.

Notice that the question Jesus asks is, *Who touched my garments?* The disciples, in their reply, make an interesting alteration: *Who touched me?* We must not think that it is the clothing of Jesus which is the source of healing power, as if we were dealing with some superstitious belief in relics. What is in question is the personal healing power of Jesus. Nor, too, must we misunderstand the exasperated comments of the disciples. For they speak the question of the crowd (and, indeed, that of Mark's readers). The impatient outburst of the disciples serves in the story to bring to light that which must not be concealed. As Jesus told them, *there is nothing hid, except to be made manifest; nor is anything secret, except to come to light* (4:22).

Knowing what had been done to her! The phrase reminds one of the divine passive, so common in Greek translation of the Hebrew scriptures. When one wanted to say, "God did X", to avoid using the Holy Name, one could say, "X was done". The fear and trembling which overcome the woman may well be due to the fact that she realises that what has happened to her, through her faith in Jesus, is beyond human capacity. One recalls the statement of Jesus: *With men it is impossible, but not with God; for all things are possible with God* (10:27). Also, fear and trembling, in Mark's perspective, seem to be part and parcel of discipleship (this aspect of discipleship will be explored fully when we come to consider 10:32).

The woman kneels before him (as did Jairus – will his prayer be answered?) and tells the whole truth. The response of Jesus continues but clarifies the ambiguity running through the story concerning being "made well". He addresses the woman as *Daughter*, that is to say, in the estimation of Jesus, she is truly a daughter of Abraham (see Luke 13:16) and may not be excluded from God's promises to her father Abraham and his descendants on the grounds of illness and its concomitant uncleanness. For, like her father Abraham, this is a woman of faith and it is her faith that has, at once, made her well and saved her.

The word "peace" (*shalom*) occurs everywhere in the Bible. It is its greatest word, signifying every blessing, wholeness, good health, prosperity, well-being. To have peace is to live in the heart of God. All the more surprising, then, to realise that Mark uses the word but once. It is on this woman of faith, and on no other, that Jesus confers the blessing of peace.

Later tradition has added to the story of this faithful woman. Among Greek-speaking Christians she became known as Berenice and was said to have been a native of Caesarea Philippi (8:27). A Church historian, Eusebius (?265 -?340 C.E.), bishop of the other Caesarea reports that there was a bronze state outside her house, depicting a kneeling woman with her hands outstretched towards the figure of a man, whose hands are extended to the woman. The Latin name for Berenice is Veronica.

A daughter restored

The story of the healing of the woman with the flow of blood will be our guide through the story of Jairus and his daughter. The seriousness of the woman's plight was such that no human remedy was of any avail. Only faith and the presence of divine power in the person of Jesus could transform the unclean outcast into the peace-filled daughter. What awaits the girl, now reported to be dead?

Jesus is not deterred by death. Jairus, who came to Jesus in faith, is urged to continue in faith, as the woman did in spite of the severity of her situation and the press of the crowds. For the woman had heard the things concerning Jesus and pressed on, even to the extent of involving Jesus in her own unclean condition. The fact that Jesus takes with him Peter, James and John is instructive. Elsewhere, these are the three disciples chosen to be present at the Transfiguration (9:2), itself a foretaste of the resurrection. They are present again in Gethsemane (14:33) on the eve of the death of Jesus. By their presence in Jairus' house they confer on the story overtones of the death of Jesus and intimations of his resurrection. They are present, too, on the Mount of Olives, when Jesus reveals to them and to all would-be disciples the final and victorious destiny of those whose faith endures and survives the terror of persecution (13:3f). The raising of Jairus' daughter is a model, as it were, of what is in store for all whose faith is in the risen Jesus who will come again.

By the time of Jesus' arrival, the mourners were assembled. Even the poorest were obliged by custom to hire professional keeners who, to the accompaniment of flute players, danced and wailed with increasing fervour: he saw a tumult, and people weeping and wailing loudly. Jesus does not share their grief nor does he join in their lamentation. Contrary to the message of those who came from the ruler's house, contrary to the tumult assembled to wail and to weep, contrary, one might imagine, to the desolation of the girl's parents he asserts that she is not dead but sleeping. At first sight, the statement of Jesus may mean no more than that he has a greater insight into the true state of the girl's condition than others; he may be suggesting that she is deeply unconscious but not yet enveloped in the shroud of death. But such a suggestion fails on two counts. First, *they laughed at him*. To those who had arrived after the announcement of death, after the mourners had assembled and begun their dismal chants, such a statement is worthy only of derisory laughter. After all, as yet Jesus has not laid eyes on the girl. Secondly, and this is more to the point, in both Old and New Testament death is spoken of as being asleep:

> And many of those who sleep in the dust of the earth shall awake, some to everlasting life, and some to shame and everlasting contempt (Daniel 12:2).

> Awake, O sleeper, and rise from the dead, and Christ shall give you light (Ephesians 5:14).

> For God has not destined us for wrath, but to obtain salvation through our Lord Jesus Christ, who died for us so that whether we wake (= are alive) or sleep (= are dead) we might live with him (Thessalonians 5:9-10).

81

In the New Testament, in order to encourage and sustain faith in the general resurrection of all, Christians spoke of those who died as having fallen asleep, that is to say, such people were truly dead but they were not prisoners of death. One day they would be with the risen Lord and share in his resurrection. It is, believed early Christians, resurrection and not death which has the final say.

Thus, with a certain amount of force (that is what the verb implies), Jesus put the faithless ones outside (outside! 3:31 and 32). Taking the father and mother and the three disciples to where the child was laid out, he took her by the hand (touching, again) and said to her, *Talitha cumi*. Mark preserves the original Aramaic words of Jesus, probably because they were in the story as he heard it. Christian tradition remembered some words of Jesus in his native tongue, usually words of particular significance (see 3:17; 7:11; 7:34; 11:9-10; 14:36; 15:22; 15:34).

Do not miss the significance of the command and its effect. Jesus uses the same word elsewhere associated with his own resurrection: *arise!* (14:28; the word is also used about John the Baptist being raised – 6:14; 6:16 – and about all the dead being raised – 12:26). The recovery of the girl is likewise described in a resurrection word: *she got up* (look up 8:31; 9:9; 9:10; 9:27; 9:31; 10:34; 12:23). The young woman (at twelve she would be regarded as "a young daughter" and at twelve and a half as "an adult"), to the utter amazement of all, arose and began to walk about and to be in need of food (details added to provide conclusive proof that we are not dealing with an illusion or a ghost and, perhaps, also to suggest baptism into the death of Jesus and its consequent Eucharist). The command to keep the matter hidden seems destined to be in vain but may also, as we shall see, have something to do with baptism.

Mark is inviting his frightened readers in Rome to see themselves as daughters of Jairus. Though all public opinion declared the girl dead, Jesus knew that death did not have the last say. The power of Jesus to restore the girl to her parents illustrates the power that is at hand ultimately to protect and bring to heavenly rest those who have suffered and continue to suffer from the demonic persecutions of a brutal empire. Nero will not have the last say. The power of the demons has been broken. It is the kingdom of God which is coming. After the teaching on the kingdom which preoccupied us in chapter four, we have four miracle stories which dramatise the ultimate effects of God's authoritative rule in creation. But this rule is exercised by Jesus of Nazareth. Who is this man?

PRAYER

The faith of the woman and the man is what carries through. Against all the odds, they believed. Psalm 119 is about someone struggling to come to and maintain faith in God. The final verses (161-176) of the Bible's longest psalm would have been a suitable prayer for the outcast woman and the distraught father. A good prayer for all whose cry is *Let me live*.

The mission of the Twelve
Mark 6:1-13

Storm clouds, as we have already observed, are never far from Mark's perspective. Black shadows, albeit lightened by the occasional burst of sunshine, cast their gloom over his pages. As we come to the end of scene two of the first act of Mark's story, we see both darkness and light, the one warning of future storm, the other of future success. What happens in the story is a pattern for all attempts to follow Jesus. For what befalls Jesus and his little band of disciples in Galilee and Jerusalem will befall all disciples even to the close of the age (Matthew 28:20). The stark lesson for Mark's persecuted brothers and sisters in Rome is that the fate of Jesus is the fate of all his disciples but that the one who endures to the end will be saved (13:13).

Careful readers will notice that 6:1-29 is a Marcan sandwich. The rejection of Jesus in his own town and by his own people and the passion of John the Baptist enfold the optimism of the mission of the twelve to preach repentance and to anoint with oil and heal the sick. The twelve are sent to serve their apprenticeship to the task that will be theirs after the death of Jesus. But Mark so places this preparatory and provisional mission of the twelve between the spurning of Jesus at Nazareth and the execution of John at the court of Herod Antipas that his readers will know that discipleship and evangelisation, in Mark's view, will always be lived between the possibility of rejection and the threat of death. Success there will be but it will be won in the eye of the storm.

Rejection at Nazareth

The rejection of Jesus at Nazareth is scarcely surprising since we have already encountered the attitude of his immediate family to his preaching and healing activity. If his family were of the opinion that he was beside himself (3:21), what are his neighbours to think? However, it is not the mere fact of rejection which concerns Mark. As ever, he is concerned with who Jesus is. When we reach the end of the Gospel, we shall see

Jesus rejected and done to death. There, too, the identity question will be to the fore (Mark 14:61, for example). As an anticipation of that rejection, the Nazareth incident will repay close attention.

READING THROUGH

There are a number of details which lie both on and beneath the surface of Mark's narrative which require attention. Thorough explanation of each of these is not possible for we do not have all the evidence we would require for certainty and we must be content with conjecture.

His own country

Luke seems to have understood that the family of Jesus, certainly, Joseph and Mary, came from Nazareth (Luke 1:26) and that his parents (Luke 2:41) went from there to Bethlehem, where the child was born. On the other hand, Matthew gives the impression, not only that Jesus was born in Bethlehem (Matthew 2:1), but that Bethlehem was the home of his family and that from there Mary and Joseph were forced to flee to Egypt. When the political situation had changed (Matthew 2:19), *Joseph took the child and his mother, and went to the land of Israel* (Matthew 2:21) but not to their home in Bethlehem. Rather, he went north, and dwelt in the city called Nazareth (Matthew 2:23). Neither Mark (1:9, 24) nor John (*Can anything good come out of Nazareth? –* 1:46) concern themselves with the matter though both speak of Jesus as the man from Nazareth. However, there would be nothing unusual in describing Jesus in terms of the village in which he grew up, even if he were not born there. This does not, however, undo the contradiction between Matthew and Luke.

Nazareth

The little village of Nazareth (not a city, as both Matthew and Luke would have it) is not mentioned in the Old Testament and it was a place of little significance. In the Book of Joshua (19:10-15), a list of the towns of the tribe of Zebulon is given but there is no mention of Nazareth. Josephus, who was responsible for military operations in the area at the outbreak of the Jewish War, gives the names of forty-five towns in Galilee, but does not say anything about Nazareth. The Talmud refers to sixty-three Galilean towns but makes no reference to Nazareth. Thus, Jewish sources, covering almost one thousand years, make no mention of Nazareth. But its proximity to the city of Sepphoris may throw some light on the early years of Jesus of Nazareth.

Herod the Great died in 4 B.C.E. and his three sons set off for Rome to beg Emperor Augustus to confirm their father's wishes and allow them to rule in the areas assigned to them by his will. While they were away, rebellion broke out in several parts of Palestine and the centre of the revolt in Galilee was the important city of Sepphoris. The city lay midway between the Sea of Galilee and the Mediterranean (the village of Nazareth was six kilometres to the southeast). The Roman governor of the area, a man called Varus, soon had matters in hand and he burned the city, selling its inhabitants into slavery.

When Herod Antipas returned from Rome to take up his inheritance, the provinces of Galilee and Perea, he decided to rebuild Sepphoris and to nominate it as his capital. Work began in 2 B.C.E. and finished about ten years later. One of his most impressive buildings was a theatre which seated up to 5,000 people. We know that the word *tekton* which is usually translated as "carpenter" may refer to a worker in metal or in stone (see below). During the growing days of Jesus, only a few miles away, was a huge building programme. Is it not likely that the boy from Nazareth did not grow up in the quiet of Joseph's workshop but rather on the bustling building site of Sepphoris? Some corroboration of this suggestion may be found in 7:6. Sepphoris had a large and fairly prosperous Jewish population.

Son of Mary

This is the only occasion that Mary, the mother of Jesus, is mentioned by name in Mark's Gospel (she is never mentioned by name in St John). It was contrary to Jewish custom to refer to a man as the son of his mother, even when she was a widow, unless an insult were intended (see 1 Samuel 26:6 and 2 Samuel 23:18 for apparent exceptions). That there were rumours that Jesus was illegitimate circulating in his own lifetime may be deduced from John 8:41 and 9:29. Whether Mark wishes to make the same reference here can only be a guess. To conclude that he is making a subtle reference to the virgin conception is to press the matter beyond all reasonableness.

rothers and sisters

We have had occasion to discuss the vexed question of the brothers and sisters of Jesus when we examined 3:31-35. The fact that Mark chooses to name the brothers here does not shed much light on the issue. However, we might note, for what it is worth, that James, the brother of the Lord (Galatians 1:19), is mentioned elsewhere in the New Testament and would appear to have played a significant role in the affairs of the christian community in Jerusalem in its earliest days (Acts 12:17; 15:13; 21:18; 1 Corinthians 15:7; Galatians 2:9,12). We might further note that when Josephus mentions this man he refers to him as the broher of Jesus. Whether the writer of the Letter of James is to be identified with James the brother of the Lord is open to question. Of the other brothers and of the nameless sisters we know nothing.

READING THROUGH AGAIN

The challenge to the people of his own town and place is the same as to others. They have heard the teaching and seen the mighty works. As in the very first visit to a synagogue (1:21-28), the teaching of Jesus elicits astonishment (a good sign in Mark) and leads to the right questions about Jesus (another hopeful sign; Mark everywhere seeks to provoke questions about Jesus: 1:27; 2:16; 2:24; 3:41; 8:27; 8:29; 9:28; 10:18; 11:28; 14:4; 14:61; 15:2; 15:9; 15:12; 15:34; 16:3). Indeed, the questions of the people of Nazareth are fundamental to Mark's presentation of the identity of Jesus: from where does the authority of Jesus come? What is the wisdom (= power) given to him? Readers will know the answers for Mark has revealed the secret on the very first page: *Thou art my beloved Son; with thee I am well pleased* (1:11). The citizens of Nazareth have asked the right questions but, because of their lack of faith, they do not come to the right answer. They are concerned with old wine and old wineskins (2:22) and their assessment of Jesus is limited by their narrowness. They know who Jesus is. He is the *tekton*. Conditioned as many are by the pieties of countless hymns and devotions that the

Greek word ought to be translated as "carpenter", a lowly social status in the days of Jesus, we should realise that the word has a wide range of meanings. It embraces anyone from a shipbuilder to a sculptor and always implies one of considerable skill. It may even be used of a physician. However, it is not the precise social standing of Jesus that is in question here. It is the unwillingness of the synagogue people, having heard and seen, to go beyond what they know and come to a knowledge of the truth (1 Timothy 2:4).

The son of Mary! The tone is disparaging, even insulting and many subsequent writers, Matthew (13:55) and Luke (4:22) among them, alter or omit the phrase. But, again, whether Mark intends his readers to see an insult in the words is not to the point. There is no insult in the obvious statement of the villagers that they know *James, Joses, Judas, Simon and the sisters (who are here with us)*. The point is that they are unwilling to go beyond what they know; they are unwilling to be led by the words and the mighty works of Jesus to discover his true identity. As ever, the question is *Who is this man?*

They took offence at him. The verb used here in time yielded our word "scandal" which means a stumbling block or a snare, something which trips a person up. Amongst early Christians the word was something of a technical term (see, for example, Romans 9:32; 1 Corinthians 1:23; 1 Corinthians 8:13; 2 Corinthians 11:29; Galatians 5:11; 1 Peter 2:8) for those who, on being confronted with the message of the gospel, found something in it (the lowly status of Jesus; his death by crucifixion; the resurrection or whatever) which prevented them from embracing Christian faith and discipleship.

One of the more acute problems for many of the first Christians was the anomaly that (some) pagan gentiles believed in the good news preached to them, while Jewish people, nurtured on the scriptures and having had Jesus among them in the land of Israel, yet, for the most part, rejected him. How can a Jew be the Messiah when the Jews themselves laugh at the very idea? The sentence of Jesus spoken to his village neighbours must have echoed throughout Christian preaching: *a prophet is not without honour in his own country, and among his own kin, and in his own house* (see John 4:44). The saying was, in one form or another, widely current in the ancient world. But notice the depressing finality of the verdict in Mark's version: his own *patria* (fatherland), among his own kinsfolk and even among his own family: The sadness of Jesus is palpable: *And he marvelled at their unbelief.*

It is not a question that Jesus cannot do a mighty work in faithless Nazareth, as if he were paralysed by its unbelief. Faith does not cause Jesus to act. Rather, the gift which Jesus brings to humanity can only be embraced by a faith which recognises its source in God. Jesus is not a magician. He is the Son to whom we must listen (9:7). What happened in Nazareth at the close of Jesus' mission in Galilee will happen at the end in Jerusalem. Failure to understand who Jesus is, is a failure to understand the God whose beloved Son he is. That a few were healed softens the impact of a depressing episode. One is reminded of the women *looking on from afar* (15:40). All is not lost.

The mission of the Twelve

In between the rejection at Nazareth and the tragic story of the murder of John the Baptist, Mark provides a ray of hope and a warning. Yes, the twelve will be successful. No, the success will not be achieved without sacrifice. The cross is part and parcel of discipleship. To those who may be inclined to think that there is such a thing as cheap grace, that the world may be brought to God by singing hymns and arias, Mark presents a rejected Jesus and the head of John the Baptist.

READING THROUGH

Just two points need detain us. The first, on the question of "the twelve", is a matter of endless speculation and conclusions will have to be tentative. The second, happily, is not a matter of dispute.

The Twelve

The twelve are mentioned eleven times in Mark's Gospel and disciples forty-six times. Are the twelve distinct from the disciples, that is, a separate group, to be distinguished from the much larger group, called disciples, which adhered to Jesus? Or are the twelve indistinguishable from other disciples, so that what may be said of the one may be said of the other? To put the matter bluntly, does Jesus intend that the twelve, and only

89

the twelve, are recipients of his teaching and are to be sent out to preach?

First, Mark calls the twelve who are sent out on the preparatory mission "apostles" (6:30), that is, "people who are sent out" (see Daniel 6:16-27), but that is the only time he uses the word. Clearly, the word was not of great interest to him. But Mark is interested in missionary activity, in preaching the gospel and, consequently, in narrating occasions when Jesus empowers people to engage in such activity. For example, the man of Gerasa is instructed to go to his friends and report what God has done for him (in stark contrast to the silence imposed on other people who are healed). Again, when John, son of Zebedee, reports, *Teacher, we saw a man casting out demons in your name, and we forbade him, because he was not following us*, Jesus pointed out that the man was to be commended and would, indeed, be finally rewarded (9:38-41).

Secondly, we should note that Mark sometimes merges the twelve with others (4:11; 10:32), he does not always differentiate between the twelve and other disciples (6:35-44; 7:17; 9:28; 10:10), and he sometimes attributes activity associated with the twelve and the disciples with people who belong to neither group (1:45; 2:15; 5:20; 7:37; 9:38-41; 14:1-9). All in all, it would seem that the twelve, in Mark, are not to be distinguished sharply from other disciples, or, indeed, from others who are engaged in furthering the gospel. What is said of the twelve may be said of all disciples and would-be disciples.

Anointed with oil

The medicinal use of oil as an emollient was familiar to the peoples of the ancient world. Isaiah speaks of God's people as afflicted with bruises and sores and bleeding wounds, which are not bound up or softened with oil (Isaiah 1:6). In the Parable of the Good Samaritan, the hero went to the unfortunate victim and bound up his wounds, pouring on oil and wine (Luke 10:34) and the Letter of James records that the elders of the church prayed over the sick, anointing them with oil in the name of the Lord (James 5:14). We can surmise that the practice of the use of oil as an accompaniment to miraculous healing goes back, not only to the instruction of Jesus to the disciples, but to the practice of the Lord himself. As the Letter of James indicates, the practice entered into the healing ministry of the Church.

There can be little doubt that Mark intended the incident of the sending out of the twelve as a model of all subsequent missionary activity. The twelve initially had been appointed to be with him and to be sent out to preach and have authority to cast out demons (3:14-15). An expeditionary mission in Galilee now takes place and it is its very peculiarities that raise it from the status of a one-off event to the model of all missionary excursions.

The authority over unclean spirits which Jesus gives to the twelve must be seen in the light of the career of Jesus as outlined so far in Mark's story. The very first of the mighty works was the casting out of a demon, a work which inspired people to speak of the authority of Jesus (1:21-28). The overcoming of demoniac power enables the healing ministry to get underway and the explanation for the sequence of events is provided (3:27). Once the strong man is overcome, the stronger one may plunder his goods. Therefore, in giving the twelve (his) authority over unclean spirits, Jesus is conferring on them all authority to plunder the strong man's goods, that is, to invite people to repentance, to invite them to shelter under the protective wing of God. That this power may be exercised only in the context of missionary activity carried on in the absence of Jesus is clear from the fact that at 9:18 the disciples are unable to cast out an evil spirit. More on this below.

The twelve were sent out two by two, a practice among itinerant preachers and their disciples and among collectors of alms who went from Palestine to importune richer Jewish communities abroad.

The instructions given to the twelve would not have helped St Paul in his great missionary journeys. They are so impractical! But what Mark's text exudes is not practicality but hyperbole, exaggeration. The twelve are instructed to take nothing for their journey except a staff; no bread, no bag, no money in their belts. A staff would provide protection and facilitate walking. But to go without bread, without a bag (the Greek word suggests a begging bag), or even the "small change" usually carried in one's belt, would hardly do for Paul, doing long tramps over mountain ranges, and *in danger from rivers, danger from robbers, danger from my own people, danger from Gentiles, danger in the city, danger in the wilderness, danger at sea* (2 Corinthians 11:26).

Sandals are permitted but only one tunic. The preachers are not to move around from (poor?) house to (richer?) house, once a mission base is established. And where a welcome is not forthcoming, they are to leave a sign which may, in God's goodtime, bring about a change of heart. For the shaking off of the dust is not to be taken as a curse but rather as a dramatic gesture to encourage the unreceptive to reconsider (the RSV translates *as a testimony against them;* it would be better to translate *as a witness for them*).

What Mark is about here in his marching orders for missioners is dramatically to convey the urgency of the mission. No detail must interfere with the all-important task in hand. The writer of the Gospel was of the opinion that the world would soon come to an end. Thus all human considerations were to be subservient to preaching the word. When Elisha wished to restore life to the Shunammite boy, he despatched his servant in haste. His marching orders to Gehazi will repay attention (2 Kings 4:29). Sometimes speed is of the essence.

The concluding verse announcing the success of the mission has the flavour of a summary statement. It is as if Mark were saying that, not only were the twelve successful, but all such endeavours, undertaken within the writ of the Lord, will meet with the same conclusion.

Once we detect the oddities, not to say the absurdities, of Mark's marching orders, we realise that he is in the business of exaggeration in order to bring home the urgency of implementing the programme of Jesus, whether in the days of Jesus in Galilee or in the turmoil of Nero's Rome. The gospel cannot be preached without personal sacrifice, the extent of that sacrifice all too visible in the rejection of Jesus in Nazareth and in Jerusalem and in the sorry fate of the one who first preached the coming of the Messiah, John the Baptist.

PRAYER

Two verses from the Book of Daniel make a fitting prayer of praise for the works that God has done in Jesus and a fitting response to those who cannot see:

92

For he is the living God,enduring for ever;
his kingdom shall never be destroyed,
and his dominion shall be to the end.
He delivers and rescues,
he works signs and wonders
in heaven and on earth (Daniel 6:26-27).

The passion of John the Baptist
Mark 6:14-29

We shall have to embark on a little history. The story of the death and burial of John the Baptist has carved itself on the imagination of poet and peasant alike. Who has not heard of Salome and the Dance of the Seven Veils? Who has not heard of her chilling request: *the head of John the Baptist*? Yet, familiar though it be, this cruel and vindictive story, as it comes to us in the Gospels of Matthew (14:1-12) and Mark, bristles with difficulties and imponderables. A journey down the byways of history will not solve every problem but we shall be the better for it.

Josephus

Joseph ben Matthais (?37-?100 C.E.) or, to give him the Latin name by which he is known to history, Flavius Josephus, was, by religious bent, a Pharisee and, by destiny, an historian. A priest of Jerusalem and well-to-do, he was born in the year Caligula became emperor and, conveniently, we may divide his life into two. His first thirty-three years were spent in Palestine as a priest, general and prisoner of war. The Jewish rebellion against Rome broke out in 66 C.E. and that is the watershed in Josephus' career for, though he had long opposed hostilities against the imperial power, as a man of public affairs, he was caught up in the turmoil of events and found himself, whether by choice or force of circumstance, commander of the insurgents in Galilee. When the army of Vespasian advanced from Antioch in the spring of 67 C.E., Josephus retreated to the town of Jotapata (not far from Cana) and endured there forty-seven days of siege. When he was captured and brought before Vespasian, he predicted that his captor would become emperor and, in short, threw in his lot with Rome. He spent the remainder of the war as an adviser to the army and, truth to tell, tried to avert the worst excesses of both sides. When Jerusalem fell, he accompanied Vespasian's son, Titus, to Rome, to begin the second phase of his career, namely, the chronicler of the Jewish wars and the apologist for Jewish history and its religious traditions. He attempted to put a good gloss on things, especially on matters to do with his own career and was, on more than one occasion, economical with the truth, but there is little doubt that, in the main, and reading between the lines, he brings us close to the events of his tumultuous times. Josephus may be said to have been a traitor, a hated deserter of his countrymen, but he saw the futility of war against overwhelming odds and sought to limit the catastrophe when it was visited upon his people. Life at home was as chaotic as that in the public domain; he was married at least three times, divorced by one wife, deserted by another.

Josephus and the Baptist

Josephus narrates the events which surrounded the death of John the Baptist in his book *Jewish Antiquities*. Herod Antipas, the political ruler of both John and Jesus, was married to the daughter of King Aretas IV of Nabatea, which bordered on Perea. On one occasion, as he journeyed to Rome, he stayed with his half-brother, also called Herod, and fell in love with his wife, Herodias, who, as it happened, was his niece, the daughter of Antipas' brother, Aristobulus. The pair decided to seek to live together. But when the daughter of Aretas heard of the liaison, she fled to her father. He was already in dispute about boundaries with Antipas and he took the opportunity of family insult to go to war. In the ensuing battle, the whole army of Herod was destroyed.

According to Josephus, to some of the Jewish people the destruction of Herod's army seemed to be divine vengence for his treatment of John the Baptist:

For Herod had put him to death, though he was a good man and had exhorted the Jews to lead righteous lives, to practise justice towards their fellows and piety towards God, and so doing to join in baptism.

Herod became alarmed as John attracted more and more people and feared that his eloquence would lead to some form of sedition. He decided that it would be better to strike first and he had the Baptist imprisoned in Machaerus and there put to death. Yet the verdict of the Jewish people was that the destruction visited upon Herod's army was a vindication of John. When we turn to Mark's account, we can see both similarities and baffling differences.

95

In the light of Josephus, we shall have to make our way carefully and many details require attention. It is exceedingly rare to have a version of a Gospel story independent of the Gospels themselves. All the more reason, therefore, to seize the opportunity offered here. There is much to be gained for our understanding of what a Gospel is, and what Mark is about, if we attend, in this instance, not only to his words but to those of his contemporary, Flavius Josephus.

King Herod

Herod Antipas was not a king. He was the son of Herod the Great (responsible, according to Matthew, for the massacre of the infants of Bethlehem), born about 20 B.C.E. and he became tetrarch of Galilee and Perea on the death of his father (4 B.C.E.). When he moved his capital from Sepphoris to Tiberias, the site of an ancient burial-ground, he showed his contempt for Jewish custom and tradition, for residence there would render a Jew perpetually unclean. Such insensitivity to Jewish religious and social contentions was equally clear in his attachment to Herodias. When that ambitious woman goaded Antipas into seeking the title king from his Roman master, the emperor Caligula promptly exiled them to the south of France (39 C.E.).

Baptist, Elijah or prophet?

The fact that people identify Jesus with the Baptist or Elijah or one of the ancient prophets come-to-life will occur again (8:28). We will postpone discussion of the matter until we reach the climax to act one of Mark, the momentous discussion on the way to Caesarea Philippi (8:27-30).

Herodias

Herodias was, as we have seen, the daughter of Aristobulus, son of Herod the Great, and so the niece of Herod Antipas. Mark tells us that she was first married to Philip. If he means Herod Philip, the tetrarch of Ituraea and Trachonitis, then he is mistaken. For Herodias was married, according to Josephus, to (yet another) Herod, son of Herod the Great and Mariamne II and they had a daughter, Salome, who was married to Philip the tetrarch. It may be that Herod to whom Herodias was married had also the name

Philip (notice that Mark does not claim that Philip was a tetrarch). It should be remembered that Herod the Great was married ten times. Herodias, by the by, was not a Jewess.

Josephus narrates that Herod Antipas had John the Baptist put to death because he feared that the latter's eloquence might excite the crowds to some form of sedition. Mark attributes the cause of death to Herodias' hatred. It is not necessary to take sides here; it may well be that each writer gives part of a complex situation. On the one hand, Antipas was determined to nip in the bud any sign of popular uprising. On the other, the Baptist, to Herodias' chagrin, preached against scandalous adultery in high places. What upset the religious sensitivity of ordinary people was not that Herodias married Antipas. It was that for a long time they flouted popular sentiment by not obtaining a divorce. They were, as the saying goes, living in sin.

The daughter of Herodias

Mark calls Herod a king. Whether he believed (wrongly) that Antipas bore that title or whether he is reflecting a local popular usage is of no great moment. But whether the daughter of Herod's wife, herself the grand-daughter of King Herod the Great, would have performed a sensual and lascivious dance before the courtiers, officers and leading men of Galilee, is another matter. The moral depravity of Herod and Herodias was, perhaps, a matter of public disgust. Nevertheless, anyone who has ever seen an eastern exotic dance may find it difficult to believe that a royal princess would so entertain the leading, and, presumably, intoxicated, men of Galilee.

READING THROUGH AGAIN

Josephus and Mark are writing from very different points of view. The historian was trying to bend history to show his people (and himself) in a good light to his Roman masters. Mark was trying to restore the faith of frightened Christians who were the victims of imperial brutality. He is not trying, as Josephus was, to appease the coercive political powers of the day; he was attempting to show that, in the divine scheme of things, such powers were coming to an end. For Mark, the kingdom of God, not of Heros Antipas, nor even of Caesar, is where real power lies.

The Passion of John the Baptist is a preview of the Passion of Jesus and, at the same time, a warning to Mark's readers that the fate of John, the fate of Jesus and their own fate are inextricably linked. If this is what happens to John, if this is what will happen to Jesus, then is not persecution, and even death, the fate that awaits all disciples?

Herod sent and seized John, just as the chief priest, the scribes and the elders will send a crowd with swords and clubs to seize Jesus (14:46). John was bound, as Jesus will be bound and led to Pilate (15:1). Herodias had a grudge against the prophet (11:32) on account of her marriage and she wanted to kill him but she could not have her way for Herod feared John, knowing that he was a righteous and holy man. Likewise, the chief priests and the scribes will seek to seize and kill Jesus (14:2; see also 12:12) but will be temporarily prevented: *lest there be a tumult of the people* (14:2). But an opportunity came when Herod gave a feast, just as an opportunity will present itself to the enemies of Jesus as he goes to the Mount of Olives, singing the hymns of the feast of Passover (14:26). Herod, seduced by the lascivious charms of Herodias' daughter, offered her whatever she wished, even to half his kingdom. Pilate, too, will make an offer: *Now at the feast he used to release for them one prisoner whom they asked* (15:6). Herodias persuaded her daughter to ask for what Antipas did not want to give. In like manner, the chief priest will stir up the crowd to frustrate the efforts of Pilate (such as they are) to release Jesus: *but the chief priests stirred up the crowd to have him release for them Barabbas instead* (15:11) and the King of the Jews will be handed over to be crucifed on a cross. The disciples of John came and took his body and laid it in a tomb. The disciples of Jesus will desert and flee but an unknown stranger, *Joseph of Arimathea, a respected member of the council, who was also himself looking for the kingdom of God,* will take Jesus down from the cross and wrap him in a linen shroud and lay him in a tomb (15:46).

The fate of John the Baptist is, then, told by Mark with his eye firmly fixed on the fate of Jesus. But there is more. As ever, Mark is aware of echoes in the scriptures and he is able to relate the death of John (as he will that of Jesus) to the great reservoir of God's word to be found therein. The plotting of Herodias against John recalls the attempts of Jezebel, the wife of King Ahab, to bring about the death of Elijah (and, in Mark's view, the Baptist is Elijah – 1:6; 9:13) because of his preaching against the royal house (1 Kings 19 and 21). The story of Esther must also have been in Mark's mind. When she came before King Ahasuerus, she found favour in his sight and he asked what she most desired, promising that she would receive her wish, *even to the half of my kingdom* (Esther 5:1-3). The offer is repeated in the context of a feast but, unlike the daughter of Herodias, Esther asks, not for death, but for the lives of her people (Esther 7:1-3). Mark's readers are invited to compare and contrast the great stories of the past with the tale he has to tell. Just as the will of God worked its way through the old stories, so, in Mark's perspective, it works its way through the story of Jesus of Nazareth. Herein lies the difference between Josephus and Mark, between historical propaganda and gospel-making. One is trying to chart the events of history in a given time and place; the other is trying to discern the finger of God in the fate of Jesus and in the community called to be his disciples.

Herod Antipas jumped to the conclusion that Jesus was John the Baptist come back to life. We, the attentive readers of Mark, know that this is not so. From the beginning we know Jesus to be the Messiah, the Son of God (1:10). Nonetheless, we know John to have been a man of God, a prophet sent to prepare the way of the Lord and we must be shocked by his cruel end. So, too, with Jesus. As we journey through the first act of Mark's story, we are, again and again, confronted with the question of the identity of Jesus and we have a host of witnesses to guide us. Yet the clearer we become in our understanding of who he is, the more anxious we become as to his destiny. The more clearly the image of God shines in the face of Jesus, the more we can see the hand of God in his actions and hear God's voice in his words, the more we feel the cross casting its ominous shadow.

PRAYER

Perhaps, in memory of that great and fearless man, we might pray the prayer of John the Baptist's father and thank God for the one who went before the Lord to prepare his way. Zechariah's prayer will serve for those who sit in the shadow of death and guide our feet in the way of peace (Luke 1:67-79).

The banquet of Jesus
Mark 6:30-44

The last scene of the first act of Mark's Gospel rushes through a series of amazing events to the open declaration at Caesarea Philippi that Jesus is the Messiah. Thus will be completed the first part of Mark's programme (1:1). Yet we will not flood into the foyer for our half-time drink with an easy mind. Too many questions remain unanswered, too many enigmas unsolved. As we move ahead, we shall find ourselves looking over our shoulders with apprehension. Recalling the fate of John the Baptist, we will be anxious for Jesus. As we leave the tomb of John, we may feel that the spectre of another tomb looms large. And, indeed, it does. But there is gospel, good news, too. We shall glean what it is if we pay attention to particulars and read between the lines.

READING THROUGH

The story of the Feeding of a Multitude is the only miracle to be recounted in all four Gospels. It must, therefore, have had a particular hold on the imagination of early Christians. Moreover, Mark and Matthew, strange to tell, relate the story twice but we must not think that Jesus fed the crowds on two distinct occasions (6:30-34 and 8:10; Matthew 14:13-21 and 15:29-39). That beggars belief. Rather, we must grapple with the fact that the first two gospel-makers were so taken by the feeding of so many people with so little food that they offer two versions of one event. Yet the writers are not guilty of mere repetition. Each telling differs in numerous details and subtle nuance. To ferret out what Mark is about we must pay attention to particulars.

Apostles
The word "apostle" is used only here in Mark (3:14 is of doubtful authenticity) and it means one who is sent out, an emissary or representative who has the right to speak on behalf of

the sender. The selection of a special group within the community of disciples began with the call of Simon and Andrew to be fishers of people (1:16-20), continued with the setting apart of the twelve to be with him and to be sent out to preach (3:13-15) and culminated in the brief missionary excursion now concluded. Just as the death of John is associated with the sending out and successful return of the apostles, so the death of Jesus will be the prelude to the sending out of all disciples for *the gospel must ... be preached to all nations* (13:10).

It is often suggested that the disciples of Jesus are here called "the apostles" to distinguish them from the disciples of John the Baptist who came to bury the decapitated body of their master (6:29). But there may be more to it than that. In 6:7, Jesus began to send them out, two by two. The verb "to send out", from which our word "apostle" derives, is twice used in the story of John's tragic end. Herod had *sent* and seized John (6:17) and, again, the king *sent* a soldier of the guard to see to the beheading. There is a clear contrast, therefore, between those whom Jesus sends to cast out demons and heal the sick and those "apostles" of King Herod who are emissaries of death.

The desert

Modern translations are not always kind to Mark's understanding of the desert. The *Good News Bible* translates the same Greek word as "desert", "a lonely place", "lonely places", and even "some place" (6:31). *The Jerusalem Bible* offers "wilderness", "a lonely place", "places where nobody lived" (6:31). The *Revised Standard Version* has "wilderness", "a lonely place" and "in the country". What is missing is the consistency and surprise which characterise the vocabulary of Mark. He uses one Greek word unerringly and provocatively. For Mark's desert has more to do with imagination than geography.

A round up of Mark's use of the word is instructive. The desert is the place where the way is to be prepared (1:3). It is the place where John preaches a baptism of repentance (1:4). It is the place where Satan tests and angels minister (1:12-13). The desert is a place for prayer (1:35), a place of retreat (1:45), a place of rest (6:31). It is a place where the shepherdless are taught and fed and satisfied (6:32-35). Mark's desert, as we shall see, resembles more the desert of the Book of Exodus than a lonely place in Galilee or Judea.

Sheep and shepherd

In the Book of Numbers Moses prays that God will appoint a leader over the people of Israel in order that *the congregation of the Lord may not be as sheep which have no shepherd* (27:17). The Lord instructed Moses to appoint Joshua to the task and, of course, that name when translated into English is Jesus.

The image of the ruler as shepherd of the sheep is frequent in the Old Testament. The Judges were appointed by God *to shepherd my people Israel* (2 Samuel 7:17). The kings were to exercise that care over their people that a good shepherd lavishes on his flocks. Even a pagan king who helps to restore the fortunes of Israel fulfils God's purpose. Thus of Cyrus, the liberator of the exiled people of Judah, God says *He is my shepherd* (Isaiah 44:28). Judith beguiles the braggart, Holofernes, with the promise that he will lead the Jewish people like sheep, adding *let no dog bark* (Judith 11:19). However, the appointed kings of Israel and Judah were more often rapacious wolves and are roundly condemned. Indeed, worthless kings, priests and prophets, negligent of their divine-given responsibilities for the flock are angrily dismissed. Their kings, their princes, their priests, and their prophets (Jeremiah 2:26) are stupid *and all their flock is scattered* (Jeremiah 10:21). *The shepherds have no understanding* (Isaiah 56:11) of the high office bestowed on them and they impoverish rather than protect the people. Therefore,

> "Woe to the shepherds who destroy and scatter the sheep of my pasture!" says the Lord. Therefore thus says the Lord, the God of Israel, concerning the shepherds who care for my people: "You have scattered my flock and driven them away, and you have not attended to them. Behold, I will attend to you for your evil" (Jeremiah 23: 1-2).

Again, the word of the Lord concerning Israel's evil rulers came to Ezekiel:

> Son of man, prophesy against the shepherds of Israel, prophesy and say to them, even to the shepherds, thus says the Lord God: Ho, shepherds of Israel who have been feeding yourselves! Should not shepherds feed the sheep? You eat the fat, you clothe yourselves with wool, you slaughter the fatlings, but you do not feed the sheep. The weak you have not strengthened, the sick you have not healed, the crippled you have not

bound up, the strayed you have not brought back, the lost you have not sought, and with force and harshness you have ruled them. So they were scattered, because there was no shepherd; and they became food for all the wild beasts. My sheep were scattered over all the mountains and on every high hill; my sheep were scattered over all the face of the earth, with none to search or to seek them (Ezekiel 34:1-6).

Small wonder, then, that the prophets began to look forward to the day when Israel would no longer look to human agencies for its wellbeing and protection. God himself would be the shepherd of the flock. Such was the vision of Ezekiel:

For thus says the Lord God: Behold, I, I myself, will search for my sheep, and seek them out. As a shepherd seeks out his flock when some of his sheep have been scattered abroad, so I will seek out my sheep, and I will rescue them from all places where they have been scattered on a day of clouds and thick darkness. And I will bring them out from the peoples, and gather them from the countries, and will bring them into their own land; and I will feed them on the mountains of Israel, by the fountains, and in all the inhabited places of the country (Ezekiel 34:11-13).

While the religious overtones of Israel's longing for God's will to be done, for his kingdom to come, must not be overshadowed, the military and political dimensions must not be played down. When the Old Testament uses the image of shepherd for human leaders, it has in mind kings and princes whose duties are to protect from invaders, to go to war against aggressors and so to conduct their dominion that the poor and wretched are not excluded from the political agenda. Jeremiah's denunciations of false shepherds refer to social injustice and when Ezekiel cries for a better future he has in mind one where people do not live in exile, do not live in fear, but are fed on justice (Ezekiel 34:16; see also Zechariah 12 and 13).

READING THROUGH AGAIN

The return of the twelve, with the report of all that they had done and taught, elicits Jesus' concern for their welfare and he invites them to repair to a desert to find rest from the pressing

103

crowds. The precise location towards which the disciples set sail is not mentioned and need not concern us for it is the significance of the desert that concerns Mark. That God provides rest for his people in the desert is a recurring motif in the Bible. Indeed, the rest which God provided in the desert became the foretaste of the rest, that is, peace, which would prevail when the people came to the land flowing with milk and honey: *the Lord gives rest to your brothers as to you* (Deuteronomy 3:20). Indeed, the prophets look to the time of Israel's young days in the desert as a symbol of the final rest promised to all. For Isaiah, the Spirit of the Lord which gave rest to the people of the Exodus, would give peace in the future (Isaiah 63:14). Jeremiah, confident in his belief that the people of the Exodus *found grace in the wilderness, when Israel sought for rest* (Jeremiah 31:2), is convinced that God's everlasting love will again be shown to all, that there will be universal peace and joy, that the day will come when all will *go forth in the dance of the merrymakers* (Jeremiah 31:4).

When, therefore, Jesus calls his disciples to the wilderness and when the crowds flock there to hear his teaching, we are invited to imagine a fulfilment of the ancient prophecies. The ancient people received the Torah (= Teaching) in the desert, they were fed with manna and were satisfied. The new people of God who will also be taught in the desert, will receive a new manna; and they will, likewise, be satisfied. The ancient desert people had cried out *O that we had meat to eat!* and Moses complained to God: *Where am I to get meat to give to all this people?* Mockingly, the great prophet taunts God: *Shall flocks and herds be slaughtered for them, to suffice them? Or shall all the fish of the sea be gathered for them, to suffice them?* With infinite patience, the Lord replied, *Is the Lord's hand shortened? Now you shall see whether my word will come true for you or not* (Numbers 11:4, 13, 22). Nor is the hand of Jesus shortened in the desert. Who, then, is he?

Another strand of biblical story-telling to influence Mark is an incident in the ministry of the prophet Elisha. Once Elisha was brought twenty barley loaves and he ordered that they be set before his followers. But his servant protested, *How am I to set this before a hundred men?* The prophet, however, knew well that the Lord would provide: *Give them to the men that they may eat for thus says the Lord, "They shall eat and have some left"* (2 Kings 4:22-44).

Yet another insight into the intricate patterns being woven by Mark in his telling of the Feeding of the Five Thousand Men may be won by paying attention to its context. Following on what may be called "The Banquet of Herod" comes "The Banquet of Jesus". In the latter case, Jesus is the host who fulfils all the host's responsibilities. He bids the people to sit down by companies, a word that denotes "a company of guests". He speaks the blessing, fulfilling the stringent rule that nothing should be eaten without thanking God. As host he breaks the bread and offers it to his servants (the disciples) to give to the people, his honoured guests. And, as a generous host, he offers more than is required: *And they took up twelve baskets full of broken pieces and of the fish.*

Jesus-disciples-crowds

The Christian reader of the Feeding of the Five Thousand will no doubt be led to think of the Last Supper and of the Eucharist. The very words of Mark press such thoughts on the mind: *he looked up to heaven, and blessed, and broke the loaves.* But it is unlikely that Mark wishes to present his story as an anticipation of the Last Supper or of the celebration of the Eucharist. To lift the face heavenwards is a natural posture of prayer; the breaking of bread and its distribution by the head of the family or the host were normal customs and the saying of a blessing was an obligation: *And when he had said this, he took bread, and giving thanks to God in the presence of all, he broke it and began to eat* (Acts 27:35). The quotation describes the normal practice of a Jew about to eat, in this case, St Paul (see also Romans 14:6; 1 Corinthians 10:30; 1 Timothy 4:3).

Mark's first point of interest is, as always, Jesus. Jesus calls the disciples to the desert which, we have seen, is always a place of notable happening or teaching in Mark. Jesus teaches the crowds, he has compassion on them, he provides for their needs. In all of this, given the words Mark uses and the scriptural stories to which he obliquely refers, we can see that he is presenting Jesus as God is presented in the ancient story of the Exodus and in the expectations of the prophets of old. The Jesus of Mark's story is not another Moses, not another Joshua; astoundingly, he fits readily into the description of God which emerges from the Law and the Prophets.

In both tellings of the Feeding of a Multitude Jesus has

compassion on the crowds who are like sheep who have no shepherd. They are the only two works which Jesus does for the benefit of the multitude. Clearly, Jesus is concerned about the hungry people. That concern is expressed in two ways: he teaches and he feeds. Perhaps, it is here that Mark's readers would have discerned a lesson for themselves. They, too, whose eucharist is a proclamation of the gospel and a sharing of the bread, must reach to the crowds; they must nourish them with the word of the gospel and feed them with the bread of life.

It is clear that Mark lays much stress on the role of the disciples in both feeding stories, rather more in the first than the second, perhaps, but in both they are prominent. The role of the disciples in these stories is of immense importance to Mark for he will come back to it and make it the basis for a discussion between Jesus and his disciples (8:14-21). It is as if Jesus submits them to an examination concerning the meaning of what has taken place. We shall postpone a full investigation of the matter until we have examined the second feeding story and its sequel. In the meantime, we will have to keep a close eye on the disciples.

PRAYER

The psalms speak of God as the Shepherd of Israel (Psalm 80:1) and the prophets looked to the day when God's shepherding would provide justice and peace for all peoples. While Psalm 23 is a very personal prayer, it is not difficult to pray it as a prayer of our world, a prayer of all people who walk through the valley of the shadow of death. Nor, in the praying of it, is it difficult to imagine the one who had compassion on the multitude who were like sheep without a shepherd.

Walking on the waters
Mark 6:45-56

Guesswork. Reading between the lines. Hazardous occupations. But reading a pamphlet which is nigh on two thousand years old, written by we know not whom, in a language other than our own and in circumstances we little understand, must involve an element of surmise. For example, does Mark call Herod Antipas a king in order to mock the pretensions of a petty tyrant or because he doesn't know any better? When he describes people as sheep without a shepherd, is he bemoaning a congregation without a spiritual leader or is he making the more dangerous political claim that his people are like an army without a general, a nation without a national leader? Our attempts to probe the strange story of Mark may, in the end, depend on no more than a wing and a prayer.

The incidents to which we now turn bristle with problems and, lacking any concrete evidence, we are driven to guess and surmise. And, of course, where so much is vague and incomprehensible, one guess is as good as another. We will return to the story of the Feeding of the Multitude to pick up some threads of what appears to be an impenetrable spider's web.

Mark reveals that those who ate the loaves and fishes were five thousand men. If the great throng had gone seeking Jesus in the desert for mighty works of healing, we would expect women and children to appear on the scene. Yet the word *men* is conspicuously placed at the end of the sentence and is strongly emphatic. Five thousand men do not assemble in the desert, waiting for the appearance of a leader, without good cause (*they ran there on foot from all the towns, and got there ahead of them*).

Jesus began to teach the five thousand men who had rushed to the desert, like sheep without a shepherd. What did he say? He *commanded them all to sit down by companies, by hundreds and by fifties*, a combination of number and orderliness which suggests not so much a dining arrangement (in the desert!) as a military formation. And the grass was green. If we are to think of Mark's desert in realistic terms, then it would have had a light coating of grass only at Passover time, a time of the year charged with messianic expectation and often scarred by nationalistic revolts. Where better to assemble for mischief than the desert: *Are you not the Egyptian, then, who recently stirred up a revolt and led four thousand men of the Assassins out into the desert?* (Acts 21:38). Josephus bemoaned the regular excursions to the desert to ferment rebellion. Impostors and deceivers called upon the mob to follow them into the desert, *For they said that they would show them unmistakable marvels and signs that would be wrought in harmony with God's design* (*Antiquities* XX.8.6). Was Jesus, after the death of his relative and friend, John the Baptist, tempted to lead an uprising in the desert? Were there public disturbances after the demise of John, disturbances which sought to solicit the support of Jesus, another young prophet who had already become a thorn in the side of the religious and political establishments (3:6)?

When John recounts the Feeding of the Multitude (John 6:1-15), he relates that such was the effect of the sign that the people were about to come and take Jesus by force to make him king, only Jesus, perceiving their intent, withdrew to the mountain by himself.

READING THROUGH

As we read through the last verses of chapter six we shall have to be aware of the guesses and surmises which are forced upon us by a text which raises more questions than it answers.

Bethsaida

There is some confusion here. Bethsaida, slightly to the north-east of the lake, was rebuilt by Herod Philip who raised it to the status of a city. The criss-crossing of the lake would lead one to believe that the disciples were now headed for the western shore and this would seem to be borne out by the fact that they land at Gennesaret (6:53), a fertile plain to the southwest of Capernaum. The matter is of no great pith or moment but it serves notice on readers that Mark's grasp of geographical detail cannot be relied upon.

Into the hills

Mark actually says that Jesus went up the *mountain*. He does not specify which mountain, anymore than he does the mountain of the Transfiguration (9:2). But, as in the case of his desert, he may have more in mind than at first appears.

When evening came

When the multitudes assembled in the wilderness, Jesus taught them, and, when it grew late, the disciples urged Jesus to send them away. After the feeding, the disciples embarked and when evening came the boat was out on the sea. Jesus came to them about the fourth watch of the night. The Romans divided the night into four quarters for the purpose of keeping watch. The Jews divided the night into three watches. The fourth watch of the night was between three and six a.m. Time references in Mark often appear to be very precise but, sometimes, on examination, turn out to be more decorative than instructive.

Ego eimi

There are some phrases of Mark's Gospel that may be grasped only by attending to the original Greek. Such a phrase is *Ego eimi*, which means *I am*.

Various names are given to God in the pages of the Bible. Some, such as "good shepherd", "father", "king", because they have human associations, are not too difficult to understand. But when Moses asked God to reveal himself, to tell his name, the reply was, I AM WHO I AM (Exodus 3:14). The phrase has not proved to be very revealing and scholars have endlessly debated its meaning. Some have suggested that it means that God is the one who always is, the eternal one, and that may be as close as we can get to the matter. Isaiah would appear to support such a suggestion:

I, the LORD, the first
and with the last;
I AM (Isaiah 41:4).

"You are my witnesses," says the LORD,
"and my servant whom I have chosen,
that you may know and believe me
and understand that I AM..." (Isaiah 43:10).

However, the matter assumes an even deeper significance for Christians. In the Gospel according to John, the phrase is used with great emphasis:

I AM, the one speaking to you (John 4:26).
I AM; do not be afraid (John 6:20).
I AM the bread of life (John 6:35).
I AM the living bread (John 6: 51).
I AM the light of the world (John 9:5).
I AM the good shepherd (John 10:11).
I AM the resurrection and the life (John 11:25).
I AM the way, the truth and the life (John 14:6).

Of course, one might translate these statements less dramatically, as indeed, do most English translations. We might say, to take the first two as examples, "I who speak to you am he" and "It is I; do not be afraid". That such translations fall short of the significance attached to them in John's writing is clear from the fact that he provides us with a key by which we may unlock the hidden treasure in his enigmatic texts:

"You are not yet fifty years old, and have you seen Abraham?" Jesus said to them, "Truly, truly, I say to you, before Abraham was, I AM" (John 8:57-58).

When we read in Mark, *I AM; do not be afraid,* we ought to pay as much attention and give as much weight to the statement, as if it were in the Fourth Gospel, the more so as Mark has also provided a key (14: 62) to his meaning.

READING THROUGH AGAIN

The command of Jesus to his disciples to get into the boat is much more than a polite request. It is an order. He compels them to go on board. From the days of one of the earliest commentators on Mark's forceful verse, Origen (?185 – ?254 C.E.), a Christian scholar from Alexandria, to the present, people have sought to explain the abruptness with which Jesus constrained the disciples to embark by reference to the dangerous situation indicated by Mark 6:14. Jesus hurried the disciples on ship in order that they might not catch the revolutionary fervour which was sweeping through the crowds after the meal in the wilderness.

The desert played no small part in uprisings against the Romans in the first century and, indeed, it was on the desert fortress at Masada that the century's greatest defeat was inflicted on the Jews. It is not surprising that there was excitement in the air after such an unexpected feeding in such an evocative location. That the words with which Mark tells the story of the Feeding of the Multitude reflect a military and political background is clear enough. But this is a far cry from saying that either (a) Jesus was tempted to lead a revolt against Rome or (b) that he was forced to discourage an enthusiastic bunch of rebels who sought to make him king and storm the barricades. At least, that is not, in my view, what Mark is about.

What Mark is about is to present the Jesus who announces the coming of God's kingdom. The feeding illustrates that, whereas political jackanapes such as Herod Antipas, a minion and time server of Roman imperialism, serve up death, even at their festive meals, Jesus, like God in the days of Moses, is in the desert teaching and feeding the people. If Jesus is to be found, then the question of his identity comes to the fore and it is this question which will be answered in the Walking on the Waters.

In the beginning, in the middle and at the end of Mark, Jesus is to be found at prayer. When many who were sick were healed, Jesus retired to the desert to pray (1:35). After the multitude are fed, Jesus retires to the mountain to pray (the mountain was the place where Moses communed with God in the Exodus story); and it is on the Mount of Olives, some distance from his disciples, that Jesus prays to his Father (14:32-36). In each case, Jesus is away from his disciples and in each case he returns to them. In each case, on his return, he reveals a matter of great import. On the first occasion, he reveals that the purpose of his coming was to preach: *Let us go on to the next towns, that I may preach there also; for that is why I came out;* the second, he reveals his identity: *I AM – do not be afraid;* on the third, he reveals his destiny: *the Son of man is to be betrayed into the hands of sinners* (14:41). In other words, the dismissal of the disciples and the retreat to prayer are preparatory to great revelations, indeed, to the perfect summary of his life: to preach, to reveal his identity, to be put to death. It is only thus that the power of the kingdom will come. Mark may use the vocabulary of kings and princes, of military and political conversation, but it is only to serve a greater king and a greater kingdom.

He wanted to pass by them

The Calming of the Storm (4:35-41) provides all the background to enable us to understand the Walking on the Waters. That the wind and the sea obey him, we already know. What further revelation will come in the midst of the second storm on the Sea of Galilee?

Though Jesus saw that his friends were distressed in rowing, he wanted to pass by them. This statement raises some baffling questions. Aware of their danger, Jesus came to them; why, then, does he mean to pass by them? Why does he bother to come, if he intends to pass by? Why get into the boat, if he intended to pass by?

The answer, as ever, lies in the Old Testament and there we shall find that the phrase, *he meant to pass them by,* is not at all what it seems. The Book of the Exodus provides the first clue:

Moses said, "I pray thee, show me thy glory". And (the LORD) said, "I will make all my goodness pass before you, and will proclaim before you my name" (Exodus 33:19).

And the LORD descended in the cloud and stood with him there, and proclaimed the name of the LORD. The LORD passed before him, and proclaimed, "The LORD, the LORD, a God merciful and gracious, slow to anger and abounding in steadfast love and faithfulness" (Exodus 34:5-6).

Likewise, the First Book of Kings:

And, behold, the LORD passed by, and a great strong wind rent the mountains, and broke in pieces the rocks before the LORD ... (1 Kings 19:11).

The verb "to pass by" is used in an odd way in these quotations but we can see why. Because of God's glory, nobody, not even Moses or Elijah, can see him face to face and live. Yet God is determined to reveal himself to them. Therefore, God is said "to pass by", that is, to keep his divine nature hidden, while at the same time, the witness catches what we might call a "side-on view" of him.

The same is true of Mark. Jesus' walking on the sea is a manifestation, an epiphany, of God's power, God's presence, which is active in the person of the Son of man (consider again 2:6-7 and 4:41). By "passing by", Jesus is revealing to the disciples, and yet concealing from them, the innermost nature of his being.

And there is more. A second clue, this time from the Book of Amos:

> Therefore thus says the LORD,
> the God of hosts, the LORD:
> "In all the squares there shall be wailing
> and in all the streets they shall say,
> 'Alas! Alas!'
> They shall call the farmers to mourning
> and to wailing those who are skilled in lamentation,
> and in all the vineyards there shall be wailing,
> for I WILL PASS THROUGH the midst of
> you", says the LORD (Amos 5:16-17).

At this point, the prophet Amos is discussing God's final intervention in history, as he sees it, and he is concerned with those who are opposed to God's will, to what Mark would call, God's kingdom. Some folk, he declares, will get their comeuppance (see also Exodus 12:12; Ezekiel 14:17). The phrase *I will pass through* indicates that the passing of the Lord will be a disaster. Conversely, to pass by, in Amos, indicates salvation. God will not pass by little Jacob (the Jewish people). *I will not pass by* them means, in effect, *I will save them* (see the occurrences of the phrase in Amos 7:8; 8:2). We may conclude that when Mark says that Jesus intends to pass by, but does not, that he is saying that Jesus intends to save them.

Bringing the two strands of Old Testament language together, we can surmise, with some confidence, that Mark means that the passing by of Jesus, on the one hand, is an intention to reveal who he is to the disciples in the boat and, on the other, to save them from the distress in which they find themselves.

That Jesus was walking on the sea is reminiscent of the awesome apparitions of God to his people. Job attempts to express the almighty nature of God by proclaiming that God alone stretched out the heavens, and trampled the waves of the sea (Job 9:8) and walked in the recesses of the deep (Job 38:16). Enough has been said by Mark to prepare us for the revelation: *I AM; have no fear.*

That the readers of Mark, if not the disciples in the midst of a storm, ought to understand what is afoot here, is clear from the trial of Jesus. Here is Mark's key to the *I AM* enigma. The high priest, exasperated by a trial that was falling to pieces, puts the

113

question: *Are you the Messiah, the Son of the Blessed?* (14:61).
To which, Jesus replies, *I AM*. At the end of the day, when his
enemies have cornered him and baited him with the ultimate
question as to his identity, Jesus proclaims that he can say, as
God said to Moses, *I AM*. That is what Mark wishes us to know
as he recounts the mysterious walking on the waters. The Jesus
who rescued the distressed disciples on the sea is the one who
can speak, can identify himself, as the God who passes by to
reveal and to save.

And he got into the boat with them and the wind ceased. The
persecuted little church in Rome, yet again, is assured that Jesus
is not absent but that he is in the boat of the Church , to reveal, for
assurance, to save, as a pledge.

That the disciples did not understand about the bread will call
for deep reflection when we come to the second feeding story
and its sequel. For now, we note that the ministry of Jesus in
Galilee is coming to an end. Mark provides us with a useful
summary of what was done there: the sick were assembled and
the sick were healed.

PRAYER

Psalm 136 has a refrain, repeated twenty-six times, to the
effect that God is the one whose steadfast love endures for ever.
It is a psalm to pray to remind ourselves that I AM is, in the case
of God, just another way of saying I LOVE.

Jesus and the Pharisees
Mark 7:1-23

The football commentator does not know the result of the match. He can only follow the run of play, note the superiority of one side to the other, and, with the help of experience and his knowledge of past form, speculate on the outcome. But there are few certainties in this life and sport, not less than life, is full of surprises.

Such was the position of those who followed Jesus through the hills of Galilee. The disciples, no less than the crowds, were amazed (1:27; 2:12), afraid (4:40), astonished (6:2), utterly astounded (6:51), and, amidst all the wonder and awe, lacking in understanding ((8:21). What disciples and people lacked was a key to open to them the meaning of the events which so captured their imaginations and bewildered their hearts. Not so the gospel-makers. Unlike the sports commentators trying to make sense of the rush of events from one end of the file do the other, they knew the result. They knew that Jesus was raised from the dead, that the death in Jerusalem was not the tragic end of the young prophet who had set out from Galilee, preaching the kingdom of God. Far from it. Now everything, or almost everything, was clear. Where before wonder, amazement, even fear, were the order of the day, the gospel-makers were able to see patterns, stratagems, plans, designs, all hidden from those who journeyed to Jerusalem with the man from Nazareth. The resurrection was the key which unlocked the meaning of the story. What a difference it makes to know the final score. How different the game is when judged by its outcome.

When we read the Gospels we must be aware that they were written by people who knew the end of the story. They tell the story through the prism of the resurrection and their telling is everywhere coloured by their knowledge. Thus, it is never a simple matter to decide in considering any event in the Gospels, what actually happened on the day, during the game, as it were, for the resurrection, the end-game, controls how the story must now be told. A simple example will serve to make the matter clear.

Early Christians soon came to call Jesus Lord. Such was the name given to God in the sacred books they received as their Jewish inheritance. The resurrection convinced the frightened and bewildered disciples that God had so vindicated Jesus that everyone could believe that *Jesus Christ is Lord, to the glory of God the Father* (Philippians 2:11). Because God had highly exalted the one who died on a cross, his true identity is revealed and before him *every knee shall bow*.

But the Greek word for Lord simply means "Sir". It is the form of address a slave would use to his master, a citizen to the emperor and, indeed, a wife to her husband. When in the Gospels a woman addresses Jesus by this word, are we to understand that she is simply being polite (*Yes, sir; yet even the dogs under the table eat the children's crumbs* – Mark 7:28) or is she making a leap of faith (*Yes, Lord*), without the knowledge of the resurrection, and acknowledging Jesus as Lord? A third possibility would be that the gospel-maker, in the light of what he knows about the resurrection, insists, with hindsight, that everyone, even before the death of Jesus, confesses that he is Lord.

THE PAGAN PROBLEM

The luxury of being wise after the event bears on another area of early Christian life. By fair the most significant controversy in the history of the Church was the first one. You might think that the breaking up of the unity of Christendom in the ninth century or the fragmentation of European Christianity in the sixteenth were moments of great (and disastrous) consequence for the Church's mission in the world and so they were. But the decision confronting the very first Christian communities was greater still.

The first Christian groups were entirely Jewish. Peter, Andrew, James and John, Mary, Joanna, Susanna, Tabitha and all who were called by Jesus were Jews. Just as Jesus had faithfully followed the teaching and practice of his religion upbringing so, too, did his followers before and after the death of their Teacher. But there were some, notably St Paul, who realised that the meaning and message of Jesus were meant, not just for those descended from Abraham, but for all God's children. Pagans, too, must be invited to the Lord's Supper.

The arguments were fierce and the scars are plain to be seen on the pages of the New Testament. Peter was on the side of the traditionalists: the message of Jesus was for Jews alone; you must not cast pearls before swine. It took a heavenly visitation to move the mind of the fisherman from Capernaum (Acts 10:9-48). Then (but only temporarily) the penny dropped:

Truly, I perceive that God shows no partiality, but in every nation any one who fears him and does what is right is acceptable to him (Acts 10:34).

From the beginning of his missionary activity, Paul was determined that the message was for all humanity and he managed to force an agreement out of *those who were reputed to be something* (Galatians 2:6) to the effect that

I (= Paul) had been entrusted with the gospel to the uncircumcised (= the pagans), just as Peter had been entrusted with the gospel to the circumcised (= the Jewish people), for he who worked through Peter for the mission to the circumcised worked through me also for the Gentiles.

This meeting with Peter and James (*those reputed to be great* – Paul didn't have much time for anyone who got in his way) may very well be the gathering in Jerusalem of senior Church figures to which Luke refers in Acts 15. The matter would appear to have been settled there in favour of opening out to the peoples of the world. But there were back-sliders, among them Peter (Galatians 2:11-23), who wanted to keep Jesus and his message within the confines of the Jewish faith. Had Paul and his supporters lost the argument there would have been no universal Church, and Christianity, if it had survived at all (an unlikely event) would have remained a sect with Judaism. But the Pauline understanding won the day, not, however, without a price.

Jewish Christians, overwhelmed by the influx of pagans into the Jesus movement and beset by the terrors of the war against Rome (66-74 C.E.), returned to the fold of the traditional Judaism ("the faith of our fathers") and, sadly, there was a parting of the ways. It was a parting that was bitter, a bitterness that grew like a canker in Christian hearts and which spewed out its poison in pogrom and holocaust to this very day. The bitterness is all too obvious in the pages of our Gospels.

An example will help to illustrate how the quarrels among

Jewish Christians and especially with non-Jewish Christians affect the way matters are presented in the Gospels. According to all the Gospels, the Pharisees were bitterly opposed to Jesus and engaged in many sharp and acrimonious exchange with him. On occasion, there are disputes with the priestly cast, the Sadducees, but it is with the Pharisees that most of the quarrels occur. This is strange for a number of reasons. First, of all the groups within Judaism at the time, Jesus most resembles the Pharisees. Secondly, Jesus was a staunch upholder of the Law as were the Pharisees and differed with them, for the most part, on how the ancient Law was to be applied on their day. Indeed, there were differences among Pharisees themselves about interpretation of certain prescriptions of the Law (on divorce, for example) and Jesus sometimes takes sides but this is hardly outright hostility, more like a disagreement within the family. Thirdly, though there is plenty of acrimony between the Jesus of the Gospels and the Pharisees, nowhere is it suggested that the Pharisees took any part in the trials, sentencing and execution of Jesus. To be sure, Mark records that *the Pharisees went out, and immediately held counsel with the Herodians against Jesus, how to destroy him* (3:6) and John records that *some officers ... of the Pharisees* (18:3) went with other to arrest Jesus, but these references are isolated and historically suspect. When one reads the accounts of the passion and death of Jesus, one is struck by the absence of the religious group most frequently mentioned in the rest of the gospel story. It is the priestly authorities and the venal Pilate who destroy Jesus.

How are these matters to be explained? If we recall that there was a break-up between Judaism and Christianity and if we further remember the defeat of Israel by the Romans in the war (66-74 C.E.), the explanation is not hard to find. The growing acrimony between Jewish authorities and Christians was well apace at the outbreak of the war. The war saw the destruction of the Temple and the powerful aristocratic clergy in Jerusalem became redundant. The Jewish religion, if it was going to survive, would do so through the work of adaptable teachers of the Law, not conservative, out-or-work priests. The Pharisees were the one group within Judaism with the skills to ensure its survival. And they succeeded. Judaism today is, for the most part, the child of the Pharisees. What the Gospels reflect is, not so much the quarrels of Jesus and of his contemporaries, but the years of growing estrangement and of final rapture.

118

There are a number of issues which must concern us here and we shall have to have out wits about us if we are to appreciate how difficult and, at least, on the surface, how contradictory Mark's material is.

Pharisees

The Books of Maccabees record a sorry time in the history of the Jewish people. The successors of Alexander the Great (356-323 B.C.E.) sought to impose themselves upon the little country of Judah and a particularly nasty specimen, Antiochos IV (215-164 B.C.E.), not only pursued military domination, but attempted to impose Greek culture and its pagan ways on the people. The Maccabean revolt was the local response. Many brave people preferred death to defiling themselves with loathsome pagan practices (the kind of thing imposed may be gleaned from 1 Maccabees 1:41-53). Those who remained faithful to the Law and the temple were called Hasidim and the Pharisees emerged from these heroic people.

The name Pharisee probably means"those who are separated", and, indeed, the Pharisees separated themselves, not only from the pagan world, but also from any group within Judaism they regarded as less than zealous for the strict observance of the Law. In order that the Law might be the more punctiliously obeyed, the Pharisees paid particular attention to the interpretations of the Law's commands by wise teachers down through the ages, for they appreciated that the Law must be expanded and explained in order to be applicable in different times and circumstances. The objective of the ancient interpretations (and that was why the Pharisees so reverenced them) was to enable all the people to attain that holiness promised to those who heard the world of God and wished to keep it. The tradition of the elders was regarded as a fence around the written Law which enabled ordinary people to grow in holiness.

The Pharisees were not a very numerous party within Judaism at the time of Jesus but they were exceedingly influential. Able to adapt to changing circumstances, their flexibility enabled them to provide a way ahead (religiously) for the Jewish people after the destruction of the temple.

Ritual washings

The washings to which Mark here refers is not concerned with bodily hygiene. What is at issue is the matter of ritual cleansing, that is, cleansing which indicates the holiness of the person and the action about to be performed. The matter is clear in the original injunction in the Law:

> The Lord said to Moses, "You shall also make a laver of bronze, with its base of bronze, for washing. And you shall put it between the tent of meeting and the alter, and you shall put water in it, with which Aaron and his sons shall wash their hands and their feet. When they go into the tent of meeting, to burn an offering by fire to the LORD, they shall wash with water, lest they die. They shall wash their hands and their feet, lest they die; it shall be a statute for ever for them, even to him and to his descendants throughout their generations" (Exodus 40:12-15).

The word "holy" originally refers to "that which is different", "set apart", "other". God is holy because God is other, different and distinct from that which is created. Certain stones (altars) are holy because they are set apart for specific religious activity; certain buildings are holy (temples) because they set apart as dwellings for the gods: and certain people (priests) are set apart, made holy, because they participate most intimately in the worship and supplication of the gods on behalf of the community. This setting part (ordination) usually involved a special public ceremony.

> Then you shall bring Aaron and his sons to the door of the tent of meeting, and shall wash them with water, and put upon Aaron the holy garments, and you shall anoint him and consecrate him that he may serve me as a priest. You shall bring his sons also and put coats on them, and anoint them, as you anointed their father, that they may serve me as priests: and their anointing shall admit them to a perpetual priesthood throughout their generations (Exodus 40:12-15).

Before the priest exercised his sacred functions, he would wash himself, according to the command of Exodus 30:17-21, quoted above.

What is clear, of course, is that the ordination-anointing and the ritual washing concerned priests, not lay people. But some two hundred years before the time of Jesus, many Jews, perhaps remembering the words, *You shall be to me a kingdom of priests and a holy nation* (Exodus 19:6 and see 1 Peter 1:9) sought to extend the holiness of the priests to all the people. Thus they assumed voluntarily the practice of washing hands and feet before praying (and, like the priests, before eating) and accompanied their ablutions with a prayer: *Blessed are you, O Lord God, king of the universe, who has made us holy by your laws and commanded us to wash our hands*. And there we have the matter in a nut-shell. Deeply religious people sought to extend to the whole community the otherness, the "apartness" of the priesthood. It was a noble attempt to sanctify ordinary life by promoting priestly practices for layfolk. The Pharisees adopted this pious endeavour and sought to extend the priestly code of ritual washing to all; in effect, they believed in "the priesthood of all the faithful" intending thereby to demonstrate that all Israel was devoted to God and his Law. The Pharisees sought to fulfil God's ancient command: *You shall be holy to me; for I have separated you from the peoples, that you should be mine* (Leviticus 20:26). We may well ask what Jesus found to complain about in such noble an pious objectives.

Corban

The word *Corban* is a Hebrew word which occurs, in one form or another, about eighty times in the Old Testament but only in the books of Leviticus, Numbers and Ezekiel. It would appear to mean "a gift" "an offering" but it is never used to denote a gift to a human being. Thus, it would appear that that gift which is described as *Corban* becomes holy, separate from the human domain and no longer available for ordinary use. It is transferred, as it were, to the divine sphere. In the situation envisaged in Mark's story, a man vows to reserve his wealth for God, thus depriving his parents of their rightful claim on their son for sustenance in their old age. The son did not, of course, hand over his goods; he merely promised to do so. That was enough to cut off the parents without a penny. Jesus was unlikely to approve of such sleight of hand and cynical manipulation of religion. But, then, as we shall see, neither were the Pharisees.

A question of identity: Who is Jesus?

The discussion concerning certain Jewish practices may seem to be of little relevance to the gospel reader of today. Ancient squabbles about what is clean and unclean, disputes about ritual washings and scrubbed or unscrubbed pots hardly seem the stuff to set hearts burning within. But when we realise that every line of Mark's story is shot through with the identity question, with who Jesus is, we will ask of these distant quarrels what they tell us about Jesus. We must confront them with the question which lies at the heart of all gospel stories: who do you say that I am?

READING THROUGH AGAIN

While the twenty-three verses now claiming our attention form a unified whole, for the sake of examination we will divide them into manageable units and, hopefully, we shall not miss the wood in our preoccupation with the trees.

Attack

Mark begins by assembling the cast, as he usually does, without any reference to what has gone before and without any details which would indicate when and where the incident occurred. The opponents of Jesus, in this case the Pharisees and some scribes from Jerusalem, are always waiting in the wings, ready to come on stage when Mark calls them. Mark says bluntly that the Pharisees gathered around Jesus. A moment's reflection will make us realise that Jesus was not surrounded by the thousands of Pharisees who lived in Palestine. What is of interest to Mark is the religious pratice of a large and highly influential group, a group supported by some, but by no means all, of the scribes.

The Pharisees and the scribes have noticed that some of the disciples of Jesus were eating with unwashed hands. It follows, therefore, that some were observing the practice of washing recommended by the strict traditions of the Pharisees. It is intriguing to speculate on how many and to what extent the disciples of Jesus were adherents of the Pharisees but Mark does not dwell on the matter; he presses on to the issues involved in the controversy.

122

The Pharisees and, indeed, all the Jews, according to Mark, undertake certain ritual washing of themselves and pots and pans used in cooking. It does not appear to be historically correct to state that all the Jewish people observed such rituals at the time of Jesus. Here, as elsewhere in his Gospel, Mark is concerned with issues relevant to his own time and place rather than with issues of the past. The groups which we find in Mark's pages symbolise groups of people within his own actual world. Mark fights against opponents of his own day; he defends christian practices current in his time, whatever the situation may have been in the days of Jesus. In the controversies of Mark's Gospel we glimpse the quarrels which beset Jews and Christians, not in the Galilee of Jesus, but in the Rome of Mark.

The Pharisees and the scribes have two questions. First, why do the disciples of Jesus not behave according to the traditions of the elders and, secondly, why do they eat with unclean hands?

Counter attack

Jesus does not immediately address himself to the questions of his interrogators; rather, he attacks the basis of their criticism. He call his opponents *hypocrites*, a word which originally meant an actor and so one who is merely playing a part. Jesus attacks the very integrity of those who claimed to speak with an authoritative voice in religious matters.

The quotation which Jesus uses as a battering ram to down his antagonists is not taken from the Hebrew Bible but from its Greek translation, familiar to Mark but hardly to Jesus. Here is what the original Hebrew says:

> … this people draw near with their mouth
> and honour me with their lips,
> while their hearts are far from me,
> and their fear of me is a commandment of men
> learned by rote … (Isaiah 29:13).

The original text referred to people who pay lip service to God, whose worship does not go beyond mere words and whose reverence for God owes more to routine convention than to heartfelt conviction. It does not refer to people who pay more attention to human tradition than to divine command, the very point that Jesus wishes to make. It may be that Mark uses the Greek version of Isaiah because that was the one familiar to his

Greek-speaking readers. But the fact remains that the original quotation is not an appropriate response to the challenge of the Pharisees, whereas the Greek version is. It may be that Jesus quoted Isaiah in another context and Mark has tailored his words to suit the present controversy. Be that as it may, what is clear is that Jesus accuses his opponents of putting their religious practices above the very laws of God. Traditions handed down by (some) religious teachers have been put on a pedestal over the commandments of God.

An illustration

In order to press home his broad-fronted attack, Jesus provides a telling illustration of how his opponents reject the commandments of God in favour of their own interpretations. The law of God, expressed in the teaching of Moses, God's spokesman, is clear: Honour your father and your mother (Exodus 20:12). So serious is the divine obligation to honour one's parents that the Torah itself (again, God's solemn pronouncement) decrees that whoever curses his father or his mother, shall be put to death (Exodus 21:17). It is true that, in the time of Jesus, the death penalty was not carried out; nevertheless, the seriousness of caring for one's parents is reinforced by the teaching of Moses.

A recent discovery helps to unravel some of the difficulties which surround Mark's text. The word *corban* has been discovered on an ossuary lid found in a tomb dating from the time of Jesus. The inscription reads: *All that a man may find to his profit in this ossuary is an offering (corban) to God from him who is within.* The inscription may have been an attempt to ward off grave robbers. In any case, the meaning is clear: any valuables found in the ossuary belong to God. Similarly, in the case of Mark's story, the son dedicates his wealth to God and avoids the duties so plainly emphasised in the Bible. It may very well be that the man simply swore an oath that his wealth was dedicated to God but did not actually hand it over to the Temple treasury. In such a case, his oath, were it upheld by the religious authorities, would be regarded as binding and his parents would be left to fend for themselves. In this way, the commandment of God was set at nought.

The illustration is not without difficulty. If Jesus is saying that a commandment of the Torah must not be set aside in favour of an oath of dedication, then what about the Torah's insistence that an oath is binding?

> When a man vows a vow to the Lord, or swears an oath to bind himself by a pledge, he shall not break his word, he shall do according to all that proceeds out of his mouth (Numbers 30:2).

Strictly speaking, then, the dilemma posed in Jesus' illustration is not a question of choosing between what is laid down in the written Torah and what is found in the traditional teaching of the rabbis handed down from one generation to the next. But Jesus is surely right to emphasise that one cannot play off one law against another in order to avoid one's bounden obligations.

Another difficulty presents itself. Would the Pharisees and some scribes (the recognised experts in interpreting the Torah and oral tradition) have agreed that the force of a vow must take precedence over a commandment of God? There is some evidence that the matter was discussed among rabbis and so there must have been disagreement and differing opinions. But it is far from clear that the Pharisees, down to the very last man, as it were, would claim that their traditions came before the clear and unambiguous word of God.

Defilement

The Pharisees had opened their attack on Jesus because they had observed that some of his disciples ate with defiled hands. This, of course, does not mean that they ate with dirty hands. What is at stake here is not hygiene but religious ritual. The washing is a sign of dedication, of belonging to a people described as a kingdom of priests and a holy nation (Exodus 19:6). The disciples, by neglecting to perform the prescribed religious rite, make themselves ritually unclean, that is to say, unacceptable to God. That, at least, is the point of view of the Pharisee.

The crowd, always waiting in the wings to be summoned when required, is called to hear Jesus' views on the matter. People are not made unacceptable to God by what they eat; it is not external things which make for uncleanness in the religious sense. It is what comes out of the human heart, from defilement within, that is evil. There is a degree of exaggeration in the way Jesus expresses himself here, rather as on the occasion when he tells his disciples that they must hate father and mother and wife

125

and children and brothers and sisters (Luke 14:26). Can you imagine Jesus hating Joseph and Mary? The exaggeration is to make us sit up, to shock us into serious reflection. Jesus does not mean that ritual purity is of no consequence whatsoever. He is claiming that there are matters of far greater importance. As long ago and as far away as the days of Noah, the word of God had declared that the imagination of the human heart is evil from youth (Genesis 8:21).

The teaching of Jesus, as so often in Mark, becomes more specific when he enters into the privacy of the house and the disciples question him on the rather puzzling statement made to the crowd. In the face of their lack of understanding (by now a commonplace in this Gospel), Jesus explains that food cannot defile since it does not enter the human heart (we would say human spirit) but merely the stomach and is evacuated. What truly defiles, what truly makes us unacceptable to God are those actions which spring from the evil desires of the human spirit: evil thoughts, fornication, theft, murder, adultery, coveting and the rest.

Mark puts in a word of explanation: thus he declared all foods clean. One of the most divisive debates in the early Church was on the question of food. Should the Gentiles have to accept all the dietary laws of the Jews, as laid down in the Book of Leviticus where whole pages are given over to listing what you may and may not eat (try Leviticus 11), or should they not? The debate caused Paul and Peter to have a row (Galatians 2:11-21) and forced early Christians to come to a compromise decision on the matter (Acts of the Apostles 15:1-21). Mark has no doubts. But the teaching of Jesus can hardly have been as unambiguous as he would have us believe. Once again, Mark is reflecting the state of affairs in his day rather than in the days of Jesus of Nazareth. But Mark's unambiguity raises another problem. Jesus condemns the Pharisees for placing their traditions above the Torah. But Jesus himself, by setting aside all the Torah's divine legislation concerning clean and unclean food, is taking upon himself the power to change the Torah itself, to undo the clear commandments of God. Who is this man?

Jesus has been attacked for inconsistency. He condemns the Pharisees for down-grading God's commandments in favour of their traditional teaching, yet he abolishes a whole swathe of divine law concerning food. Later on, we shall see that Jesus changes the clear teaching of the Bible on divorce. By what right does he undo the commands and ordinances of God?

In chapter one we were told that the people were astonished at the teaching of Jesus. They were amazed at one who spoke with unique authority. Jesus did not teach as the scribes who handed on what had been passed down. The crowds in the synagogue recognised an altogether more powerful voice (1:21-28). As we journeyed through the pages of Mark, the origin and nature of that voice has become clearer. With astonishment the people of Capernaum heard the claim that the Son of man had authority on earth to forgive sin and saw for themselves the living proof of the matter in the paralysed man who took up his bed and walked (2:1-12). We have listened to the claim that the Son of man is Lord even of the sabbath and learned that his authority is no less than that of King David (2:23-28). More than that, for the authority of the Son is greater than that of the king, we have seen the storm calmed, the Legion destroyed, sickness overcome and death defeated (4:35-5,43). Such authority can only come from God. If Jesus is doing that which only God can do, who, then, is he?

Jesus refines and even re-interprets the divine command-ments. Not only does he challenge the interpretation of the Torah offered by the scribes and Pharisees but he confronts the Torah itself. Such a thing is impossible – unless, of course, Jesus has a mandate from God so to do. And that is what Mark believes and teaches. Jesus is not a scribe who debates the meaning of the Torah. He is one entrusted by God to declare his own command-ments. Behind the authority of Jesus stands the authority of God.

PRAYER

The Books of the Chronicles are not everybody's cup of tea. But they do contain some of the most beautiful prayers in all of Scripture. Here is one which sings God's praises and we can so easily apply its words to Jesus for in the teaching and works of the Son we can see the face of the Father:

Blessed are you, O Lord, the God of Israel our Father, for ever and ever. Yours, O Lord, is the greatness and the power, and the glory, and the victory, and the majesty; for all that is in the heavens and in the earth is yours; yours is the kingdom, O Lord, and you are exalted as head above all. Both riches and honour come from you, and you rule over all. In your hand are power and might; and in your hand it is to make great and to give strength to all. We thank you, our God, and praise your glorious name (1 Chronicles 29:10-13).

The Syrophoenician woman
Mark 7:24–8:10

The discussion concerning defilement was a burning issue in the early years of the Church. The first Christians were Jews but when the idea that non-Jews might be admitted to the new movement began to gain currency, the question arose as to what extent, if any, Gentiles had to accept Jewish laws and customs on a whole host of issues. We have seen how Peter and Paul quarrelled over the matter and how a group of influential Christians, meeting in Jerusalem, tried to reach a compromise on the issue (Acts 15:1-21). The compromise did not hold and, by the time Mark came to write his story, he was convinced that in the matter of defilement and purification rituals there was no obligation to accept the prescriptions of Jewish law and tradition. That is why he placed his discussion on the matter where he did (7:1-23). It stands as an introduction to three miracle stories by means of which the ministry of Jesus is extended to Gentiles.

In Mark's perspective, Jesus declares that purification is unnecessary and food regulations superfluous before he sets out to instigate a ministry among pagans. Once again, the dispute and contentions of Mark's day dictate not only what he narrates but also the shape he gives to his story.

The three miracle stories which are now to engage our attention are closely bound to each other because they take place in pagan territory. It will be convenient, however, to examine each separately but we must be careful to remember that what Mark has joined together we must not set asunder. We will begin with the story of a remarkable woman – a daughter of a most remarkable people, the Phoenicians.

We have met the region of Tyre and Sidon before (3:8) but a closer look at the economy of the area will be fruitful. Mark's description of the woman as a Greek, a Syrophoenician *by birth*, will also repay careful scrutiny.

Tyre

Tyre was a rich commercial city on the Mediterranean seacoast but it depended on the lands of Upper Galilee for its food supplies. There were many Jewish villages in its hinterland and these were overshadowed by the economic wealth of the great trading city. The rich city dwellers were able to buy up the available produce of the Jewish peasant farmers of Galilee who were, as a result, forced to make do with an inadequate diet. Accordingly, there was little love lost between the urban and pagan rich and the rural and God-fearing poor (look up Acts 12:20).

A Greek, a Syrophoenician

By informing his readers that the woman was a Greek, Mark is not referring to her nationality but to her social status. The woman was one of the well-educated, wealthy and free citizens of the Roman empire who enjoyed privileges not extended to the under classes and slaves (recall how proud St Paul was to possess full citizenship; see Acts 22:28). Belonging to the oppressor rather than to the oppressed, the woman's background was such as to excite the hatred and disdain of impoverished Jewish peasants. And, of course, in their eyes, she had a further disability. She was a woman.

The Phoenicians were the great traders of the ancient Middle East. Mark identifies this pagan woman as a Phoenician from Syria. The other Phoenician community in the Mediterranean basin was in Libya and its chief city was Carthage.

READING THROUGH AGAIN

Jesus makes his way into the pagan world, most likely to the Jewish villages which straddled the borders of Syrophoenicia and Galilee. The attempt to remain anonymous is thwarted by the fame which had attracted people to him from this very region (3:8). A woman comes to the house. Mark's readers will have noted that people who come seeking Jesus in a house are presented sympathetically and receive the reward of their faith in the man from Nazareth. After Simon's mother-in-law was healed in the house, the whole city was gathered about the door and he healed many who were sick with various diseases, and cast out many demons (1:29-34). The four men who lowered their paralysed friend through the roof of the house had their friend restored to good health (2:1-12). But the one who approaches Jesus in the region of Tyre is from a wealthy, oppressive and pagan people.

The woman falls at the feet of Jesus. This is a good sign. The reader will recall that the woman with the haemorrhage fell down before him and she received what she most desired (5:33). The man who was possessed by a legion of demons fell down in worship before Jesus and he received what he most needed (5:6). The fact that the man in the country of the Gerasenes was a pagan augers well for the woman of Tyre. But the interview with Jesus gets off to a frosty start.

The initial reply of Jesus to the woman's request, *Let the children first be fed, for it is not right to take the children's bread and throw it to the (little) dogs*, has caused embarrassment to many of Mark's readers, for the term "dog" was in common use among Jews as a term of contempt for Gentiles. To suppose that Jesus rebuffed the woman with the customary rudeness of his fellow Jews is too much for some and they take refuge in the fact that Mark actually uses a Greek word which means "little dogs", and go on from that observation to surmise that Jesus spoke the words whimsically and gently, with the intention of testing the woman's faith. However, there is no indication in the story as to what tone of voice Jesus may or may not have used and to be called a little dog is hardly less insulting than to be called a dog.

If we are not to sweeten the reply of Jesus, neither are we required to see it as a gruff and cruelly crushing remark. The matter may be clarified by recalling a scene in the Gospel according to John. In the course of his conversation with the marvellous woman of Samaria the question of where one ought to worship God comes up. Is it right and fitting for Samaritans to worship God in their temple on Mount Gerazim or are the Jews right in saying that the temple in Jerusalem is the only place where one can truly worship? Jesus accepts neither position, pointing out that true worship is that which will be instigated by the Holy Spirit which is to be given to the disciples by the Risen Lord. Jesus explains that the Samaritans, like everyone else, must realise that salvation is from the Jews, that is to say, that the new community of God, what we would call the Church, is founded on the spiritual heritage of Judaism. Jesus is not being harsh with the woman but he does insist on explaining the order God laid down for his plan of salvation (John 4:20-24). As St Paul puts it, God gives salvation to everyone but in his own way, that is to the Jew first and then to the Greek (= Gentiles) (Romans 1:16).

What, then, Jesus wishes to establish is the order of priority which governs his ministry. What saves the statement from being an arrogant put down is the word "first". It is that word which changes its character. Jesus is not saying that pagans are never to be served with bread from the table. He is saying that they are to be served but not first. It is this optimistic view of things that the woman seizes and turns to her advantage.

The woman begins her reply to Jesus by addressing Jesus as Lord. The Greek word used here was the ordinary word employed by an inferior when addressing a superior; for example, a slave addressing his master or a citizen addressing the emperor. "Sir" would be the appropriate translation in such cases and, indeed, most English translations put *Yes, Sir* on the woman's lips. But the word was adopted by Christians and applied to Jesus to express their faith in his unique status as Son of God. It seems very likely that Mark intends the woman's greeting to have its full Christian force. Since this is the only occasion on which Jesus is addressed as Lord in Mark's Gospel, we may be surprised to find it on the lips of a pagan woman. But that is the way Mark does things. We will be further surprised to find a rough, pagan soldier, routinely completing a messy crucifixion, declare of the victim, *Truly this man was the Son of God* (15:39). Mark wishes us to know that the woman showed true insight into the identity of Jesus and that, as a consequence, she rightly understood the priority of his ministry among his own people. But she is equally insistent that the Gentiles are not to be excluded permanently from the Lord's table. They , too, are his concern.

The saying of the woman, *yet even the dogs under the table eat the children's crumb*s, while it acknowledges the position of pagans in the divine order of things, nonetheless lays claim to attention. In acknowledging that Jesus is Lord and in recognising the priorities in his ministry, she expresses her faith and, accordingly, the heart of Jesus is moved to grant release to her daughter.

The story of the Syrophoenician pagan woman mirrors the story of the development of Christianity. The ministry of Jesus was exercised, for the most part, among his own people. But Jesus made sufficient excursions into the world of pagans to convince many influential Christians, such as Paul and Barnabas, that the gospel could not be confined to one people. The woman's story exemplified for those who fought for the universality of the gospel that there is not one chosen people; all people are chosen.

Accordingly, the story of this remarkable woman endeared itself to christian hearts. She was given the name Justa and one writer records:

> There is among us a certain Justa, a Syrophoenician ... whose little daughter was tormented by a serious disease, and who came to our Lord, calling upon him and begging him to heal her daughter ... and she obtained healing for her daughter, as she asked... (But), with her daughter, she was driven out from her home by her husband, whose sentiments were opposed to hers.

Tradition gave the little girl a name: she was called Berenice.

The second of the three miracles which extend the ministry of Jesus to the lands and peoples of the world outside Israel is the story of the healing of a deaf man who also suffered from a serious speech impediment (7:31-37). Mark tells the story in his usual brisk manner but, again as usual, there is a depth to his tale which is not immediately apparent.

READING THROUGH

English translations tend to tidy up the rather confusing geographical details which preface the story of the deaf man. An accurate, unpolished rendering yields *And again going out from the region of Tyre, he went through Sidon to the Sea of Galilee through the region of Decapolis*. The confusion is apparent to the reader who has a good map. Taken at their face value, these geographical details imply that Jesus, intending to return to the lake, that is, to travel south-east, sets off directly north for Sidon, twenty miles further up the coast, goes through the city, then turns east and somehow manages to get to the Decapolis region without first coming to the lake. Such confusion will not trouble those who come to Mark's Gospel to learn who Jesus is rather than the niceties of the geography of the near-east. But Mark's vagueness may be an indication that he was not familiar with the regions traversed by Jesus, except in the most general way. In other words, his rather patchy geographical awareness may indicate that Mark's Gospel was written far away from the land of Jesus.

Ephphatha

The first tellers of the gospel were Palestinian Jews whose language was a form of Hebrew (Aramaic). When the good news of Jesus spread beyond the confines of Israel, preachers adopted the *lingua franca* of the Mediterranean world which was Greek. But some words of the language spoken by Jesus on particularly impressive occasions lingered on and were lovingly preserved. Of the four gospel-makers Mark is most careful to hand on the very words of Jesus himself. It is both convenient and instructive to draw them together:

Talitha cumi = Little girl, arise (5:41).
Corban = Given to God (7:11).
Ephphatha = Be opened (7:34).
Abba = Father (14:30).
Eloi, Eloi, lama sabachthani = My God, my God, why have you forsaken me? (15:34).

In these words we can hear the very sounds uttered by Jesus of Nazareth.

READING THROUGH AGAIN

Whatever the vagaries of Mark's geography, there is no doubt that he intends the healing of the deaf man to take place on the eastern shore of the Sea of Galilee, in a region whose inhabitants were predominantly pagan. Mark does not identify the people who bring the man to Jesus or the man himself as Gentiles but the fact that he places the story in the Decapolis region strongly suggests that they were.

Not only was the man deaf but he suffered from an impediment of speech. The word used to describe his speech impairment is exceedingly rare. It occurs only here in the New Testament and only once in the Greek version of the Old Testament.. By using such a rare word Mark is surely pointing his reader to the text in the prophet Isaiah which speaks of the time when God's glory will be made manifest in the healing of all human weakness and distress:

Then will the eyes of the blind be opened
and the ears of the deaf unstopped.
Then will the lame leap like a dear,
and the mute tongue shout for joy (Isaiah 35:5-6 [NIV]).

By means of his subtle biblical reference Mark provides his readers with yet another clue as to the identity of Jesus. The divine intervention in human affairs promised in Isaiah is taking place in the ministry of Jesus.

Jesus takes the man aside. We know withdrawals from the public gaze (6:31; 9:2; 9:28; 13:3) mark occasions which are of particular importance. The gestures used by Jesus – placing his fingers in the man's ears, touching his tongue with spittle, looking up to heaven, sighing (as Jesus often did in the face of human distress) – confirm the solemnity of the occasion. Bringing the power of God's salvation into the world of the Gentile is a matter of the greatest moment.

To state that *his tongue was released* misses the point. Mark says that *the bond of his tongue was loosed*. Running through all the ancient world was the belief that a human being could be bound or fettered by demonic influences. Luke records a question of Jesus to a synagogue official who was annoyed that he healed on the sabbath: *Ought not this woman, a daughter of Abraham whom Satan bound for eighteen years, be loosed from this bond on the sabbath?* (Luke 13:16). That, too, is Mark's view. He means to tell his readers that not merely was a deaf mute made to speak but that a demonic power had been broken and a work of Satan undone.

The instruction to keep silent is, as elsewhere, disregarded and the great deed is proclaimed. *Astonished beyond measure,* the people declare, in words which re-echo Isaiah 35:5, their confidence that in the deeds of Jesus the salvation of God is brought to distressed human beings.

The third miracle crowns the work of Jesus among the pagans. A woman has her possessed daughter restored to her; a man has his hearing and speech restored; now a great crowd will be fed in the desert (8:1-10). The blessings showered on the people of Israel are poured out on the Gentiles.

READING THROUGH

The Feeding of Four Thousand is surely a second version of the story we encountered in 6:30-44. There are many similarities between the two. Both incidents take place in the desert. In both Jesus has compassion on the people. The question: *How many loaves have you?*, recurs, as does the command to sit on the ground. In both the disciples are given the food to distribute, the people eat and are satisfied, the fragments are gathered. In each the dismissal of the crowd is followed by a journey in the boat. While there are differences between the two accounts, the substantial similarities make it certain that we have here two versions of a single event. Is it not impossible to believe that the disciples could so quickly have forgotten the first feeding?

We may make a number of guesses as to why Mark chose to repeat the story. We have reached a point in his story where the disciples come under close scrutiny and are found lacking in understanding. The feeding stories will soon become a subject of discussion between Jesus and the disciples and they are upbraided for their failure to see the significance of the events in which they had played so prominent a role (8:14-21). We will note the disciples lack of understanding as we proceed.

It has long been suggested that the first feeding symbolises the giving of the bread of life to Jewish people and the second to the pagans. But while it is fairly clear that one takes place in Galilee and the other outside the land of Israel, we cannot be sure that Mark wishes to make that fact the significant point of his narratives. The emphasis in each would appear to be on the location (desert), the inability of the disciples to deal with the problem, the action of Jesus (breaking, reciting the blessing, giving to the disciples), the satisfaction of the crowds. We shall attend to these matters below.

Dalmanutha

Dalmanutha is unknown and Matthew, when he came to tell the story, mentions *the region of Magadan* (15:39). If such a town or region existed, it has left no mark on the pages of history.

READING THROUGH AGAIN

The second feeding, like the first, takes place in the desert. Mark wishes his readers to recall that God fed the people of Israel in the desert. The account of the matter in Numbers 11 has surely influenced him. Failing to understand God's purpose, Moses poses faithless questions:

> Why hast thou dealt ill with thy servant? And why have I not found favour in thy sight, that thou didst lay the burden of all this people upon me? Did I conceive all this people? Did I bring them forth, that thou shouldst say to me, "Carry them in your bosom, as a nurse carries the suckling child, to the land which thou didst swear to give their fathers?" Where am I to get meat to give all this people? For they weep before me and say, "Give us meat, that we may eat". I am not able to carry all this people alone, the burden is too heavy for me (Numbers 11:11-14).

Put Mark's disciples in the place of the complaining, faithless Moses. They are in a desert; they are confronted with the problem of feeding a multitude of people; they expressed their incredulity that they should be expected to meet such a challenge: *How can one feed these people with bread here in the desert?*

Moses is rebuked for his lack of trust in God's promise to take care of all the people and is assured that *The Lord will give you meat, and you shall eat* (Numbers 11:18). In the feeding of thousands in the desert Jesus is seen to be doing what God had done in ancient days. Once again, we are forced to confront the identity question: Who is this man?

Mark's readers will, of course, have noticed that the words and gestures of Jesus resemble closely the words and gestures which were part of their celebration of the Eucharist. Indeed, the word which is translated *having given thanks* is *eucharistesas* from which is derived the word *eucharist*. No doubt the Feeding of the Four Thousand (and the Five Thousand) will have been seen as a sign of things to come. Just as Jesus miraculously fed a multitude in the desert, so after the resurrection and in the life of the Church he will continue to feed all who come to him and they will be satisfied.

PRAYER

When a disciple asked Jesus to teach his followers to pray, Jesus replied, *When you pray, say:*

Father! Hallowed be thy name! Thy kingdom come! Give us each day our daily bread. Forgive us our sins, for we ourselves forgive everyone who is indebted to us. And lead us not into temptation.

This, of course, is not the "Our Father" most familiar to us. This is Luke's version and we should not neglect it entirely, if only for the reason that it is almost certainly closer to the actual prayer of Jesus than the more florid edition to which we are accustomed (see Matthew 6:9-13). Luke will certainly have wished his prayer for our daily bread to be understood as a prayer for that bread from heaven by which the Lord sustains his disciples on their journey of faith (see Luke 24:35). It is a prayer which reminds us of God's care in Jesus for all. He is the father of all, Jew and Gentile.

The leaven of the Pharisees
Mark 8:11-26

The three miracles performed in pagan territory, if not exclusively for pagans (the areas had sizeable, if minority, Jewish populations) provide a typical Marcan arrangement. A woman comes to Jesus, a man learns to hear, people are fed. The order of the three stories reflects staging posts on the journey into discipleship: come to Jesus (a woman heard of him, and came and fell down at his feet – 7:25), learn to hear (and his ears were open – 7:35), share in the bread of the Eucharist (and they ate and were satisfied 8:7). Deftly, Mark has sketched the pattern of discipleship for all ages: come, listen, share. Not all, of course, who come to Jesus, remain to pray. The next three incidents in Mark's story are of a more sombre hue.

READING THROUGH

We have met the Pharisees and Herod before. Twice in Mark's Gospel the Pharisees combine with Herod's supporters to oppose Jesus (3:6; 12:13). Leaven, a substance that produces fermentation in dough, is taken by Matthew (16:5) to mean teaching, by Luke (12:1) to refer to hypocrisy, but generally was taken as a symbol of the evil tendencies and inclinations of the human heart. St Paul speaks of the leaven of malice and evil (1 Corinthians 5:8).

The attitude of the Pharisees and the Herodians is consistently hostile to Jesus throughout Mark's story and the leaven of malice and evil seems an appropriate description for these implacable opponents of Jesus.

Bethsaida

We have met Bethsaida before (6:45). There is some dispute as to whether Mark is referring to a town on the western shore of the lake or to one on the northeastern shore, Bethsaida Julias, the capital of Gaulanitis, in the territory of Herod Philip. The later is more likely since Mark places it *on the other side* (8:13), a term reserved for the eastern shore.

READING THROUGH AGAIN

Unlike the distraught pagan woman who came and fell down at his feet, the Pharisees come to argue, not for the purpose of enlightenment, but in order to test Jesus, the very thing that Satan sought to do in the desert (1:13). As ever, the Old Testament will prove to be an indispensable guide to what Mark is about.

The Pharisees demand a sign from heaven (that is, from God). The story of the ancient people of Israel, delivered from slavery in Egypt by *all the signs which I have wrought among them* (Numbers 14:11) is the story of people never satisfied by the great wonders the Lord has done to bring them to freedom. A psalm writer urges the people of his generation not to behave in the hard-hearted and faithless ways of their ancestors:

> Harden not your hearts, as at Meribah,
> as on the day at Massah in the wilderness,
> when your fathers tested me,
> and put me to the proof,
> though they had seen my work (Psalm 95:8-9).

What the Book of Deuteronomy calls *a perverse and crooked generation* (Deuteronomy 32:5) constantly plagued Moses for further proofs of God's loving concern, so that the great prophet complained, *Why do you find fault with me? Why do you put the Lord to the proof?* (Exodus 17:2). The Pharisees who come to Jesus demanding *a sign from heaven* (that is, from God) are like the faithless generation of old. The great wonders wrought by Jesus are not enough to convince those who will never be convinced: there are none so blind as those who will not see.

When the man with the withered hand appeared before Jesus in the synagogue at Capernaum (3:1), Jesus asked whether it was lawful to do good on the sabbath. The silence of the congregation provoked him to anger and grief, anger at their unwillingness to put people before precept, grief at the hardness of heart which refuses to accept what God is offering them in the work of the prophet from Galilee. The Pharisees who had so clearly rejected what they had witnessed in Capernaum are not now to be awarded with a further sign. Anger and grief return to the heart of Jesus. No sign will avail in the face of such unbelief. No sign, therefore, will be given. As if to emphasise his rejection of their demands, Jesus embarks once again and heads for the eastern shore, the gentile side of the lake.

No sign shall be given to this generation. But the phrase *except the sign of Jonah* will come into the minds of many readers who will recall the words from Matthew (12:39; 16:4) and Luke (11:29). Just as Jonah was in the belly of the great sea-beast for three days and three nights (Jonah 1:17) so Jesus will remain in the tomb and, after three days, will rise again as a sign that God has vindicated his life's work and established his identity as *my beloved Son* (9:7). But the sign of the risen Jesus is not an option Mark wishes to adopt. He is, of course, aware of the resurrection but he does not wish to stress it. For Mark the witness which bears weight is the vigorous defence which Jesus makes before the Sanhedrin and, finally, the agonising death on the cross which leads even pagan soldiers to acknowledge the plainest truth of all: *Truly this was the Son of God* (15:39). For Mark's readers, caught up in Nero's persecution and its aftermath (*they will deliver you up to councils; and you will stand before governors and kings for my sake, to bear testimony before them... and brother will deliver up brother to death, and a father his child...* [13:9-12]), the witness that they may be called upon to make, the sign they may be forced to give, is steadfastness in the face of trial, persecution and even death.

Only one loaf

After the teaching of the day of parables (chapter 4), the disciples and Jesus set out across the lake to the eastern shore. On the way, a great storm is calmed but the disciples fail to answer the question which the incident provokes: *Who then is this, that even the wind and sea obey him?* On landing, Jesus heals the man possessed by a legion of demons.

After the first feeding of a multitude of people, Jesus sends the disciples across the lake, again from west to east, but shortly appears to them walking on the water. The disciples, yet again, fail to understand the significance of what they have witnessed. On landing, Jesus heals many sick people who are brought to him.

Now, for the third time, after the exchange with the Pharisees concerning the demand for a sign, Jesus and the disciples set out from west to east. During the voyage a significant conversation takes place which highlights the disciples' lack of understanding. On arrival at Bethsaida, Jesus heals a blind man.

The pattern is clear: Jesus and his disciples set out to cross the sea from Galilee to the pagan east shore. On the way, a significant event (storm, walking on water, deep conversation) takes place which reveals the inability of the disciples to understand who Jesus is or what he is about. On coming to land, Jesus exercises his ministry of healing, as if to demonstrate by deed what the disciples fail to understand.

Paying attention to Mark's pattern in the telling of the criss-crossings of the lake helps to pinpoint what he wishes to empha-sise: the disciples do not understand who Jesus is or what he is about. Though in a privileged position as his constant compan-ions and recipients of private and detailed instruction (*privately to his own disciples he explained everything* – 4:34), the disciples of Jesus prove themselves unable to grasp the truth concerning his person or the importance of hearing his word.

Ignoring the anger and grief of Jesus in his dismissal of the unbelieving Pharisees, the disciples, having apparently learned nothing from the feeding of two large crowds with a few loaves and fishes, are concerned that, except for one loaf, they had forgotten to bring bread. The attempt of Jesus to bring their minds to bear on more important matters proves to be futile and exasperating. One can detect the annoyance and frustration of Jesus in his many unanswered questions.

The attitude of the Pharisees and of Herod toward Jesus is undisguised hostility. Even a tiny amount of leaven (yeast) will cause the loaf to rise. The disciples are warned to avoid the slightest taint of the corrupting disbelief of the Pharisees and Herod and his ilk. They continue to argue with one another over their lack of provisions. The Pharisees refuse to see the hand of God in the miracles of Jesus; the disciples fail to see or even to remember that *he has done all things well; he even makes the deaf to hear and the dumb to speak* (7:37), not to mention feeding hungry people. Six of one and half a dozen of the other.

Listen to the disappointment and exasperation in the voice of Jesus:

Why do you discuss the fact that you have no bread ? Do you not yet perceive or understand? Are your hearts hardened? Having eyes do you not see? Having ears do you not hear? Do you not remember? When I broke the five loaves for the five thousand, how many baskets full of pieces did you take up? And the seven for the four thousand, how many baskets full of broken pieces did you take up?

There are only two passages in all of the New Testament which speak of the hardness of heart of Jesus' most intimate companions – here and at 6:52. If the disciples in Mark are portrayed as they are in order to warn Mark's readers of the challenges of discipleship in their time and in their place, then the warning is couched very forcefully indeed. Mark's readers would be familiar with the idea of the boat as an image of the Christian community, they would realise that one loaf (Jesus, the Eucharist) is sufficient, and they would understand the importance of listening to the word of Jesus, to listen to him and to share the bread of life. Once again, the process is remarkably like that by which a convert finds the way from paganism to instruction, from instruction to baptism and from baptism to a place at the table of the Eucharist.

A blind man sees
The boat pitches up at Bethsaida on the eastern shore and there follows an incident of healing which bears such a remarkable resemblance to the cure of the deaf man (7:31-37) that Mark is surely compelling his readers to pay attention. Identical phrases occur in each account: *And they (people) brought him... and they besought him... and he spat.* Notice, too, that in each there is a request to touch the afflicted persons, a request which is fulfilled, there is a taking aside privately, and, finally, a demand for secrecy.

The story of the deaf man follows a failed attempt by Jesus to overcome the intransigence of some Pharisees and scribes to come out of their narrow ways and give an open and generous hearing to what he has to say. But they, no less than the disciples, have hardened hearts and stopped ears. It is left to the pagan woman of Syrophoenicia to come to beg, to listen and to believe.

In like manner, the story of the blind man follows hard on the heels of the account of the Pharisees who come to argue, and who, like faithless generations of old, to seek a sign, to put Jesus to the test. No less than these, the disciples fail to understand, to grasp the significance of what they have seen and heard. They, too, have hardened hearts.

The detail with which the story of the blind man is told now becomes clear. The Lord must take the man in hand, he must lead him to where he can be with him privately. He must summon all his powers to overcome the blindness and restore sight. He spits, he touches. But the man sees but partially: walking men look like trees. The Lord must renew his efforts: *then again he laid his hands on his eyes.* And at last, *he saw everything clearly.* It is not too difficult to see in all this a parable of the career of the disciples. They as yet do not see. Much remains to be done and said. More failure lies ahead. But the resurrection will come. For the moment, they are like the half-cured man, stumbling about and bumping into trees.

Mark's readers will not have missed the point as far as their own position is concerned. They, too, are in danger of shallow discipleship, of misunderstanding, of myopia. If Peter, Andrew, James and John and the rest, can prove to be so incapable of reading the signs and hearing the words, what of themselves?

Half-way

We have come half-way. We have reached the end of the first act of Mark's drama. There is much that is already clear, yet much that is shrouded in semi-blindness and hardness of heart. The pivotal incident on the way to Caesarea Philippi, next to engage our attention, will conclude an act which has been characterised by blurred spiritual vision. It will set in train a time of darkness, unfold a journey from the green hills of Galilee to the place of the skull (15:22). But despair is not the final word. The blind man of Bethsaida at first saw people that *looked like trees.* But that isn't the end of the story for the blind man or for the disciples.

PRAYER

The disciples are going to need much attention if they are to shape up and become what they have been called to be. A more faithful reliance on Jesus will be needed, if they are to face what

144

lies ahead in Jerusalem. Once again, words from Psalm 22 might well be their prayer and, indeed, the prayer of all would-be disciples:

> [Lord] thou art he who took me from the womb;
> thou didst keep me safe upon my mother's breasts.
> Upon thee was I cast from my birth,
> and since my mother bore me thou hast been my God.
> Be not far from me,
> for trouble is near
> and there is none to help (Psalm 22:9-11).

Jesus the Messiah
Mark 8:27-30

The question of identity is everywhere present in Mark's story. Who is this man? Where does he get his authoriy – to forgive sin, to rule over the sabbath, to call the wind and the sea into obedience, to restore the sick to health, to penetrate the very portals of death?

On the way, skirting the villages of Caesarea Philippi, the question will be brought into the open. The disciples, hitherto bewildered and confused, will be asked directly to confront the issue which must be addressed by Christians of every place and time: *Who do you say that I am?*

READING THROUGH

The blind man saw partially and only when Jesus had laid his hands upon his eyes a second time did he see everything clearly. The man mirrors the state of confusion and limited understanding of the disciples. The journey to the villages of Caesarea Philippi yet again reveals them to be blind to the identity of the one who goes with them.

Caesarea Philippi

The city of Caesarea Philippi, in the district of Iturea to the north of Galilee, was situated in an area of great natural beauty near the source of the Jordan at the foot of Mount Hermon. Herod the Great had built a temple there in honour of Caesar Augustus beside a grotto consecrated to the Greek god Pan. Herod's son, Philip, built extensively in the area and renamed the city in honour of Tiberias Caesar and himself (to distinguish it from the other Caesarea on the Mediterranean coast). The city was the regional capital and a centre of Greco-Roman culture. Its population was largely pagan. It is here in this gentile territory that Peter, a Jew, declares Jesus to be the Messiah. At the end of the

146

story, a pagan Roman soldier, in the holy city of Jerusalem, will declare Jesus to be the Son of God (15:39).

On the way

Mark frequently mentions that people, disciples, or whoever, are *on the way* (*on the road* in some translations). Early Christians sometimes spoke of their new faith journey as the Way (the Acts of the Apostles speaks of people *belonging to the Way* – 9:2; see also 18:25; 19:23). Bearing this in mind, we might suspect that when Mark uses the word "way", he has two meanings in mind. On the one hand, of course, he wishes to refer to an ordinary journey, a geographical movement from A to B (for example, 6:8). On the other hand, he wishes to suggest that the journey is a journey of faith, a journey into discipleship. The way taken by Jesus and the disciples is, indeed, a journey from Bethsaida to the villages of Caesarea Philippi. But it is at the same time a way of learning, a journey into understanding, if the disciples are capable of understanding. But there is more. Mark wishes his readers to journey with Jesus and his friends, to listen and learn. The question of the identity of Jesus, and the other questions to which Mark's story gives rise, must be attended to by all, in every generation, who would seek to journey with Jesus, to become a disciple, to follow him wherever he goes.

Elijah

We have met Elijah before. The location of his ministry, his dress and eating habits, marked out John the Baptist as Elijah returned (1:4-6). Jews believed that the prophet Elijah would one day return to earth to prepare for and to witness to a new and final act of God on behalf of suffering and sinful humanity. Such belief arose because, according to the Second Book of Kings 2:2-11, the prophet did not die but *went up by a whirlwind into heaven.* The ascension of Elijah, people surmised, must be part of some great design of God. Thus grew the belief that Elijah would return and the very last verses of the Old Testament promise,

> Behold, I will send you Elijah the prophet before the great and terrible day of the Lord comes. And he will turn the hearts of fathers to their children and the hearts of children to their fathers ... (Malachi 4:5-6).

147

The Book of Ecclesiasticus, otherwise known as the Wisdom of Jesus the son of Sirach, provides a summary of the career of the fearless man from Tishbe:

Then the prophet Elijah arose like a fire, and his word burned like a torch. He brought a famine upon [the Israelites], and by his zeal he made them few in number. By the word of the Lord he shut up the heavens, and also three times brought down fire. How glorious are you, O Elijah, in your wondrous deeds! And who has the right to boast which you have? You raised a corpse from death and from Hades, by the word of the Most High; who brought kings down to destruction, and famous men from their beds; who heard rebuke at Sinai and judgments of vengeance at Horeb; who anointed kings to inflict retribution, and prophets to succeed you.

You were taken up by a whirlwind of fire, in a chariot with horses of fire; you who are ready at the appointed time, it is written, to calm the wrath of God before it breaks out in fury, to turn the heart of the father to the son, and to restore the tribes of Jacob (Sirach 48:1-10).

The full account of the exploits of Elijah will be found in 1 Kings 17–2 Kings 2.

One of the prophets

That speculation concerning the identity of Jesus should turn to the possibility that he was *one of the prophets* is hardly surprising. Not only would the authority with which he spoke and the deeds he performed for the weak and the infirm suggest to many that Jesus was heir to the great prophetical tradition, but there was also the belief that one day God would send a mighty prophet of the stature of Moses *and I will put my words in his mouth, and he shall speak to them all that I command him* (Deuteronomy 18:18). It is to be expected, therefore, that some people should judge that in Jesus of Nazareth they were face to face with the prophet promised long ago.

Messiah

The opening verse of Mark's Gospel proclaims Jesus as the Messiah, the anointed one. We have seen that the word signifies a special role in God's care of his people. Prophets, priests and kings were anointed to indicate that they were entrusted with particular responsibilities for the people. Some Jews believed that the long-awaited final act of God for the wellbeing of humanity would be entrusted to one individual, anointed to bring about the outpouring of God's mercy which would restore Israel to freedom and bring salvation to the world. It is clear from Mark's opening verse that he is keen to establish that Jesus is the Messiah, the anointed representative of God. Nonetheless, he uses the title sparingly (see 1:1; 8:29; 9:41; 12:35; 13:21; 14:61; 15:32) for it carried (at least, for some people) political and militaristic overtones, suggesting the overthrow of the Roman imperial power by force of arms.

READING THROUGH AGAIN

The question asked by Jesus *on the way* to Caesarea Philippi and the reply given by Peter bring to an end the first act of Mark's drama. The opening verse of Mark's prologue declared Jesus to be the Messiah, the Son of God. We have come half-way on our journey into the identity of Jesus. We need to take stock.

To the question, *Who do people say that I am?*, the disciples report the speculations mentioned earlier (6:14-15). John the Baptist, Elijah or one of the prophets of old has come to life. The question, however, cannot be satisfactorily answered by appeals to popular rumours. If the disciples are to be disciples, if they are to be found worthy to journey *on the way,* they must answer the question for themselves: *But who do you* (plural) *say that I am?*

Peter answers enthusiastically on behalf of the others: *You are the Christ.* We cannot be sure what exactly he might have meant by his declaration but it would be fair to Peter, and in keeping with the deeper knowledge that we, the privileged readers, have concerning the identity of Jesus, to say that he is right but much more needs to be said. Unlike Peter, we have Mark's word for it, and that of the heavenly voice and the supernatural demons, that Jesus is God's Son. Peter has yet to learn what we already know.

What had Peter and the others to go on? They will have seen demons driven out, leprosy cleansed, the storm calmed, a dead daughter restored to grieving parents, and much else besides, such that the crowds of ordinary folk were astonished beyond measure and declared, *He has done all things well; he even makes the deaf hear and the dumb speak.* Yet though this display of extraordinary power provoked the question of the source of the authority of Jesus, his true identity remained hidden, even from the disciples. For there were other forces at work. His association with sinners, his flouting of received religious conventions, above all his disregard for notions of what was and was not acceptable on the sabbath, had provoked opposition to such an extent that the leaders of public opinion and religious orthodoxy regarded him as possessed by the prince of demons (3:22) and even went so far as to take steps to have him destroyed (3:6). In view of such conflicting speculation, Peter's confession, on the face of it, has much to commend it. But as we shall see, his understanding of the messiahship of Jesus is far removed from that of his master.

After Peter's acknowledgment of the messiahship of Jesus (limited though it be), the disciples are warned not to tell anyone about Jesus. This is the first time in the story that secrecy is enjoined on the disciples. Clearly, what Peter had proclaimed is, on the one hand, of the utmost importance and, on the other, is so open to misunderstanding, that silence is the order of the day. As yet the disciples are not equipped to proclaim the true identity of Jesus and his destiny for they do not know him (*Do you not yet understand?* 8:21). It will take all of the second act of Mark's drama to school the disciples and even then they will all run away at the end (14:50).

The first act has come to an end. Our exploration into the identity of Jesus and the nature of discipleship to which that identity gives rise has come a long way. There is much more which needs to be said and done, if we are to grasp who Jesus is and how we are to follow him. But we have seen and heard enough to know that there are storm clouds about. The life of Jesus is under threat. Death stalks the pages of Mark with a fearful intensity. The second act of Mark's drama is likely to be a bloody affair.

PRAYER

Dark clouds hover over Mark's story. But there is much joy and we must hold fast to faith which assures that Good Friday is followed by Easter Sunday. However, we must not rush from death to resurrection, as if the death may be passed over. Praying Psalm 22 will keep us at the foot of the cross long enough to learn what it means.

ACT TWO

A QUESTION OF DESTINY:
MARK 8:31–15:39: DEATH ON A CROSS

SCENE 1: The Way of the Cross for Jesus and Disciples: 8:31–10:52
SCENE 2: The Fate of Jesus, Disciples and Jerusalem: 11:1–13:37
SCENE 3: The Passion reveals Jesus to be Son of God: 14:1–15:39

The prediction of suffering
Mark 8:31–9:1

At the end of the first act of Mark's Gospel one part of the secret has been established. Jesus is the Messiah, the divine messenger whose task it is give to humanity the Holy Spirit (1:8), to overcome the demons of evil which convulse and terrorise people (1:26; 5:3-4), to bring forgiveness of sins (2:10), to heal all "who were sick with various diseases" (1:34). Above all, Jesus is the preacher of the kingdom of God (1:14-15), the revealer of the kingdom's secret (4:11), the one who tells of a God who is determined to save, to rule over his creation with tenderness, to show us, in his words and deeds, a God who has compassion on the crowds of bewildered humanity, on the sheep who have no shepherd (6:34). But we have yet to understand the greatest secret of all: Jesus is the Son of God. To be sure, Mark has told us of this in his opening verse: "The beginning of the gospel of Jesus Messiah, Son of God" (1:1). We have heard the demons cry out "I know who you are, the Holy One of God" (1:24). But we have yet to understand how this man, whose family think he is mad (3:20), who is alleged by religious authorities to be "possessed by Be-el'zebul", the prince of demons (3:22), who "eats with tax collectors and sinners" (2:16), is yet none other than God's Son. How are we to grasp this astonishing truth, how are we to become so convinced of it that we will throw in our lot with him and become his disciples? The second act of Mark's drama will take us from Caesarea Philippi, where we learned that Jesus is God's Messiah (8:27-30), to the place of the skull, to Golgotha (15:22), where we find Jesus on a cross and hear a soldier declare, "Truly this man was the Son of God" (15:39). How can it be that a man can come to the most profound understanding of the person of Jesus only at the foot of a cross? The great dark shadow across the stage of the second part of Mark's story is the shadow of the cross. If we stand in that shadow, paradoxically, we will come to the light.

Strength in weakness

Have you noticed how human the Jesus of Mark's story is? Mark's Jesus is an emotional man. Consider these statements:

> he was moved with pity (1:41);
> Mhe sternly charged him (1:43);
> he looked around at them with anger, grieved at their hardness of heart (3:5);
> he marvelled (6:6);
> he sighed deeply in his spirit (8:12);
> he was indignant (10:14) ;
> he loved him (10:21);
> he was greatly distressed and troubled (14:33).

Mark's Jesus is not always in control, doesn't always know the answer. Consider these statements:

> Jesus could no longer openly enter a town (1:45).
> What is your name? (5:9).
> Who touched my garments? (5:30).
> He could do no mighty work there (6:5).
> How many loaves have you? Go and see (6:38).
> He would not have anyone know it; yet he could not be hid (7:24).
> Do you see anything? (8:23).
> What are you discussing with them? (9:16).
> How long has he had this? (9:21).
> What were you discussing? (9:33).
> He went to see if there was anything on it ... he found nothing but leaves (11:13.14).

Throughout his story Mark emphasises the weakness, the vulnerability and human limitations of Jesus (Matthew, who may very well have had a copy of Mark's Gospel in front of him as he wrote, omits every single one of the above statements). But from 8:31 onwards he presents a Jesus not alone subject to human frailty but destined for death, the ultimate human weakness. Hitherto, Mark hints at the sorry destiny of Jesus (see 2:20; 3:6; 3:19) but now the matter is out in the open (8:31-2; 9:31; 10:33-34). Strangely, the more we are drawn into understanding the fate of Jesus, the more we come to realise that, truly, this man is the Son of God. The nearer we come to the cross, the nearer we come to the truth.

Three times in the second act of Mark's drama we are warned of what lies ahead (8:31-32; 9:31-32; 10:32-34). We are told that Jesus insisted on teaching the disciples of his fate and we are left in no doubt that the disciples fail to grasp the point. A suffering, dying Messiah is beyond their ken. How could God permit the ignominious death of his anointed one? Of course, each statement ends with a declaration that Jesus will rise again but that does not make the death less terrible. Even Jesus himself would have preferred not to have had to face the terrors of crucifixion (14:36). Clearly, we will have to take the death of Jesus seriously. We will not hear what Mark wants to tell us if we run away from the horror of Good Friday to the joys of Easter Sunday.

Before we examine 8:31–9:1 in detail, there are some general questions that need to be addressed. Four come to mind as the most pressing:

1. How is it that the human, fallible Jesus of Mark's Gospel knows so clearly what is going to happen to him?
2. How is it that the disciples fail to grasp what Jesus is trying to tell them about his fate?
3. Who is responsible for the death of Jesus?
4. What does "he will rise" mean?

We will attend to these matters in turn.

Knowing the future

We have noted above that Mark presents a Jesus who has his limitations. When we consider the matter historically, we must remember that the Gospels were written after the death and resurrection of Jesus and were written in the light of these momentous events. During the time Jesus spent with his disciples the question of his confrontation with authorities must have come up. No doubt Jesus could foresee that he was on a collision course with some of the religious rulers of his day and that the likely outcome would be violence and death. Any shrewd observer, watching the career of Jesus, would have come to the same conclusion.

The gospel-makers were in an altogether different position. They had the benefit of hindsight and were able to put on the statements of Jesus a precision that they did not originally have.

Remember the writers were writing for Christians who knew the story and its outcome. The writers are not trying to prove to their readers that Jesus died and rose; they knew that already. They are trying, each in his own way, to delve into the meaning of these events. Mark, for example, is so precise in the detailed predictions of Jesus' passion and resurrection, particularly in 10:33-34, that the last three chapters of his Gospel follow what has been foretold down to the smallest detail.

Consider an odd fact. Mark's is a short story. He has sixteen short chapters (as the divisions stand in our modern Bibles). Yet six of these chapters (11-16) are devoted to the last week of Jesus' life. You might think that this is out of all proportion. Would we not wish to know more about the life of the Lord? But Mark wants us to understand that we will have no understanding of the life without a profound realisation of its end. Thus the end of the story colours everything Jesus does and informs everything he says.

Disbelieving disciples

Our second question is closely linked to the first. Mark presents the disciples in a bad light. Not only do they fail to grasp what he tells them but, at the end, one of them betrays him (14:43), they all run away (14:50) and Peter, the first to be called and privileged to witness the Transfiguration, with a great deal of cursing and swearing, denies he ever knew the man (14:71). Again, whatever the precise historical detail, Mark is deliberately underlining the failure of the disciples for the benefit of his readers. As we shall see, Mark is offering good news, gospel news. His good news is that even failed, betraying, denying disciples are not written off. Disciples may abandon Jesus. He does not abandon them.

Responsible persons

Who was responsible for the death of Jesus? Mark lists elders, chief priests, scribes and, finally, Gentiles in his three predictions. What is important to note is that the Jewish people were not responsible for the death of Jesus. Some of the religious authorities in Jerusalem (important priests, elders and some, but by no means all, scribes, made up the Sanhedrin or governing council in Jerusalem – see 14:55) moved against Jesus and handed him over to a Roman civil servant named Pilate. Pilate alone had the authority to put Jesus to death and he duly did so. We must be very careful not to fall into the outrageous crime of blaming the Jewish people for the death of Jesus of Nazareth.

Rising from the dead

As we make our way through the second act of Mark's drama, we shall have occasion to notice that the matter of rising from the dead is to the fore in many discussions. We would do well to ask ourselves what a contemporary of Jesus (let us say a thoughtful neighbour in Nazareth) would understand by resurrection from the dead. We might even ask what we understand when we declare that Christ is risen or what we mean by declaring in our Creed that we believe in "the resurrection of the dead". There are some surprises in store for us in Mark's second act!

READING THROUGH AGAIN

The second act opens with an astonishing revelation. The Messiah *must* suffer and be killed. That *must* indicates that what is about to happen is in accordance with the Scriptures, that is to say, in accordance with God's will. It is, indeed, astonishing that the Messiah will be put to death; it is well-nigh past belief that this violent death is sanctioned by God. As we move nearer and nearer to Jerusalem and to the place of the skull, Mark will reveal why this should be so. We must look for clues not only to how Jesus will be done to death but why.

Jesus speaks plainly but Peter will have none of it. He *rebukes* Jesus. We have met this word before. It is the very word with which Jesus confronts demons and shatters their power (1:25; 4;39; 9:25). It is with this strong word that Peter rejects the word of Jesus. But Jesus, seeing his disciples and, perhaps, realising that they, too, may want to join in the rebuke, turns on Peter with equal vigour. The man who had been nick-named Peter (the rock) is given yet another name, Satan! To reject a suffering and dying Messiah is to fly in the face of God. It is to miss God's purpose and align oneself with the ways of the world.

Suffering is not the fate of Jesus alone. It is the possible fate of all would-be disciples. Jesus calls on the crowd (that multitude of potential disciples which peoples Mark's stage) to follow him on the way of the cross. Mark's frightened community, trying to rebuild itself in the aftermath of terrible persecution and betrayal, is reminded that discipleship and the cross go together. And Jesus is not speaking in metaphors. He is not advocating self-denial. For many in Mark's community, to take up the cross and follow Jesus meant precisely that, to die by crucifixion.

Just as Jesus will be restored to life by a God who will not allow death an ultimate and everlasting victory, so the disciple who endures to the end will participate in God's final triumph. How foolish it would be to cling on to human life at the cost of missing out on the fullness of life offered to all when the Son of man comes in glory. When, in the fullness of time, the Son of man comes with the glory and authority of God to call creation to its ultimate destiny, those who in this life reject the way of humiliation and suffering, reject fellowship with Jesus, will, in turn, be rejected by him.

The statement in 9:1 is difficult. Certainly, some of the first generation of Christians believed that the so-called second coming of Jesus would take place quickly and in their lifetime. This is the view express by St Paul himself in the First Letter to the Thessalonians. Paul is trying to reassure the Christians of Thessalonika that those who have died will fare the same as those who are alive when Jesus comes again. They, too, will share in the general resurrection. Notice what he says:

For this we declare to you by the word of the Lord, that we who are alive, who are left until the coming of the Lord, shall not precede those who have fallen asleep [= have died]. For the Lord himself will descend from heaven with a cry of command, with the archangel's call, and with the sound of the trumpet of God. And the dead in Christ will rise first; *then we who are alive*, who are left, shall be caught up together with them in the clouds to meet the Lord in the air; and so we shall always be with the Lord (1 Thessalonians 4:15-17).

It may well be that Mark is comforting his harassed community with the thought that their suffering would be short-lived. If so, he can't have been very successful. We are still praying for the coming of the kingdom of God!

It seems better to take the words of 9:1 as applying to the story of the Transfiguration which follows immediately. Then

160

three of the disciples ("there are some standing here") will witness the revealing of the true glory of Jesus, the glory that will be revealed to all at the second coming.

PRAYER

Perhaps the prayer which Jesus taught his disciples would be a fitting response to the words of Jesus which call on disciples to do God's will, not their own. The version found in St Luke is sadly neglected. Here it is:

Father, hallowed be thy name.
Thy kingdom come.
Give us each day our daily bread;
and forgive us our sins,
for we ourselves forgive
everyone who is indebted to us;
and lead us not into temptation (Luke 11:2-4).

The transfiguration
Mark 9:2-13

Looking back and looking forward. That is the way Mark tells his story. He reaches back to the traditions of his people, especially to those written down in the scriptures, in order to enlighten his readers on the significance of what Jesus does or says. In the very beginning of his drama he called on the words of Isaiah (and other old-time prophets) to point the reader to the true origins of his story. It is none other than the story foretold in ancient times (1:2-3). John the Baptist appears, not out of the blue, but out of the promises of God, written in the scriptures, that a new way would be prepared, a new salvation offered. Isaiah is called upon again to strengthen the teaching of Jesus and to illustrate that when he speaks we hear the voice of God (7:6-8). The past is recalled to explain the present.

And looking forward. Mark does not hesitate, as he unfolds his story of Jesus, to hint of things to come. The predictions of the death and resurrection of Jesus are, of course, more than hints. But Mark is not always so forthcoming. Sometimes his hints for the future (the future of Jesus and of would-be disciples) have to be ferretted out. Readers have to have their wits about them. The story of the transfiguration of Jesus looks back and looks forward. The Roman god entrusted with the protection of doorways, passages, and bridges was called Janus and in art he is depicted with two heads facing opposite ways, the better to enable him to keep a sharp lookout. Mark's readers could do with a similar advantage!

READING THROUGH

A few features of Mark's narrative need clarifying. The rather odd "after six days", and the word "transfigured" demand attention. We need, too, to refresh our memories on some of the details of the careers of Elijah and Moses and to explore the business of the over-shadowing cloud.

162

After six days

At first glance, it would appear that "after six days" means just that. But Mark is not usually given to providing exact time details, at least, not until he is telling of the passion and death of Jesus (see 2:1 – the vague "after some days"; 2:13 – "he went out again" but he doesn't say when; 3:1 – "again he entered the synagogue" but no mention of when or where; examples are endless). When he is precise we suspect that something is afoot.

Look back. Look back to the Book of Exodus, the story of the great escape of God's people and their epic trek to freedom. The people come to Mount Sinai and Moses is called by God to ascend the mountain to receive the tablets of stone on which are written "the law and the commandment". Moses obeyed and this is what happened:

> Then Moses went up on the mountain, and the cloud covered the mountain. The glory of the Lord settled on Mount Sinai, and the cloud covered it for six days; and on the seventh day he called to Moses out of the midst of the cloud. Now the appearance of the glory of the Lord was like a devouring fire on the top of the mountain in the sight of the people of Israel. And Moses entered the cloud, and went up on the mountain (Exodus 24:15-18).

Moses spent six days of preparation on the mountain and, after six days, that is, on the seventh day (Exodus 24:16), God spoke to Moses and revealed his glory to him (Exodus 33:17-23). Of interest, too, is the fact that Moses separates himself from the people at the foot of the mountain and takes with him seventy elders and a special group of three people whose names are given: Aaron, Nadab, and Abihu (later we are told that Moses went up the mountain accompanied by Joshua only – Exodus 24:13). Add to this that he places his scene on "a high mountain" and we can be in no doubt that Mark is looking back to the story of the Exodus and using that ancient tale to clarify his own.

Transfigured

The story of the metamorphosis or change to the appearance of Jesus has been called the Transfiguration since the days of St Jerome (347-420 C.E.) who translated the Bible into a famous Latin version (called the Vulgate or common edition because it soon became the most popular translation in the western churches). In his translation he uses the latin phrase *transfiguratus est* to describe the luminous change witnessed by Peter, James, and John. Mark, unlike Matthew (17:2), does not specify that the face of Jesus was altered though he would seem to imply as much by saying that Jesus was transfigured. Like Matthew, he calls attention to the transformation to the garments of Jesus. Once again, looking back will elucidate.

In St Paul's second letter to the Christian community in Corinth the apostle has a rather peculiar passage concerning Moses, peculiar, that is, to our minds but not to the mind of a Jew steeped in the scriptures. Paul is arguing that the covenant which is given through Christ is superior to that given through Moses. Here is what he says:

> Since we have such a hope, we are very bold, not like Moses, who put a veil over his face so that the Israelites might not see the end of the fading splendour. But their minds were hardened; for to this day, when they read the old covenant, that same veil remains unlifted, because only through Christ is it taken away. Yes, to this day whenever Moses is read a veil lies over their minds; but when a person turns to the Lord the veil is removed. Now the Lord is the Spirit, and where the Spirit of the Lord is, there is freedom. And we all, with unveiled face, beholding the glory of the Lord, are being changed into his likeness from one degree of glory to another; for this comes from the Lord who is the Spirit (2 Corinthians 3:12-18).

Paul is attempting to point up the privileged position of those who are baptised. To do so he turns to the story of Moses. When Moses had spent forty days and nights on Mount Sinai communing with God, he came down from the mountain, with the two tablets of stone on which were written the commands of the Lord. But, the text explains, Moses did not realise that his face shone because he had been talking to God and when the people saw him they were afraid to come near him. Moses had to put a veil on his face:

> ... whenever Moses went in before the Lord to speak with him, he took the veil off, until he came out; and when he came out, and told the people of Israel what he was com-

manded, the people of Israel saw the face of Moses, the skin of Moses' face shone; and Moses would put the veil upon his face again, until he went in to speak with him (Exodus 34:34-35).

We have seen that the glory of God had settled on Mount Sinai (Exodus 24:16) and that Moses entered into this divine manifestation. The story of the veil is meant to show that only Moses was privy to the divine apparition. The reaction of the people to the reflected glory shining on the face of Moses is in line with Old Testament thinking that no one can see the face of God and live. Paul uses the story to show that all Christians are, through Jesus, brought into the divine sphere and may dwell in the divine presence without fear. Similarly, the transformation in the appearance of Jesus is an indication that through him divine glory, divine presence, is being revealed to Peter, James and John.

Elijah and Moses

A number of features in the careers of Elijah and Moses help to explain why they are in the story. First, both are associated with Mount Sinai in the Old Testament and both experience the presence of God on that mountain (in the case of Elijah, read 1 Kings 19:4-14 and note that Horeb is another name for Sinai). Secondly, Moses represents the Torah and Elijah the prophetical tradition and it is fitting that they should be present in the story of Jesus, the one who is seen as the fulfilment of both. Thirdly, both were severely tested and suffered much in their appointed vocations. Their presence on the mountain with Jesus is a reminder of the sufferings of the Son of man (see Luke 9:30). Fourthly, as we shall see, the presence of Elijah and Moses points to the future.

A cloud

The cloud is a symbol of the presence of God. During the journey through the desert to the land flowing with milk and honey God was with his people, guiding and protecting: *And the Lord went before them by day in a pillar of cloud to lead them along the way, and by night in a pillar of fire to give them light that they might travel by day and by night* (Exodus 13:21). There seems to have been some expectation that the cloud of the Exo-

165

dus story would return at the end of time. We shall return to this matter.

READING THROUGH AGAIN

The Transfiguration, like many stories in Mark, looks backward and forward. It is clear that Mark has elected to tell this strange tale with the help of images which come from the Exodus story and other stories of the Old Testament. The very high *mountain* is not named but it is identified: the hint of *after six days*, the presence of *Elijah and Moses,* the overshadowing *cloud*, the voice from *out of the cloud* all point to Mount Sinai. In other words, Mark's mountain is a theological mountain; he is not concerned with the historical site.

Taking with him Peter, James and John (as he will do again – 14:33 and see 13:3), Jesus leads them up a high mountain in order to be *apart by themselves* (Mark emphasises the privacy of the occasion). Jesus is transfigured before them. It is not clear what this means and we do not know exactly what happened. Even Mark can't convey the awesomeness of the event. The best he can do is to say that the clothing of Jesus began to glisten and became intensely white. Clearly, Mark is out of his depth. His statement that the whiteness was as *no fuller on earth could bleach them* is hardly informative. Shakespeare would have done better. But because he tells his story in the images and vocabulary of the Old Testament we can grasp his meaning. Peter, James, and John saw a transformed Jesus, one who for a short time appeared in heavenly glory. Just as the glory of God's presence surrounded Moses on Mount Sinai and spoke to Elijah on the same mountain, so the glory of God is now revealed in the person of Jesus. It is no less than *the glory of his Father* (8:38), the divine glory with which he would be possessed after his resurrection and exaltation to heaven and with which he would be made manifest at his coming again. That event is now anticipated and the disciples are made privy to the final destiny of Jesus. They will have to learn that Jesus will suffer and die but now they are given a vision of the triumphant end of the story.

The significance of the presence of Elijah and Moses is not easy to determine and many suggestions have been made (see above). There seems to have been a belief that the symbols and signs which surrounded the Exodus would return at the consummation of the world. Look how Mark describes the return of Jesus (the so-called Second Coming): *And then they shall see the Son of man coming in clouds with great power and glory* (13:26). When Isaiah looks to consummation of all creation, he reaches back to the language of the past to describe the future:

> Then the Lord will create over the whole site of Mount Zion (= the temple area) and over her assemblies a cloud by day, and smoke and the shining of a flaming fire by night; for over all the glory there will be a canopy and a pavilion. It will be for a shade by day from the heat, and for a refuge and a shelter from the storm and rain (Isaiah 4:5-6).

There is a curious passage in the Second Book of the Maccabees which narrates that the prophet Jeremiah hid the ark of the covenant in a cave and that *the place shall be unknown until God gathers his people together again and shows his mercy.* The writer continues: *And then the Lord will disclose these things, and the glory of the Lord and the cloud will appear, as they were shown in the case of Moses* ... (see 2 Maccabees 2:4-8). In both Isaiah and Maccabees, the images of the past are employed to remove the veil from the future. That, too, is what Mark is doing. Elijah and Moses not only recall the past. They point to the future.

It is entirely to be expected that Peter should offer to provide three booths or tents. Again, in the Exodus journey, Moses had a special tent (the Tent of Meeting) which he used to pitch outside the encampment of the people and within which he communed with God (Exodus 33:7-11. The imagination of Israel frequently pictured salvation in terms of God's pitching his tent in the midst of his people as he had done in the wilderness days (Ezekiel 37:27; Zechariah 2:10-11) and, indeed, the end-time is pictured as God and his people tenting together (Revelation 21:1-3). Peter is aware that he is in the divine presence. But his request is inappropriate. The end is not yet. First, there is Golgotha and the preaching of the gospel, for the world-to-come will be reached only by way of suffering. Not only do Peter, James, and John fear in the divine presence, they do not know what to say; as yet they have failed to understand the way of the cross.

The great commandment in the Bible is to listen (Deuteronomy 5:1; 6:4), such that listening is the first movement in

Israel's prayer. Where previously we had been directed to listen to the Torah and to find there the mind and heart of God, now we are directed to the beloved Son. To use the words of another gospel-maker, the word is now flesh. Looking around the three saw only Jesus. All that God wishes to reveal on the mountain is in Jesus.

Elijah re-visited

It is entirely in keeping with Mark's understanding of Jesus that the first words the three disciples are required to listen to as they descend the mountain concern the destiny of the Son of man. The momentous revelation of the glory of Jesus is not to be broadcast until the resurrection. The suffering must come first. The disciples ponder on what rising from the dead might mean. The point here is not that they did not understand what resurrection in general might mean. The idea of resurrection was well-known in first-century Judaism, though not everyone believed in it (see 12:18-27). What the disciples cannot understand is what resurrection has got to do with the Messiah since it implies his death. They demonstrate yet again that they have failed to understand his words about the inevitability of suffering.

The question of Elijah arises naturally out of the transfiguration scene. The scribes did, indeed, teach that Elijah would return in the days of the Messiah and that he would be instrumental in identifying God's anointed one for such is the teaching of the Scriptures:

> Behold I will send you Elijah the prophet before the great and terrible day of the Lord comes. And he will turn the hearts of fathers to their children and the hearts of children to their fathers (Malachi 4:5-6).

Jesus takes the opportunity to return to the theme of suffering. Elijah has, indeed, come. He was none other than John the Baptist whose passion and death we have attended (6:14-29). We shall attend another passion and death before this story is done.

PRAYER

The Transfiguration is at the centre of Mark's Gospel and the centre of christian faith for it reveals the very identity of Jesus as God's beloved Son. Such good news should be received with joy. Psalm 96 sings of the glory of God and of the great salvation he intended for all peoples.

A boy possessed
Mark 9:14-29

Mark is not given to long stories. At least, not much. He will extend himself when he comes to the end of his story. It comes as something of a surprise to realise that the last few days of Mark's story of Jesus takes up six chapters (11:1-16:8), well over one third of his whole text. Up to that point, Mark has been content to paint in brisk and brief strokes. But there are exceptions. The story of the man possessed by a legion of demons (5:1-20) and that of the passion and death of John the Baptist (6:14-29) are narrated in some detail. Their length is an indication of their importance. The Gerasene story not only reveals important information as to the identity of Jesus but it also shows unambiguously that the mission of Jesus was not confined to Jewish people. The terrible fate of John is presented in bloody detail for it points to the fate of Jesus himself. Thus, the length of the tale of the boy possessed by an evil spirit would seem to indicate that it is of particular importance. We shall see.

READING THROUGH

Notice how Mark's organisation of his material here resembles his introduction of Jesus at the beginning:

Baptism of Jesus	You are my Son	Conflict with Satan
Transfiguration	This is my Son	Conflict with a Demon

Clearly, Mark wishes us to understand that the fight against the powers of evil is at the root of the mission of the beloved Son. He is the stronger one who enters into the kingdom of Satan and plunders all his goods (3:25-27).

Confusion
The story of the boy with the *dumb spirit* is full of confusion. In the first place, the crowds are highlighted: it is a great crowd

which runs up to Jesus and greets him. But later in the story we are told that a crow*d came running together* (verse 25). We are not told how the crowd reacted to the miracle as we are on other occasions (1:27; 1:45; 2:12; 4:41; 5:42). The scribes are introduced but instantly drop out of the story. Another confusion is caused by two descriptions of the boy's illness (verses 17-18 and verse 22). The symptoms given in verses 18, 20 and 22 have nothing to do with dumbness (verses 17 and 25) or deafness (verse 25). Mark does not give us an exact medical description such as we might find in a medical text-book but the details given and the words used provide a very vivid picture of the seizures which have endangered the boy's life from his earliest years and leave us in no doubt that he suffered from a major form of epilepsy. Of course, to conclude that the boy suffered from epilepsy is not to deny that his illness was due to demon possession. Epilepsy is a symptom and not a disease.

The confusions in the story may be due to the fact that Mark has twisted a straight-forward miracle account in order to emphasise for his disciples (and readers) the importance of faith and the necessity of prayer, lessons lost on the hapless disciples.

The house

There are frequent references to "house' in Mark's Gospel. While many of these are an integral part of the story and excite little comment (1;29; 6:4; 10:29; 12:40; 13:15), some would seem to be significant. We know that the first Christians met in each other's houses. These so-called "house-churches" are mentioned frequently in the New Testament. At the end of his Letter to the Romans, St Paul sends greetings to his old friends Prisca and Aquila and adds a further greeting to *the church in their house* (Romans 16:5 and see also 1 Corinthians 16:19). There are many references in the Acts of the Apostles (Acts 2:2; 2:46; 8:3). Acts 5:42 is of particular interest: *And every day in the temple and at home [the apostles] did not cease teaching and preaching Jesus as the Messiah.* In Mark, we find that a house is often a place of instruction. In 3:20 the house serves to separate the disciples from the milling crowds and there they receive teaching. The same is true of 7:17: *And when he entered the house, and left the people, his disciples asked him about the parable.* Similarly, in 9:28 and 10:10, the house offers a haven from the crowd and a place of instruction. This pattern in Mark has suggested to scholars that he was linking the activity of Jesus with the practice of early Christians. As they met in their house-churches (and as Mark's Gospel would have been read to them), they would receive instruction in the true meaning of disciple-ship. Just as Jesus took his disciples apart from the pressing crowds into the privacy of a house, so his words, as they are read and discussed, continue to nourish the lives of Christians assembled in their house-churches.

READING THROUGH AGAIN

Since we left Caesarea Philippi and the proclamation there that Jesus is the Messiah, we have seen Jesus primarily concerned to instruct his disciples, particularly about the suffering and agony which lie ahead. This intense teaching will continue throughout the second part of Mark's story until we come to Gethsemane. Sadly, for the disciples prove to be inattentive and obdurate pupils, little is achieved: *And they all forsook him, and fled* (14:50). The story of the epileptic boy highlights the failure of the disciples to understand the way of Jesus.

Jesus and the three come down the mountain to the waiting disciples and encounter a great crowd and some scribes. An argument is in progress but it is not clear what about. It would appear to be about the failure of the disciples to heal the possessed boy. The amazement and the enthusiasm of the crowd are noted but to no purpose. The father explains that he brought his son to Jesus (*I brought my son to you*) but it is the disciples who are asked to heal the lad. Thus it is the failure of the disciples which is highlighted. Certainly, it would seem that it is the disciples who are called a *faithless generation* and the father, by contrast, is portrayed as having some faith and praying for a strengthening of his faith. The theme of faith and its importance is underlined by the emphatic statement of Jesus: *If you can! All things are possible to one who believes.*

Faith plays an important role in Mark's story. It is the faith of his friends which moves Jesus to heal the paralytic (2:5); it is faith which saves blind Bartimaeus (10:52); it is faith which heals the woman with the haemorrhage (5:34). Most startling of all, it is faith which brings life to a dead girl: *Do not fear, only believe* (5:36). And, sadly, it is the disciples who do not have faith: *Have you no faith?* (4:40). It is these very disciples who are set apart *to be with him, and to be sent out to preach and have authority to cast out demons* (3:14; 6:7). But, as we shall see, they are pre-occupied with power and position and they little realise that to be with Jesus, to share in his authority over unclean spirits, only one thing is necessary: the discipline of prayer (9:29).

The story of the failure of the disciples to cast out the evil spirit is told at considerable length and in great detail because it warns the *faithless generation* (the disciples!) to pray. The urgency and importance of the warning is underlined by the fact that Jesus speaks privately to the disciples in the house. But the warning goes unheeded. The faithlessness demonstrated at the foot of the mountain of transfiguration will have a sorry outcome at the foot of another mountain. At Gethsemane, the foot of the Mount of Olives, these same disciples will sleep. They are warned to pray (13:18) and to watch (13:37) but they do not listen. And so disaster comes: *Watch and pray that you may not enter into temptation* (14:38). But it is sleep, not prayer and watchfulness which concern Peter and the rest. And the consequences? *They all forsook him and fled* (14:50).

PRAYER

Do not be too hard on the disciples. Throwing the first stone is best left to those without fault. The truly faithful one in the Bible is God. Our prayer must be that our little faith be sustained and helped by the faithfulness of the one who is faithful *in all his words*. Psalm 145 speaks of the source of all faith and the wonders which flow from it.

Who is the greatest?
Mark 9:30-50

Mark is very fond of the word *way*. He uses it no less than sixteen times. Modern English editions employ a number of words to translate the single Greek word used by Mark throughout his little book: way, road, path. But it would be more than helpful if there was consistency here for there is more to Mark's *way* than meets the eye. Consider the quotation which first introduces the word:

> Behold, I send my messenger before thy face,
> who shall prepare thy way;
> the voice of one crying in the wilderness:
> Prepare the way of the Lord,
> make his paths straight (1:2)

It is quite clear that Isaiah is not referring to a new M25 motorway across the desert. His thoughts are not on concrete and steel. He is speaking of a spiritual reform which will be brought about by the Lord's messenger as he prepares the people for God's coming. John the Baptist does not build a road; he calls the people to confess their sins and he preaches *a baptism of repentance for the forgiveness of sins* (1:4). The way of the Lord is the way of spiritual renewal.

On the other hand, Mark uses the word simply to mean a path or a road. The sower who went out to sow scattered some seed on the path through his field (4:4). Nothing mysterious there. But consider this sentence:

> And they were on the way, going up to Jerusalem,
> and Jesus was walking ahead of them;
> and they were amazed,
> and those who followed him were afraid (10:32).

Clearly, Mark is telling us that Jesus is on the road, journeying to the city of Jerusalem, walking ahead of his followers, some of whom were amazed and some afraid. But is he doing anything more here? Does not the sentence, when looked at more carefully, suggest a description of what it means to be a follower of Jesus? To follow Jesus in the way of discipleship is to follow him on the way of the cross and to do so in amazement and a deal of trepidation. And, of course, we know that in some christian circles, people who followed Jesus, who became disciples, were called the Way (Acts 19:9; 19:23; 24:14; 24:22). When we meet the word *way* in Mark , we ought always to ask ourselves whether he is referring solely to road or path or whether he his hinting at another journey, the journey into discipleship. When Mark tells us that Bartimaeus follows Jesus *on the way* (10:52), do you think he means only that he ran down the road after Jesus? Is he not also hinting that the once blind man, now that he can see clearly, follows Jesus into discipleship, that he not only follows Jesus but becomes a follower of Jesus?

READING THROUGH

The first difficulty which confronts us in this section is that it does not appear to be held together by any logical development of thought. The whole passage seems to have been stitched together by means of catch-words and phrases: *name* (verses 37, 38, 39, 41); *receive* (verse 37); *child/little one* (verses 36, 37, 42); *it would be better* (verses 42, 43, 45, 47); *stumble* (verses 42, 43, 45, 47); *fire* (verses 43; 48; 49); *salt* (verses 49; 50). But there is a clear thread running through the bits and pieces of this passage. Mark is laying down some of the conditions of discipleship. The instructions given by Jesus are applied to the community for whom Mark is writing.

Disciples and the Twelve
The instruction concerning the death and resurrection of Jesus is given to the disciples. But a little way down the page Jesus calls the Twelve and it would appear that the rest of the chapter is devoted exclusively to them. This gives rise to a difficult question. Are the Twelve a distinct group within the larger group of disciples? Following the call of Simon and Andrew and James and John (1:16-20), those who follow Jesus are called disciples (2:15; 2:16; 2:18; 2:23; indeed, some forty-four times in the Gospel). At 3:7, *Jesus withdrew with his dis-*

ciples to the sea but then he goes up a mountain and *called to him those whom he desired, and they came to him, and he appointed twelve to be with him* (3:13-14). All told, the Twelve are mentioned ten times (3:14; 4:10; 6:7; 9:35; 10:32; 11:11; 14:10; 14:17; 14:20; 14:43) and some of these verses would seem to make a distinction between the Twelve and the group called disciples. Does Mark wish to assert that there is a special group who receive special teaching and are given special authority, not granted to the generality of disciples? This is hardly the case. For one thing, the important teaching of chapter 13 is given to Peter and James and John and Andrew (13:3). Is it for them alone? Indeed, no. The chapter ends with Jesus saying, *And what I say to you I say to all* (13:37). The young man at the empty tomb asks the frightened women to tell his disciples and Peter that the Lord will meet with them in Galilee (16:7), whereas that promise had been made exclusively to the Twelve in 14:28. The matter may be resolved by realising that Mark is putting together material which he has found in various strands of tradition, some of which, we may surmise, spoke of disciples and some of an intimate group referred to as the Twelve. But there is no reason to think that, for Mark, Jesus conferred a special status or confided a special teaching to the Twelve. The overwhelming impression of the Gospel is that discipleship (not twelveship) is what counts.

Gehenna and hell

The word *hell* occurs only in this section of Mark. It is not a very common word in the New Testament (three times in Mark, seven in Matthew, once in Luke and once in the short letter of James). Actually, the word translated as *hell* is Gehenna, the name of a valley to the south of Jerusalem. In view of the rather flamboyant views one hears about hell, an explanation may not go amiss.

One of the more horrendous practices of some ancient peoples was child sacrifice. The people of Israel turned their back on such barbarism. But, on occasion, it occurred in their midst from time to time. The prophet Jeremiah bemoans the fact that some of God's people have turned to such evil:

> And they have built the high place of Topheth,
> which is in the valley of the son of Hinnom,
> to burn their sons and their daughters in the fire;

which I did not command, nor did it come into my mind (Jeremiah 7:31).

The writer of the Second Book of Kings tells that the evil king Manasseh had *burned his son as an offering* (2 Kings 21:6) and that a later and religious-minded king, Josiah by name, destroyed the altar on which such abominations took place *in the valley of the sons of Hinnom* (2 Kings 23:10). The valley of Hinnom (called Gehenna in the days of Jesus) was turned into a dump for the offal and refuse of the city. It was a constantly smouldering reminder to the citizens of the godlessness of the past. It became an image of the punishment which the prophets warned would befall the enemies of God. The very last verse of the Book of Isaiah speaks of the men who have rebelled against God and warns that *their worm shall not die, their fire shall not be quenched, and they shall be an abhorrence to all flesh,* a verse quoted by Mark. What should be clear is that the Bible's use of figurative language and fanciful images to speak of divine punishment should not encourage speculation on "eternal damnation". The future, and its secrets, belong to God.

The reader should note that verses 44 and 46, found in some English translations, are to be omitted. They are not found in the best ancient manuscripts and, in any case, are identical with verse 48.

READING THROUGH AGAIN

The second prediction of the death and resurrection is, as the first, for the ears of the disciples only. Peter misunderstood the first plain statement of Jesus concerning his destiny (8:32). The three who were witnesses of the transfiguration of the Lord were also bewildered about the teaching on the resurrection (9:10). Likewise, all the disciples are confused and lack understanding and are afraid to ask for an explanation.

The inability of the disciples to comprehend what the destiny of Jesus will be and what that destiny means is everywhere in Mark's Gospel. As we have seen only the death itself will reveal who Jesus really is. Until we stand at the cross and see the broken body we will not know that this man is the Son of God. The disciples will run away from the place of the skull. They will not see the death. Does this mean that Peter and the rest are permanently excluded from the company of Jesus? We shall see. But things don't look too good.

The greatest

So far are the disciples from understanding who Jesus is and what he is about that their chief concern is which of them will be the greatest among them. Their concern is for position and power. Their ambition is to lord it over everyone else. The reader will notice that the discussion takes place *on the way*. The temptation to seek power is a constant temptation to disciples. All who follow Jesus on the way, in every age and clime, are vulnerable to the lure of power, to the corruption peculiar to power-seekers. Jesus will have none of it.

When he was in the house – a location that alerts readers to the importance of what is said for their own Christian living. Jesus calls the Twelve. The lesson about power is especially for the chosen intimates but all disciples must take heed of what is said here.

When Jesus healed Peter's mother-in-law, she got up and served Jesus and the disciples who were with him (1:31). The word there used for "served' gives us in English our word deacon. We might say that the woman "deaconed" to Jesus. That is the word which is used here: the one who is last must be *the servant* of all. What characterises discipleship in all ages is service. Being last is a condition of discipleship. Jesus turns the power game on its head. The one who is first in God's estimation is to be found among the servants.

Children

The twentieth-century Western world has, generally speaking, a very romantic view of children and our culture is, to a considerable extent, child-orientated. This was not the case in the culture which nurtured Jesus of Nazareth. That culture idealised the mature adult rather than the child. St Paul says that a child is no better than a slave (Galatians 4:1). The child is someone to be trained and educated before it is of any significance. The child is someone unimportant. All the more surprising, therefore, that Jesus should embrace a child and inform the disciples that they must be ready to receive such unimportant and insignificant people and be their servant. Even more astonishing is the fact that, in receiving such nobodies, the disciple will be receiving Jesus and the God of Jesus.

A *closed shop?*

After each of the predictions of the suffering and death of Jesus, Mark inserts a response of one of the inner group of disciples. In each case, the disciples manage to get it wrong. Peter goes so far as to rebuke Jesus (8:32); James and John will so miss the point that they wish to sit on the right and left of Jesus when the kingdom comes (10:37). Only one statement is allotted to John, the brother of James, in Mark's story and, typically, he, too, reveals a lack of understanding. Notice, too, that he speaks in the plural. He speaks for all the disciples and he conveys the failure of all to understand.

From the declaration of the messiahship of Jesus at Caesarea Philippi Mark's story presents Jesus teaching his disciples and, as we have noted again and again, to little avail. We have also come to realise that this teaching is not exclusively directed at the group of followers gathered around Jesus in Galilee. Mark speaks to disciples and would-be disciples in his own Christian community. The voice of Jesus bridges time. What he says in the house at Capernaum must be applied to the community in Rome. We are, then, permitted to ask what conditions in Mark's community called for the necessity to remind it of the teaching about outsiders who acknowledge Jesus but are not his followers.

We might guest that a group with common aims and a strong sense of fellowship, as Christian communities had from the beginning, would tend to erect a barrier around itself so that it can more easily define itself over against those who do not belong. We might surmise that Mark's community was excessively exclusive, too much of a closed shop and it needed to be reminded that Jesus demanded a more generous attitude.

The Acts of the Apostles tells of an itinerant group of Jewish exorcists who sought to cast out demons through the power of Jesus (19:13-17). It may be, then, that the man casting out demons in the name of Jesus (that is, invoking the power of Jesus) was not as rare as we might have anticipated. John is all for reprimanding such exorcists who do not belong, who are not disciples. The attitude of Jesus is more welcoming. Anyone who gives even a cup of water to anyone who belongs to Christ, will be rewarded. In times of persecution, as Mark's community had good reason to know, anyone who is not against us is for us. Jesus also suggests that anyone who does a mighty work by invoking the power of Jesus will not soon speak evil of him. The suggestion is that the outsider may soon become an insider.

Stumbling

Verse 42 would appear to move on to a new topic. But if we take it that *little ones* does not refer to children but rather to those outsiders who *give you a cup of water to drink, because you bear the name of Christ*, then the connection with the previous verse is clear. Those who cast out demons in the name of Jesus, those who come to the aid of Christians with but a cup of water, are not to be scandalised. They are not to be caused to stumble, caused to fall, have hindrances put in their way. Mark wants to emphasise that a too exclusive Christian group which snubs those whom it regards as "not one of us" is far from the Christian way. Such attitudes are stumbling-blocks to the true spirit of Jesus.

It is not only narrow sectarianism which is to be condemned. Anything which causes the Christian to stumble, anything which hinders doing God's will is to be avoided like the plague. The destruction of the offending hand, foot and eye is, of course, not to be taken literally. The colourful language of Jesus serves to highlight the seriousness of the matter. It is better *to enter life* maimed, *to enter life* crippled, *to enter the kingdom of God* with one eye than to go to Gehenna. The phrase *to enter life* means the same as *to enter the kingdom of God*. We have seen, in considering 1:15, that the kingdom of God refers to the doing of God's will. If we would be where the will of God is being done, then we must be serious in our discipleship. The sternest measures may be required to remove all stumbling-blocks we may encounter on the *way*.

The image of the smouldering city dump provides Mark with a vivid and terrifying picture of a destruction which continues endlessly. It is interesting to note that when the passage from Isaiah 66:22-24 was read in the synagogue, verse 23 was repeated so that the reading was brought to a conclusion with a word of comfort. Mark is not so sanguine.

Salt

The mention of fire turns Mark's thoughts in another direction. The disciple must be salted with fire, that is, must become a sacrifice for God. St Paul addresses the church in Rome to the same effect:

> I appeal to you therefore, my brothers, by the mercies of God, to present your bodies as a living sacrifice, holy and acceptable to God, which is your spiritual worship (Romans 12:1).

The Book of Leviticus, the rule-book for Temple sacrifice, lays down that all sacrifices must be seasoned with salt (Leviticus 2:13). Mark is thinking of the persecutions which will, as it were purify, not to say toughen up, all disciples. The community in Rome had experienced the trial of bitter persecution. They had witnessed members burning as human torches in the gardens of Nero. Mark's grim warning that disciples must endure such terrors to purge away anything contrary to God's will will have been an all too painful reminder of the cost of following Jesus in the way of discipleship.

The final word of Jesus to those in the household of the Church (9:33), to those who were discussing *along the way* who would be the greatest among them, is a word of peace. Discipleship must be free of discord and rivalry. Power dominates the way of the world. Peace is the way of discipleship.

PRAYER

Mark's grim text needs a counter-balance. The second last verse of the Book of Isaiah is as much part of Scripture and the last verse. Psalm 121 presents a timely reminder that *the Lord will keep you from all evil.*

A question of divorce
Mark 10:1-12

Divorce, like the poor, is ever with us. It is of epidemic propor-
tions in modern western societies and, indeed, it was very common in the society in which Jesus lived and in the wider
environment of the Roman empire. Then as now, divorce was a
social and economic catastrophe, especially for women: prostitu-
tion fed on the victims of divorce.

No one, at least, no sensible person, is in favour of divorce.
The pain and anguish visited on husband and wife, parents and
children, caught up in the throes of divorce, are an everyday
experience. The fragility of human love is nowhere more poign-
antly revealed, nowhere more publicly suffered, than in our divorce courts. The terrors of divorce may be read in faces of
countless children.

It is, therefore, of the utmost importance that, no matter how
we interpret the teaching of Jesus on divorce (and there is room
for discussion and diverse opinions), we must not lose sight of
the unanimity which is clear to all. Jesus saw divorce as a
tragedy. Any divorce denotes a failure, not only of human love,
but, because it is just that, it is a failure of divine purpose, for
those God has joined together in marriage should not be separated. There is no such thing as a good divorce. The discussion
that follows must be judged in the light of that bed-rock truth.

Before we proceed with an attempt to understand the teaching
of Jesus on this most sensitive of subjects we need to be aware of
a number of matters which would have been taken for granted by
participants in the debate with Jesus.

First, and this may seem superfluous, it is essential to be clear
on what was understood by the term divorce. Does divorce
assume the right to remarry or does it assume only the right to put
away one's spouse and be separate? That divorce can be understood as involving separation without subsequent remarriage is
obvious. But did the common understanding of the word in the
milieu of Jesus assume the right to remarry? This question, in

view of the evidence available to us, is to be answered in the affirmative. The essential part of a Jewish writ of divorce consisted of the words "You are free to marry anyone". This is how St Matthew understood the question (Matthew 19:9). St Paul, when he wishes to make a distinction between separation and remarriage, is constrained to spell out the matter clearly (1 Corinthians 7:10-11). "Divorce" in the texts of the Bible, unless the contrary is made clear, should be understood as assuming the right to remarry.

Secondly, the biblical text which permits divorce needs to be recalled for it is the basis on which the Pharisees question Jesus. The text is to be found in the Book of Deuteronomy:

> When a man takes a wife and marries her, if then she finds no favour in his eyes because he has found some indecency in her, and he writes her a bill of divorce and puts it in her hand and sends her out of his house, and she departs out of his house, and if she goes and becomes another man's wife, and the latter husband dislikes her and writes her a bill of divorce and puts it in her hand and sends her out of his house, or if the latter husband dies, who took her to be his wife, then her former husband, who sent her away, may not take her again to be his wife, after she has been defiled; for that is an abomination before the LORD, and you shall not bring guilt upon the land which the LORD your God gives you for an inheritance (Deuteronomy 4:1-4).

This piece of legislation takes for granted that a man may divorce his wife and that she may enter upon a second marriage, that is to say, divorce assumes the right to remarry. The main thrust of the piece is to prevent a husband remarrying a woman he had previously divorced if she had entered a second (or third or fourth?) marriage. But the religious teachers of the people of Israel looked to this text for guidance on the matter of divorce. For the rabbis the Law of Moses was clear: a man had every right to divorce his wife and to remarry. This teaching was deemed to override any suggestion to the contrary. The voice of Moses was sufficient to silence any who argued otherwise. It is to this voice that the Pharisees appeal in their dispute with Jesus.

There were other voices. The prophet Malachi mourns for the loss of marriage fidelity and for the havoc marital infidelity causes among the people:

Have we not all one father? Has not one God created us? Why then are we faithless to one another, profaning the covenant of our fathers? (Malachi 2:10).

Malachi sees in the breakdown of a human covenant of love the very unravelling of the bonds of God's covenant with his people. His call for faithfulness was, for the most part, ignored:

You cover the LORD's altar with tears, with weeping and groaning because he no longer regards the offering or accepts it with favour at your hand. You ask, "Why does he not?" Because the LORD was witness to the covenant between you and the wife of your youth, to whom you have been faithless, though she is your companion and your wife by covenant. Has not God made one and sustained for us the spirit of life? And what does he desire? Godly offspring. So take heed to yourselves, and let none be faithless to the wife of his youth. "For I hate divorce, says the LORD the God of Israel, and covering one's garments with violence, says the LORD of hosts. So take heed to yourselves and do not be faithless" (Malachi 2:13-16).

There is some evidence that the community which produced *The Dead Sea Scrolls* did not tolerate polygamy (an age-old practice, curtailed in the time of Jesus more by economic necessity than religious scruple) or remarriage after divorce. In a document called *The Temple Scroll*, in a passage concerning the duties of a king in Israel, the writer warns,

He shall not marry as wife any daughter of the [foreign] nations, but shall take a wife for himself from his father's house, from his father's family. He shall not take another wife in addition to her, for she alone shall be with him all the time of her life. But if she dies, he may marry another from his father's house, from his family (11QT 57:11-19).

In another document, called *The Damascus Rule*, the writer holds that any one who takes a second wife while the first is alive is guilty of fornication twice over. His reasons are straightforward (and rather like those of Jesus): *the principle of creation is male and female he created them.* He adds, *those who entered the ark went in two by two* (CD, IV, V). Not only do these texts outlaw polygamy but they also condemn remarriage after divorce and even divorce (separation) itself.

It is impossible to say what influence this religious sect had on main-stream Jewish life. Probably, very little. It is, however, an intriguing question to ask to what extent its teachings and practices may have influenced Jesus.

Thirdly, the grounds for divorce are not spelled out in the text from the Book of Deuteronomy. If a wife ceases to find favour in her husband's eyes *because he has found some indecency in her,* he may put her away. The word translated as "indecency" might equally well be translated as "some shameful thing" or "some unseemly thing". At the time of Jesus, two schools of thought sought to impose their understanding of the vague sentence in Deuteronomy. Whereas the school of Rabbi Shammai limited the grounds for divorce to some unchaste or indecent conduct, the followers of Rabbi Hillel were much more liberal and permitted divorce even for burning the husband's supper. Rabbi Akiba declared, "Even if he found another more beautiful than she, for it is written, *she fails to please him*".

The famous historian, Josephus, whom we have met before, reflects the practice of his fellow Jews when he states that "it is (only) the man who is permitted by us to do this [divorce], and not even a divorced woman may marry again of her own initiative unless her former husband consents" (*Antiquities* XV, 259). And it is, indeed, clear from the text of Deuteronomy that only men were permitted to divorce. Women did not have access to such privilege, as they had outside the confines of Judaism in the wider, pagan vistas of the Roman empire. However, there is some evidence that Jewish women were at certain times and places able to divorce their husbands. The most celebrated marriage in Galilee in the days of Jesus was that of Herod Antipas and Herodias. She had divorced her husband under Roman law. The matter, however, was sensitive enough to lead to the death of John the Baptist.

St Paul

Before we come to close quarters with the question of divorce in Mark, it will be helpful to notice what St Paul has to say on the matter. Dealing with a variety of marriage issues, Paul turns to the question of divorce:

185

To the married I give charge, not I but the Lord, that the wife should not separate from her husband (but if she does, let her remain single or else be reconciled with her husband) – and that the husband should not divorce his wife (1 Corinthians 7:10-11).

Here Paul makes clear that his teaching has the authority of the Lord Jesus himself. A wife should not *separate* from her husband and a husband should not *divorce* his wife. The difference between the two words should not be pressed. Both mean "to divorce". But it is something of a surprise to find Paul envisaging the possibility of a woman divorcing her husband (as Mark does, too). Equally to be noted is his effort to insist that the divorced woman should not seek another husband. Paul, therefore, qualifies the ideal of a life-long partnership in marriage by admitting the possibility of separation without remarriage among his Christian community in Corinth.

To the saying of Jesus concerning the married Paul adds his own apostolic command concerning a new situation which could not have arisen in the time of Jesus but was all too common as the Church spread among pagan peoples:

To the rest I say, not the Lord, that if any brother has a wife who is an unbeliever, and she consents to live with him, he should not divorce her. If any woman has a husband who is an unbeliever, and he consents to live with her, she should not divorce him. For the unbelieving husband is consecrated through his wife, and the unbelieving wife is consecrated through her husband. Otherwise, your children would be unclean, but as it is they are holy. But if the unbelieving partner desires to separate, let it be so; in such a case the brother or sister is not bound. For God has called us to peace (1 Corinthians 7:12-15).

Again, be it noted that Paul allows equal rights to men and women. But it is the weight which we ought to give to the phrase *the brother or sister is not bound* which is most difficult to determine. Paul clearly envisages a situation where the pagan spouse does not wish to continue to be married to a Christian and seeks a divorce. "Let it be so", says Paul. But where does that leave the Christian? Is he or she free to enter into a second marriage? Is Paul saying that such a spouse is not bound by the obligation of the first marriage but is free to enter into a second marriage? (You will notice, of course, that Paul accepts without question the validity of the pagan/Christian marriage: the children of such a union are holy.)

A good case can be made for holding that Paul allows for remarriage in the case of desertion by an unbelieving spouse. "Not bound" most probably means "free to marry". This view sits well with Paul's general view that *because of the temptation to immorality, each man should have his own wife and each woman her own husband* (1 Corinthians 7:2). A divorced wife or husband would be, in Paul's terms, equally exposed to the temptation of immorality. Not all can receive the precept of celibacy (Matthew 19:11). If *it is better to marry than to be aflame with passion* (1 Corinthians 7:9), then the deserted spouse is not bound by previous ties and is free to remarry. One would be more confident that this is what Paul means were it not for his teaching that the unmarried state is, in his opinion, preferable to the married state (1 Corinthians 7:32-35). He bases this estimation on rather shallow ground: *I want you to be free from anxieties* (7:32). Not everyone, however, will wish to be free from the anxieties of marriage!

What is especially important here is that Paul is making exceptions to teaching that apparently admits of no exceptions. Certainly he is declaring that a wife or husband may seek divorce from a pagan partner who does not wish to continue the marriage. Less certainly (but only a little less) he would allow for a second marriage. The point is that, like St Matthew, Paul is of the opinion that the view that divorce is always to be outlawed will not do.

A word on St Matthew

St Matthew twice introduces the subject of divorce (5:32 and 19:3-9). But his condemnation of divorce is not absolute. On each occasion he admits that there may be an exception to the general rule:

> It was also said, "Whoever divorces his wife, let him give her a certificate of divorce". But I [Jesus] say to you that everyone who divorces his wife, *except on the ground of unchastity,* makes her an adulteress; and whoever marries a divorced woman commits adultery (Matthew 5:32).

And I [Jesus] say to you: whoever divorces his wife, *except for unchastity,* and marries another, commits adultery (Matthew 19:9).

Both of these statements outlaw divorce but both admit of an exception. Divorce is permitted on the grounds of "unchastity". There is great difficulty in understanding what precisely we are to understand by the Greek word Matthew used and which in these statements is translated as "unchastity". In Mark 7:21 the word would appear to mean sexual immorality; it cannot here mean adultery for another word in the same sentence denotes adultery. Some have suggested (unconvincingly) that the word refers to incestuous relations which would, of course, mean that there really was no marriage in the first place. Whatever the solution to the matter may be, it is perfectly clear that Matthew seems to be saying that there are grounds (however obscure) for permitting divorce. On the other hand, Luke 16:18 admits of no exception.

READING THROUGH

We are entering a most important teaching section (10:1-52) and at a critical time. Jesus has left Galilee and entered Judea and the region beyond the Jordan. He has entered into the territory of his chiefest enemies, the region where he will be confronted by those hostile forces and brutally done to death. The chapter before us is full of teaching for the crowds but it contains refinements and expansions given to the disciples. Note: *in the house* (10:10); *the disciples* (10:13); *said to his disciples* (10:23); *the twelve* (10:32); *James and John* (10:35); *the ten* (10:41). And recall that private instruction to the disciples is Mark's way of highlighting teaching to which his Christian community ought to pay particular attention.

The question of the Pharisees concerning divorce is not asked in order to discover the truth or even to enter into honest debate with Jesus. It is asked *in order to test him.* Previously, the Pharisees had come to Jesus, arguing and seeking a sign in order to test him, in response to which Jesus *sighed deeply in his spirit* and refused the sign (8:11-12). The Pharisees and the Herodians (old cronies in deadly opposition to Jesus, according to Mark – 3:6) come to test Jesus over the thorny matter of taxation (12:15).

These testings must be seen for what they are. It is Satan who is the supreme tester of Jesus (1:13). All other testings are an outreach of that wilderness ordeal and those who participate in them are allies of Satan whose house and kingdom will not be allowed to stand (3:23-27). We must not read Mark's discussion on divorce as if it were a casual, polite debate. What is at issue is *the way of God* (12:14), *the power of God* (12:24) in its implacable opposition to Satan and those who would ally themselves with the evil one.

READING THROUGH AGAIN

The question addressed by the Pharisees to Jesus makes sense only if we understand that by divorce they mean separation and the right to remarry. The terms of their question (*Is it lawful...*) indicate that they seek to know what God permits in this matter. Accordingly, Jesus refers them to God's spokesman, to Moses, the greatest of the prophets, the one who brought the the Law of God down from Mount Sinai to the people of Israel. There could be no greater authority, could there? The Pharisees reply with a neat summary of the salient points in Deuteronomy: a man (and only a man) may write out a certificate and send his wife away.

Jesus does not deny that such is the case. What he undertakes is to explain why the divine voice speaking through Moses countenanced divorce (*he taught them as one who had authority* – 1:22). Jesus dares to interpret the mind of God! Permission to divorce was no more than toleration of human weakness (male, actually) and clean contrary to the mind of God. Hardness of heart everywhere proves impervious to God's word (6:52; 8:17). From the beginning, in the blueprint for human happiness and dignity, before any accommodation to sin and weakness became expedient, *God made them male and female* (Genesis 1:27). The making of male and female is for the making of the community of a couple. The man and woman shall leave father and mother and become one flesh, become one person. *Flesh* does not refer only to sexual union but to the wholeness of love which draws body and soul, heart and mind, into a loving and lasting coupling. What has become one remains indelibly one. No human agency can claim the right to destroy what God has created.

Jesus has spoken. But how does it work in practice? How should the christian community order its affairs so that the will of God be done on earth as it is in heaven? The discussion moves into the house and, as so often, it becomes the place of plain speaking. For Mark there are no ifs and buts. If a man divorces his wife and marries another, the second union is adulterous and the same is true if a woman does likewise. Adultery is inevitable because divorce is impossible.

As we make our way through this very chapter of Mark's story we will hear an astonishing statement:

> Jesus said, "Truly, I say to you, there is no one who has left house or brothers or sisters or mother or father or children or lands, for my sake and for the gospel, who will not receive a hundredfold now in this time…" (10:29; and see Luke 14:26, if you dare)

Does anybody seriously believe this? Do you feel that to be a disciple of Jesus you must abandon your father and your mother? Your brothers and sisters? Your children? Not Peter, not most other apostles, not the brothers of the Lord. Paul tells us that these luminaries were accompanied by their wives on their missionary journeys (1 Corinthians 9:5). Are we to believe they left their children behind? The teacher who condemned with such passion and anger the man who tried to deprive his father and mother of their due by some fancy spiritual foot-work (7:9-13) is hardly the teacher to recommend abandoning father and mother, brothers, sisters and children. If it is wrong to run out on parents and children in order to save some money, it is equally wrong to do so in order to preach the gospel. In either case the word of God (*Honour your father and your mother… He who speaks evil of father or mother, let him surely die* – 7:10) is frustrated. Must we not conclude that Jesus, as he so often does, is exaggerating in order to drive home his basic point, namely, that God will not be outdone in generosity? The evil of divorce is so great, is so contrary to God's wishes for his family, that Jesus can only express himself by means of exaggeration. Rather than lessen the importance of the teaching of Jesus on this matter, exaggerated language heightens it.

We had better decide that Jesus is exaggerating in his response to the Pharisees. The callous attitude to divorce and the plight of divorced women in the world in which he lived readily

190

explain his implacable opposition to divorce for any reason. If one thinks of the suffering and betrayal which tore apart Mark's community in Rome, one can readily understand that he would be opposed to more heart-break, more betrayal, more broken families (see 13:12).

But there remain the exceptions to a universal ban on divorce. Matthew and Paul must be heard, too. This does not in any sense mean that we can multiply *ad infinitum* other exceptions in order to permit divorce and remarriage. On the other hand, it does raise the question of whether they may be other exceptions.

It would be difficult for a Christian to countenance divorce for, even allowing for the exceptions, however they are to be explained, the New Testament insists that divorce is contrary to God's will for his people. Divorce is a failure of God's blue-print for humanity. But is it possible that it may be less of a failure than other failures?

If a wife and her children were subject to such violence at the hands of her husband that their deaths ensued, would not a question arise? Would not a divorce have been a lesser evil?

PRAYER

Perhaps, not a prayer. A romantic reading of the Song of Songs might remind us that human passion, faithfulness and love are not beyond our frailties.

A rich man
Mark 10:13-31

All four Gospels have much to say about children. The earliest Christians, who shaped the traditions they received from the first preachers of the gospel, must have regarded stories and sayings about children as of the utmost importance. As they sought to articulate, as plainly and as faithfully as might be, their understanding of the death and resurrection of Jesus, what it meant to believe that a man from Nazareth was, indeed, the man from God, Christians treasured and passed on details of Jesus' concern for children and his instructions that the little ones serve as a perfect model for perfect discipleship.

We have considered Mark 9:33-37 and we have seen that, in the ancient world, children were of little account. The discovery of childhood as a recognised developmental stage, as a process, important in its own right, is a phenomenon of our time. The biblical view of children, and this is as true, overall, of the New as well as the Old Testament, has to do with their obligation to obey their parents, in accordance with the ancient commandment, *Honour your father and your mother* (Exodus 19:12; Deuteronomy 5:16). The view of children in the world beyond the morality of the Jewish people may be judged by a letter from Alexandria, dated 17 June 1 B.C.E., which contains the following instruction from a husband to his pregnant wife: "if it is a male child, let it live; if it is a female child, cast it out".

Before tackling Mark's second story about Jesus and children, it may be fruitful to glance, however briefly, at the way other gospel-makers handle material concerning children.

St Matthew
Matthew begins his story with the birth of an infant over whom hangs the shadow of death. Though he is conceived of the Holy Spirit and is clearly God's Son, the infant is born into danger, a vulnerable child cast into exile, his safety achieved at the price of many little ones. These are heart-rending stories but

they are more than that. They warn us, at the very beginning of the child's life, what its end must be. The child born to be king will be crowned, but with thorns, will rule, but from a cross. The perilous infancy of Jesus (Matthew 1-2) not only mirrors the tragic end of the story, but provides a vivid picture of what it means to be a disciple of Emmanuel (Matthew 1:23). The disciple, too, is a child of the heavenly Father (Matthew 6:9), to whom is revealed all hidden things (Matthew 11:25). A child, in its nothingness, is a model for all would-be disciples (Matthew 18:1-4) and these "little ones" are not to be despised for *in heaven their angels always behold the face of my Father who is in heaven* (Matthew 18:10). A detail in one of Matthew's stories is highly instructive. Mark relates, as do all the evangelists, the story of the miraculous feeding of a vast number of people (Mark 6:32-44). Indeed, he is quite exact about the number: *five thousand men.* Matthew's concluding sentence of the story is at once less exact but more embracing: *And those who ate were about five thousand, not counting women and children* (Matthew 14:21). Matthew will not allow the women and the children to be sidelined. They, too, are disciples; they, too, are fed by the Lord; they, too, belong to the Christian family.

St Luke

Joy to the world! A barren woman has a child. A poor, bewildered young woman has a son. Prophets and angels dance about their cribs. Even in the womb there is dancing for joy. There is news of great joy for shepherds and peace for all the world. The whole of Luke's Gospel, not just the memorable stories of the births of John the Baptist and Jesus, is full of joy and it is a joy that is unconfined, an unabashed child-like joy. Tax collectors and sinners are Wisdom's children (7:35). Children are restored to distraught parents (Luke 9:42; 15:32). God's mercy to the weak is brought to our world in the mercy of Jesus for sinners, children who have gone astray, who must be sought, who must be found. In Luke, and only there, Jesus puts children by his side (Luke 9:47). That is where they belong.

St John

The Fourth Gospel has one story about a child (John 4:46-54). But one could say that the whole of John's Gospel is about a child, the child of the Father, the one who comes mysteriously into our world from the world of the Father, the one who returns to his Father so that the Father might become our Father. This means that believers are "children of God" (John 1:12; 11:52); they are the ones who are born again, who enter into the womb of God in order to be birthed into a new cosmos, to be born of the Spirit (3:3-16); they are the children who are reborn to love (John 13:34).

It is clear that the child of the Gospels is not merely a child. A metaphor has been born. The child has become a metaphor, an image of discipleship, a way of talking about God; gospel child-talk is gospel God-talk. It is, at the same time, a way of talking faith and fellowship; it is about how belief in the Son makes children of God and and how belief in each other makes brothers and sisters.

READING THROUGH

In this chapter we are concerned not only with the little vignette about children but about the longer and more difficult story of the man who had great possessions. It is this latter matter which requires some preliminary attention.

In the world of Jesus, the world of a tiny country in the near Middle-East, in the midst of his own people (and leaving aside the representatives of the military might of Rome which coerced them), there were essentially two groups of people, the rich and the poor. There was a small wealthy class and a large, poor, peasant and artisan class. The poor were often referred to as "the people of the land". They were subjected to the vagaries of the weather and the fluctuation of prices. The finer points of religious practice, the constant necessity to wash hands and eat from well scoured vessels and so forth, often went by the board in the face of everyday toil. Such impoverished and sore-tried people were regarded as sinners (a point to remember when considering such phrases as "tax collectors and sinners"). The wealthy classes consisted of the high-priestly classes in Jerusalem who controlled the lucrative affairs of the Temple, the Herodian family which controlled about half the land of the country, those who made good in trade or tax collecting and managed to purchase land (that most durable currency), and prosperous merchants who made their money in a vigorous export market. All of these wealthy citizens were deeply resented by "the people of the land" and, although there were religious prescriptions demanding alms-giving (alms-giving, fasting and prayer were the three pillars of Jewish piety), there was little evidence to discredit the view of one observer: *the poor you have always with you.*

The Old Testament, for the most part, saw wealth as a sign of God's favour (Job 1:10; 42:10; Psalm 128; Isaiah 3:10). The riches of the likes of Abraham, Jacob, Solomon and Job are advertised as clear proof of divine favour. This view survived into the time of Jesus but bitter experience had raised some real questions. Many people saw that wealth was often acquired by injustice and by grounding the face of the poor. The *Book of Amos* is trenchant in its criticisms of rich people who batten on the poor. The *Book of Job* tries (unsuccessfully) to unravel the connection between riches and piety. There were even some who came to believe that riches were an obstacle to righteousness but that view would have been regarded as wildly eccentric. The disciples are amazed that the rich will find entry into the kingdom of heaven well-nigh impossible. It is Jesus, not they, who champion eccentricity.

READING THROUGH AGAIN

The material concerning children in 10:13-16 is part of the wider landscape of material which is concerned with christian discipleship. Mark's second act (8:31–10:32) is preponderantly concerned with instructing the intimate disciples in the way of discipleship, particularly in the way of suffering discipleship. This is appropriate in a Gospel which emphasises so strongly that God's power is revealed in weakness and that true greatness is to be found in becoming *the slave of all* (10:44), that saving life must be the losing of it (8:35). The paradox of divine power is that the Lord does not lord it over people (10:42), that the divine playground is a riot of children to be taken in arms, divinely cuddled and blessed (10:15-16).

Mark's tenth chapter deals with profoundly important details of life in the divine playgound, life in the kingdom of God. Christian discipleship is lived in the real world, the world which brings Jesus to death, which uses burning people to illumine imperial gardens and feed imperial dogs. In this real world there are the concerns of

195

marriage (10:1-12) and children (10:13-16), of property and possessions (10:17-31), of power and privilege (10:32-45). How is discipleship to be lived in these concerns? At the end of the chapter, blind Bartimaeus will help us to see (10:46-52).

Children

The virtue of faithfulness is, as we have seen, required of those who have committed their love to the discipline of marriage. Following on that teaching, the attention of Jesus is drawn to the question of children by the insistence of the crowd in *bringing children to him, that he might touch them.* The disciples rebuke the people. That verb "rebuke", again! We have seen that it is the word by which Jesus overcomes the power of demons and disease and chastises the unbelief of Peter. The action of the disciples shows their lack of understanding. They are, indeed, *not on the side of God, but of men* (8:33). The anger of Jesus is kindled (so seriously does he take the banning of children from his presence) and, in words that precisely echo his words to John (9:39), he rebukes the disciples. As the anonymous exorcist is not to be forbidden (*Do not forbid him*), so the children are not to be excluded from their rightful place in the Christian community. Whether the words of Jesus are to be seen as supporting the practice of infant baptism is a matter of dispute.

The reason for admitting children and the explanation for the most affectionate way Jesus receives them (*he took them in his arms and blessed them, laying his hands upon them*) are to be found in the phrase, *for to such belongs the kingdom of God.* The child is, for would-be disciples, a model, an image of what a disciple should be. To be where the will of God is, to be in the realm of God, is not something to be grasped; it is not a possession which can be acquired. It is a gift. A child is a gift. To be where God is is to be as dependent as a child, to be at God's disposal, to be where *my will* becomes *your will* (14:36). To be like a child in the ancient world was to have nothing, to be nothing. To be a disciple in the kingdom is, at once, to lose everything and to gain everything, to die and to live.

Possessions

The rich man who approaches Jesus catches up with him *on the way*, a reminder of the way to Jerusalem and the way of discipleship. His greeting is respectful, not overblown. His re-

196

quest to inherit eternal life is a request to enter the kingdom (a comparison of 9:43 and 9:47 makes this plain), to be where the will of God is done. The reply of Jesus focuses on God. He reminds the man that good, all good, comes from God. That is where the commands come from.

The commandments cited by Jesus concern relations with people. The presumption is that the rich man is satisfactorily fulfilling the first three commandments which enjoin us to love God with all our heart and mind and soul. Loving one's neighbour may not come so easily to the rich.

Many commentators suggest that the man is not cut out for discipleship. It is said that his running up, his kneeling and his polite address "bespeak an impetuous character who could easily become discouraged", that "the effusive fulsomeness of the man Jesus meets on the way is in striking contrast to Jesus' own reserve and sobriety". The man's question – *What must I do...?* – is belittled for implying "a piety of achievement which stands in contrast to Jesus' teaching that a person must receive the kingdom as a gift from God in his helplessness". But this is to miss the point. The eager approach of the man, the warning that Jesus is *on the way*, the man's kneeling posture, his formal address to Jesus, the weighty question concerning eternal life, all suggest a deep-seated respect for the Teacher and, at least from Mark's point of view, a desire to join with him on the way. We should, therefore, conclude that the man did, indeed, observe all the commandments from his earliest days. It is this honest, forthright acknowledgement that wins the heart: *And Jesus looking upon him loved him.* This is the only man in Mark's story who moves the heart of Jesus to love.

The call to discipleship is a demand for renunciation. To throw in one's lot with Jesus is to throw in one's lot with God. Everywhere in the Old Testament, God is the champion of the the poor, the protector of the widow, the orphan and the impoverished immigrant. To be with Jesus is to give all. The one who will lay down his life as a ransom for all (10:45) demands no less of his followers. The fishermen were required to leave their nets; the man is required to leave his great possessions for the poor. Sadly, he went away. In the days of Abraham great wealth was a sign of God's favour. In the days of Jesus there is a new urgency. There is a time and place for riches, to be sure. But there is a time, too, for travelling light.

Camels and needles

To do the will of God, to enter the kingdom, to live eternal life, demands too much of human frailty. To be burdened with the distractions of riches adds to the difficulty. It used to be said that there was a gate in the walls of Jerusalem called *The Needle*, through which one could squeeze a camel with great difficulty. Such is not the case. Jesus means that the rich have as much chance of being where God is and where his will is done as of getting a camel through a sewing needle. What Jesus has undermined is a concept of merit, that is, in rich man's language, banking your good works. The contemporaries of Jesus believed that the rich could store up merit accumulated by good works. But the rich are obliged, like everyone else, to be little children, to be dependent on God, not on wealth or even on the undoubted good which wealth can facilitate.

When Sarah laughed at the thought that she would have a child (*My husband is old and shall I have pleasure?*), God, somewhat tetchily, asks rhetorically, *Is anything too hard for the LORD?* (Genesis 18:14). Job acknowledges to God that *I know that all things are possible, for nothing is impossible to you* (Job 10:13 in the Greek version); indeed, he confesses, *I know that you can do all things* (Job 42:2). It is to this unadulterated faith that Jesus appeals. Salvation is God's business. You cannot save yourself. There are no credit notes, no interest rates, no deposit accounts. God, in Jesus, is the saviour, and the only saviour of the world.

The answer to Peter's question is couched in hyperbole. Jesus exaggerates in order to make his point. We have already seen that it would be immoral to abandon father and mother, brothers and sisters and children and lands (!), be it even for the sake of Jesus or to facilitate the preaching of the gospel. The exaggerated speech of Jesus highlights the radical importance of giving one's all to the service of his mission and message. The exaggeration heightens the urgency of discipleship and the single-mindedness required to preach the gospel in season and out of season.

Divine generosity is not outdone. All goods things come to those who lay down their lives at the service of the gospel. With *persecutions* thrown in for good measure! When we consider chapter 13, we shall see how persecutions might be a gift.

And in the age to come eternal life. Beyond persecution, beyond service and discipleship, beyond the glimmer of being where God is as we make our way through the world, there is the promise of a completion of what we are. What we are is what we will become but what we become is more than what we are.

PRAYER

Prayer is the language of hope. Hope is the expectation that all God's children will be as his only Son:

Have this mind among yourselves,
which you have in Christ Jesus,
who, though he was in the form of God,
did not count equality with God
a thing to be grasped,
but emptied himself,
taking the form of a servant,
being born in the likeness of men.
And being found in human form,
he humbled himself
and became obedient unto death,
even death on a cross.

It is thus that suffering is transformed:

Therefore God has highly exalted him
and bestowed on him the name
which is above every name,
that at the name of Jesus,
every knee should bow,
in heaven and on earth and under the earth ...
(Philippians 2:5-10).

The blind man of Jerico
Mark 10:32-52

A famous line: *Many that are first will be last, and the last first.*
Ask when Jesus uttered the famous words, however, and confusion sets in. Didn't Jesus tell a parable about a man who was so
short of workers that he kept hiring right up to closing-time and
paid everyone, the early-birds and the Johnny-come-latelies, the
same wages? And didn't he round off his story with the telling
line about the first and the last? Yes, he did (Matthew 20:1-15).
But didn't he chide those who claimed that eating and drinking
with Jesus would ensure preferential treatment in the matter of
salvation with the put-down that some who are last would be
promoted to the first places? Well, yes, he did (Luke 13:22-30).
And didn't he conclude his teaching about the snares of wealth
and the path of self-denial demanded of would-be disciples with
the injunction that following him requires a reversal of earthly
power and position, so that the first becomes last, and the last
becomes first? Indeed, he did (Mark 10:17-31). What are we to
make of such confusion?

The easiest way out is to say that Jesus used the snappy
sentence three times. It's a pithy saying, well worth repeating. It
provides such a succinct summary of much of what Jesus had to
say that it bears repetition. The disciples, so concerned with
privilege and status, needed to hear it, and hear it again and
again.

The easiest solution will not do, however. A careful examination of the three occurrences of the saying in the Gospels will
reveal that the words are the same (not exactly so) but that the
situations to which they refer are quite different. Mark sees the
saying as a powerful summation of the teaching of Jesus concerning the nature of discipleship. If the disciples thought that
they would enter the kingdom of God by giving up today in order
to be rewarded tomorrow, Jesus shattered such a false understanding. What he demanded was a total commitment to himself
and his cause, a radical surrender to his way and, above all, a

willingness to accept the consequences of aligning oneself with Jesus. What discipleship embraces is not consolation; it is the cross. In other words, Mark gives the saying his own peculiar twist.

What seems to have happened is that a very memorable saying of Jesus persisted in the minds of early christian preachers and teachers but somehow got detached from its anchorage. The gospel-makers inherited the saying in the material that came to them but could not discover (if, indeed, they wanted to) its original setting in the preaching of Jesus. They wanted to preserve a memorable saying of the Lord. To do so, each attached it to some teaching of Jesus which seemed best suited to the meaning of the sentence as each understood it.

A useful lesson concerning the gospel-makers art may be learnt here. It is the gospel-makers who are responsible for the ordering and application of the bits and pieces about Jesus which came to them in the traditions they received from those who had gone before them. What we touch in the Gospels is not the story of Jesus but the story of Jesus as it has been reconstructed by the evangelists in order to meet the demands of the people for whom they wrote.

READING THROUGH

Excellent examples of the gospel-maker's art may be detected in the material now before us. A few preliminary remarks are required before they emerge with clarity.

Jerusalem
Jerusalem was, of course, the chief city of the province of Judea. It was not the seat of Roman administration because Pilate preferred the pleasant Mediterranean climate of Caesarea. The Temple, the centre of Jewish religious life, was located in Jerusalem and added to the prestige and economic importance of the city. But for Christians Jerusalem was the place where Jesus died. Every time the city is mentioned in the Gospels and other New Testament writings, it is the fact of the terrible death of Jesus which pre-occupies the Christian mind. That is to say, Christians looked on Jerusalem, not merely as a holy city, but as the place where God, through the death of Jesus, reconciled the

world to himself (2 Corinthians 5:18-20). For Christians, Jerusalem is not merely a geographical location; it is the city where Jesus *gave his life as a ransom for many* (10:45). For Mark, it is the place of enemies, of betrayal, of torture and death. In his story, Jesus makes his way there, not as a pilgrim but as a victim.

In your glory

The request of James and John pinpoints the extent to which the most prominent of disciples can get it wrong. What they seek is the privileged places to the right and left of the Messiah when his true splendour is revealed. It may very well be that the sons of Zebedee envisage Jesus as the all-conquering hero who will, as it were, take Jerusalem by storm and restore the throne of King David. The hapless pair thus completely misunderstand the nature of Jesus' messiahship, not understanding it as a call to suffering but as a royal power-base which would issue in benefits for themselves.

Son of David

The incident involving the blind beggar is the last of the healing miracles recorded in Mark. Bartimaeus is the last person to be healed before Jesus enters into Jerusalem, the city of crucifixion and death. The story is not just another in a long list of healings. It is a summary of much of what has gone before and demands careful attention.

Twice the blind man addresses Jesus as Son of David. These are the only occurrences of the title in Mark's story (but see 11:9-10 and 12:35-37). Some Jewish traditions looked forward to a restoration of the royal family of David, the national hero. Near contemporaries of Jesus, the people who left us *The Dead Sea Scrolls,* looked to the day when there would be *a descendant of David upon the throne,* when *the righteous Messiah, the branch of David* would come and whose rule over his people would last *for everlasting generations* (4QPBless). This kind of expectation grew out of the longings of some of the ancient prophets:

> There shall come forth a shoot from the stump of Jesse,
> and a branch shall grow out of his roots.
> And the Spirit of the LORD shall rest upon him,
> the spirit of wisdom and understanding,

the spirit of counsel and might,
the spirit of knowledge and fear of the LORD (Isaiah 11:1-2).

(Christians looked to this verse to provide them with a list of the Seven Gifts of the Holy Spirit. The Greek version adds piety to the six given here.) Jeremiah pursues the same line of thought:

> Behold, the days are coming, says the LORD, when I shall raise up for David a righteous Branch, and he shall reign as king and deal wisely, and shall execute justice and righteousness in the land (Jeremiah 23:5).

Ezekiel combines the idea of the good shepherd with the ideal king:

> I will save my flock, they shall no longer be a prey; and I will judge between sheep and sheep. And I will set up over them one shepherd, my servant David, and he shall feed them: he shall feed them and be their shepherd. And I, the LORD, will be their God, and my servant David shall be prince among them; I, the LORD, have spoken (Ezekiel 34:22-24).

We may speculate as to how the blind Bartimaeus came to know that Jesus was of the family of David (see Matthew 1:1) or, since Jesus (in Mark's story) had never passed that way before, come to understand that he was the Messiah. Further, we may wonder how he came to believe that Jesus could take away his blindness. Did he know of such prophetic words as Isaiah 35:4-5 or 61:1 were to be fulfilled in the work of Jesus? When the man comes before Jesus, he addresses him respectfully as *my master*; there is no suggestion that Bartimaeus has the kind of insight into the person of Jesus shown by the supernatural demons who know him to be Son of God and Messiah. However, here is an example of the gospel-maker's art. Whatever the blind man may have known about Jesus as he passed through the gates of Jericho, his words and actions, in Mark's telling of the story, take on a deeper and more profound meaning for the informed Christian reader. The reader knows (from the very first line of Mark's text) that Jesus is the Messiah, Son of God. The reader knows that it is this Jesus who brings into the world the mercy of God. The reader knows that it is this Jesus who goes to Jerusalem as the Messiah and that he will die there as the Messiah. The gospel-maker has a right to expect his readers to read between the lines. Bartimaeus may have been blind to the true identity of Jesus. Mark expects clearer vision of his readers.

READING THROUGH AGAIN

The journey to Jerusalem is a journey to death. But it is not only the death of Jesus which concerns Mark. The journey which Jesus makes is the journey to which disciples are called. The way of the cross is the way of Jesus and, accordingly, the way of discipleship. As Jesus makes his way to the city of destiny, he is most urgent in clarifying for his disciples the destiny to which they are called.

On the way

When he met the man of great possessions (10:17), Jesus *was setting out on the way*. The hint of the way of discipleship contained in the phrase is confirmed in the call of Jesus: *come, follow me*. Consider now 10:32:

> And they were on the way, going up to Jerusalem, and Jesus was walking ahead of them; and they were amazed, and those who followed were afraid.

To be sure, this is Mark's description of Jesus and his followers as they journeyed from the Jordan valley (10:1) to the city of Jerusalem. No doubt Jesus strode ahead, eager to reach the place of destiny. No doubt, too, those who clambered in his wake (see 10:46) were, as always, amazed. No doubt, those who followed were afraid. What would happen when Jesus went into the stronghold of his enemies?

Read the lines another way. What is discipleship? It is following Jesus; it is taking up the cross and following where he has gone before (8:34). Discipleship is knowing that Jesus goes ahead and it excites amazement, for to be with Jesus is to be amazed. But the journey is always, in Mark's view, to Jerusalem, always to the cross. Even Jesus faces the place of the skull in fear (14:33). To be afraid is not to lack courage. It is to enter into the agony of Jesus himself.

Thus we see a gospel-maker at work. What appears to be a matter-of-fact description of Jesus and his band of followers making their way to Jerusalem turns out to be, not just that, but also, for the alert reader, a perfect description of discipleship for

204

all seasons. That is what gospel-makers do. They take the words and deeds of Jesus and narrate them in such a fashion that they are brought to bear on the needs and aspirations of the people of their own time and place.

The third prediction

For the third time Jesus takes his intimate followers to one side and spells out for them in the clearest details what lies ahead. The prediction is so close to the order of events that unfold at the Gospel's end that it is likely to have been composed with hindsight. Be that as it may, the purpose behind Mark's precision is to highlight, yet again, the twelve's inability to cope with a suffering Messiah or to imagine a God who can turn death into life.

Each of the predictions of suffering and death is followed by gross misunderstanding. James and John want position and prestige. They want to be first. They want to sit on the right and left. But the seats available are to the right and left of the cross. The cup which Jesus must drink and the baptism he must undergo refer to his death (the metaphor of the cup is to be found in Jeremiah 49:12 and early Christians were fond of describing baptism as a dying with Jesus). James and John, says Jesus, will suffer a fate similar to his own. But it is not in the power of Jesus to dictate what will happen in the life to come. The future belongs to God.

The indignation of the ten hardly does them credit. They are not shocked at the outrageous hubris of the sons of Zebedee. Rather, they are fearful lest the two brothers should secure some advantage over them. Jesus is obliged to spell out what being last means.

Servants

Jesus lived in a world of power. His country was dominated (see the pedigree of this word in a good dictionary) by an imperial, coercive force. Occupying armies held the population in an iron fist. Fierce taxation devoured the produce of the land. The coins in their pockets reminded Jewish people of their plight. To give two examples, the denarius coin (see 12:16) that was used for paying taxes portrayed the emperor Tiberius (14-37 C.E.) as the divine son of the divine Augustus and his divine mother Livia; the copper coins which Jesus and his disciples would have used to buy food in Caesarea Philippi (8:27) bore the head of

Tiberius with the emperor's name and the inscription, "He who deserves adoration". It is these *great men* who rule the lives of Jesus and his people. It is these people and their minions who create terror and call it peace, who rule with a rod of iron and call it authority. It may come as a surprise to some to hear Jesus speak so disparagingly of his political masters. Notice the contempt in his voice: *You know those who are supposed to rule over the Gentiles* ... For Jesus, as we shall see, power belongs to God.

The exercise of authority among those who follow Jesus would appear to stand the world on its head. According to the principle outlined in 10:31, the last shall be first. The first is to be the servant of all. The word which Mark uses for servant is *diakonos*, the word from which we derive our word deacon. But the word does not (in Mark's text) refer to any ecclesiastical office. Superficially, it describes one whose task is to prepare and serve food, to wait on tables. From Mark's point of view, it describes the service given to Jesus by angelic powers and women disciples.

The term describing Simon's mother-in-law is a verb from the noun *diakonos*: she served them. It is clear that Mark means that the healed woman prepared and served food to her son-in-law and his companions (1:29-31). The verb has occurred before. When the Spirit had driven Jesus out into the desert to be tested by Satan, *the angels ministered to him* Mark refers to a large number of women who followed Jesus to Jerusalem and witnessed (*from afar*) his death:

> There were also women looking on from afar, among whom were Mary Magdalene, and Mary the mother of James the younger and of Joses, and Salome, who, when he was in Galilee, followed him, and *ministered* to him; and also many other women who came up with him to Jerusalem (15:40-41).

These women are of immense importance to Mark. They are going to provide his only witnesses to the empty tomb, they will be entrusted with the message of the young man concerning the resurrection of Jesus and they will bring down the curtain on Mark's drama as they run from the tomb, trembling with astonishment and silenced by fear (16:1-8). The only persons, therefore, in Mark's Gospel who follow Jesus and minister to him are women. As Jesus said, he who has ears to hear, let him hear.

The third person who is described as "deaconing" or serving

in Mark's story is the Son of man. Jesus tells the twelve that their service must be modelled on his. But the extent of his service is spelled out: *to give his life as a ransom for many*. The term "ransom" is a commercial term; it is the price which must be paid to redeem an article from the pawn-shop, the price which must be paid to buy someone out of slavery, the price which must be paid to rescue a prisoner of war or a kidnap victim. What is to be noticed is that the object in pawn or the person in slavery or captivity is powerless. Freedom can be achieved only if someone else is prepared to act on behalf of the victim. Jesus proclaims that his unique service is to offer himself as the price by which freedom is won for the many (= all). The saying in 10:45 claims scrupulous attention for it is the one verse in Mark's Gospel which provides an explanation of the death of Jesus.

A ransom for many

Any attempt to determine how Jesus understood his mission must take the ransom saying into account. Since the declaration of his messiahship at Caesarea Philippi, Jesus has been at pains to focus the attention of the disciples on his suffering and death. Apart from more veiled references, there are the three explicit passion predictions. Each of these, as we have seen, is followed by some indication of the failure of the disciples to comprehend what Jesus means and there follows further attempts to bring them to a proper realisation of what it means to follow Jesus, to take up the cross. The ransom saying comes just before the arrival in Jerusalem and it explains the reason for the journey to the holy city and the suffering that awaits Jesus there. But we may well ask why the death of one man should rescue all?

The Jewish people have never enjoyed extensive periods of freedom from foreign domination and persecution. The three hundred years before the birth of Jesus saw Palestine dominated by the successors of Alexander the Great (336-323 B.C.E.) and then by the Romans. There were many efforts to rise up and overcome tyrannical rulers, the revolt of the Maccabees (167 B.C.E.) the most successful and, accordingly, the most famous. Out of a long history of military resistance to foreign oppression grew the idea that the woes of the nation were not entirely due to the rapacity of marauding foreigners. Some came to believe that the failure of most of the people to observe God's law and live up to the religious traditions of the nation earned God's wrath and provoked divine punishment. Many of the prophets were of the opinion that Israel's woes were self-inflicted.

The sins of the many lead to the enslavement of all. If the only solution is that everyone stops sinning, the future will be bleak. The idea arose that the lives and deaths of good people could compensate for the sins of others. Especially effective in this regard was the death of one who gave his life for the people, that is, a martyr. This idea is expressed in writings concerning the careers of the Maccabee family. Here is a prayer of Eleazer:

> Be merciful to your people and let our punishment be a satisfaction on their behalf. Make my blood their purification and take my life as a ransom for theirs (4 Maccabees 6:28-29).

Another, Mattathias, on his deathbed, urged his sons to live righteously and resist oppression:

> Now, my children, show zeal for the law, and give your lives for the covenant of our fathers (1 Maccabees 2:50).

When the Maccabees resisted the most hated of oppressors, Antiochus IV, one of their number ran to what he thought was the elephant bearing the tyrant, attacked it and killed it. Unfortunately, the dead animal fell on top of him *and there he died*:

> So he gave his life to save his people and win for himself an everlasting name (1 Maccabees 6:44).

But the most famous example of one laying down one's life to atone for the sins of others is to be found in a section of the prophecy of Isaiah which deals with a mysterious servant who suffers on behalf of sinful people:

> Yet it was the will of the LORD to bruise him,
> he has put him to grief;
> when he makes himself an offering for sin,
> he shall see his offspring, he shall prolong his days;
> the will of the LORD shall prosper in his hand;
> he shall see the fruit of the travail of his soul,
> and he shall be satisfied;
> by his knowledge shall the righteous one, my servant,
> make many be accounted righteous;
> and he shall bear their iniquities.

Therefore I will divide him a portion with the great,
and he shall divide the spoil with the strong;
because he poured out his soul to death,
and was numbered with the transgressors;
yet he bore the sin of many,
and made intercession for the transgressors (Isaiah 53:10-12).

This passage is quite mysterious but it seems to suggest that a servant will endure great suffering and even death but that his death will be accounted by God as a prayer for all who have sinned and will be effective in saving the transgressors from their sins. Another passage is, perhaps, more familiar, but no less difficult on that account:

Surely he has borne our griefs and carried our sorrows;
yet we esteemed him stricken,
smitten by God, and afflicted.
But he was wounded for our transgressions,
he was bruised for our iniquities;
upon him was the chastisement that made us whole,
and with his stripes we are healed.
All we like sheep have gone astray;
we have turned every one to his own way;
and the LORD has laid on him the iniquity of us all
(Isaiah 53:4-6)

Whatever we are to make of these difficult ideas, it seems clear that within Jewish thinking there was the idea that good people could make up for the sins of others, that one good person, especially a martyr who died defending God's ways, could make up for the sins of the people and win forgiveness from them. Such ideas seem to have inspired Jesus in his reflections on the meaning of the death that lay before him in Jerusalem. Why God should have willed that all sinners should receive forgiveness because of the death of the sinless Jesus is a question we will postpone until we come to the story of the Passion.

The death of Jesus, the cross of Calvary, stands at the heart and defines the meaning of Christianity. It is the mystery which unlocks all mysteries. Christians will forever draw on the profound meaning of the cross and they will never exhaust its meaning. Mark places its meaning in the context of service. Thus he warns that service is the defining quality of Christianity. The

Christian is called to that degree of service which can be seen on the cross of Jesus. There is no room for *lording it over them* in the Christian way. Authority is not a question of power; it is a duty of service. To be a Christian is to be last. To be a Christian in authority is to be even more last!

Blind Bartimaeus

As Jesus passes out of Jericho, he is accompanied by *his disciples and a great multitude*. Bartimaeus, the blind beggar, sits along the way. Of course, Mark means that the man is sitting by the roadside, outside the city gate – a good place to attract the attention of passers-by. But Mark's use of the word "way" as a metaphor for discipleship allows readers to see the blind man as a possible disciple. His call to Jesus, *Jesus Son of David, have mercy on me!*, further reveals the identity of Jesus. Since Caesarea Philippi, Jesus has been trying to make his disciples realise that the Messiah is destined to suffer and die (to little avail). Ironically, the blind Bartimaeus recognises Jesus as the messianic inheritor of the royal family of David. Many rebuke him (note the use of this word in Mark) and try to silence him. In crying out all the more, the beggar witnesses to his faith in Jesus and is, accordingly, called into his presence. His healing quickly follows.

Faith in Jesus, faith that he could dispense the mercy of God, leads to enlightenment. It should be noted that the RSV is misleading in its translation *your faith has made you well*. What Jesus says is *your faith has saved you*. There is a world of difference. The mercy of God which comes through the work of Jesus is not only concerned with physical well-being. It is concerned with salvation.

Jesus offers Bartimaeus the freedom to depart but the man is now a man of seeing, of insight. He follows Jesus *on the way*. He throws in his lot with Jesus and sets out with his new Master (verse 51) on the way to Jerusalem and beyond.

A little detail. The blind man sprang up in his eagerness to come to Jesus. The effort required him to throw off his mantle. A mantle is a blind man's means of livelihood. Spread at his feet, it is the only means he has of collecting the coppers thrown to him. It is hardly pressing the matter too far to see in Bartimaeus one who leaves everything to follow Jesus on the way (10:28). At the end of the journey to Jerusalem, at the end of the efforts to instil into Peter and the rest the meaning of true discipleship, there is one man who understands.

Act two: scene one

The way of the Cross for Jesus and his disciples is the central concern of the first scene in Mark's second act. Time and again the fate of the Son of man is foretold, either indirectly or in the plainest possible manner. To be sure, such hints have always been accompanied by the assurance that death will not be the end, that there will be a rising from the dead. The disciples, frequently taken to one side by Jesus, all the more to concentrate their minds, are as incapable of understanding the notion of resurrection as they are unwilling to entertain the possibility of suffering and death, either for the Messiah or for themselves. The journey of Jesus to Jerusalem is now at an end. The crisis is upon Jesus and his band of followers. In the second scene of Mark's tragedy we shall see Jesus face what is to come with courage and deep faith in his God. We shall see the disciples run away. Save for the dignity of Jesus, it will not be a pretty sight.

PRAYER

The opening lines of Psalm 42 would seem to echo the heart-felt need of the blind man of Jericho, and, indeed, of all who seek true discipleship:

As a hart longs
for flowing streams,
so longs my soul
for thee, my God.
My soul thirsts for God,
for the living God.
When shall I come and behold
the face of God?
My tears have been my food
day and night,
while men say to me continually,
"Where is your God?" (Psalm 42:1-3).

211

Introduction to the passion story
Mark 11:1–13:37

St Paul was a city man. He was born in a city: *I am a Jew, from Tarsus in Cilicia, a citizen of no mean city* (Acts 21:39). He was brought up in a city: *I am a Jew, born at Tarsus in Cilicia, but brought up in [Jerusalem]* (Acts 22:3). All the communities of Christians he founded or visited were in cities: Corinth, Philippi, Thessalonica and the rest. He died in a city, the capital of the empire. For Paul what lay beyond the city walls was not pleasant, flowing countryside; it was merely desert (2 Corinthians 11:26).

Jesus, on the other hand, was a man of the countryside. He was born in the tiny village of Bethlehem; he was brought up in the obscure village of Nazareth. We may speculate on whether or not he visited any of the cities of Galilee. We may incline to the plausible conjecture that he made his living on the building sites of Sepphoris. But his language, his images, his stories are of the country. Mark, more than the other gospel-writers, keeps Jesus out of cities. To be sure, Jesus makes the village of Capernaum his home-base as he engages in his itinerant mission in Galilee. But Capernaum is on the shore of Lake Kinnereth (Sea of Galilee) and it is the lake, not the village, that attracts Jesus. Otherwise, Jesus is in the countryside around Gerasa (5:1); he lands briefly at Bethsaida (6:45), at Gennesaret (6:53); he is in the region of Tyre and Sidon (7:24) and the region of the Ten Cities (7:31); he visits the villages around the city of Caesarea Philippi and ventures south to the countryside of Judea (10:1); he comes to Jericho, only to leave it (10:46) and when, finally, his destiny forces Jerusalem upon him, he chooses to stay outside the city in the tiny suburban village of Bethany (11:11).

Jerusalem is the only city to have any prominence in Mark's Gospel. It is, as we have noted, the place of enemies and the place of death. If the risen Lord is to meet with his disciples it will be in Galilee, not in the city of the crucifixion (16:7) Throughout his story, Mark does not disguise his hostility to Jerusalem

212

and, particularly, to its Temple. In the second verse of his text he so edits his quotation from the prophet Malachi to avoid any suggestion that the Messiah would make his appearance in the Temple. In striking contrast to the other gospel writers, Mark never mentions the Temple until Jesus arrives in the city and begins a critical and hostile campaign against it. The Temple will loom large in the last days of Jesus.

The teaching and preaching of Jesus in Galilee, in the region of the Decapolis, in the villages of Caesarea Philippi, in the region of Judea and beyond the Jordan, have occupied but ten chapters of Mark's Gospel. The last five days of his life in Jerusalem occupy five chapters (chapters 11-15). Clearly, the death of Jesus and the events immediately leading up to his death, are of immense importance for Mark. We have seen that the cross looms large on every page of his story and noted that the true identity of the man from Nazareth cannot be revealed until he has breathed his last (15:37-39). It may come as a surprise to many that the Gospels spend far more time contemplating the suffering and death of Jesus than they do his resurrection. This is especially true of Mark who omits any account of the risen Lord and is content merely to report the fact of the resurrection to frightened women.

Before making our way through his account of the last days of Jesus in Jerusalem, we will review the extent to which the death of Jesus casts its shadow over all of Mark's story and we will seek the motives which may have led him (and, indeed, all gospel-makers) to dwell so long at the foot of the cross.

The shadow of the cross

From the very beginning of Mark's story there are signs that it will end in tragedy. Sometimes Mark's hints of the disasters to come are quite broad; on other occasions, he is subtle and requires our careful attention. Such is the case of his use of a verb which occurs twenty times all told, the first of which is in 1:14 and concerns John the Baptist. There we are told that *after John was arrested, Jesus came into Galilee*. It is the Greek word that is translated *was arrested* which demands our attention. This word is translated by a number of English words: to arrest, to hand over, to give into the hands of another, to surrender treacherously, to hand down, to deliver up.

If, however, we settle on one translation, to *hand over*, then

Mark's pattern emerges. Consider the sentences in which the word occurs:

1:14 Now after John *was handed over*, Jesus came into Galilee, preaching the gospel of God.

3:19 and Judas Iscariot, *who handed him over.*

9:31 The Son of man *will be handed over* into the hands of men, and they will kill him …

10:33 Behold, we are going to Jerusalem; and the Son of man wi*ll be handed over* to the chief priests and the scribes, and they will condemn him to death, and *hand him over* to the Gentiles.

13:9 But take heed to yourselves; for they w*ill hand you over* to councils; and you will be beaten in synagogues; and you will stand before governors and kings for my sake …

13:11 And when they bring you to trial and *hand you over,* do not be anxious beforehand what you are to say …

13:12 And brother *will hand over* brother to death, and the father his child, and children will rise against parents and have them put to death …

14:10 Then Judas Iscariot, who was one of the twelve, went to the chief priests in order *to hand him over* to them …

14:11 And when they heard it, they were glad, and promised to give him money. And he sought an opportunity *to hand him over.*

14:18 And as they were at table eating, Jesus said, "Truly, I say to you, one of you *will hand me over,* one who is eating with me".

14:21 For the Son of man goes as it is written of him, but woe to that man by whom the Son of man *is handed over*! It would have been better for that man if he had not been born.

14:41 And he came the third time, and said to them, "Are you still sleeping and taking your rest? It is enough; the hour has come; the Son of man *is handed over* into the hands of sinners."

14:42 Rise, let us be going; behold, my *hander-over* is near.

14:44 Now *the hander-over* had given them a sign, saying "The one I shall kiss is the man; seize him and lead him securely".

15:1 And as soon as it was morning the chief priests, with the elders and the scribes, and the whole sanhedrin made consultation; (and) binding Jesus, they led him away and *handed him over* to Pilate.

15:10 For he perceived that it was out of envy that the chief priests *had handed him over*.

15:15 So Pilate, wishing to satisfy the crowd, released for them Barabbas and having scourged Jesus, he *handed him over* to be crucified.

Notice how Mark has made a very profound point by knitting his material together with this one word:

John the Baptist is *handed over*
Jesus of Nazareth is *handed over*
Disciples of Jesus are *handed over*

John the Baptist prepares the way for Jesus. He is a witness to the man who comes from Nazareth to the Jordan. He points to Jesus so that other people may come to know him. John the Baptist is handed over and he is put to death.

Jesus of Nazareth comes into Galilee, preaching the gospel of God. He heals the sick and overcomes the power of Satan. He calls disciples to follow his way. He is handed over and he is put to death.

Disciples of Jesus are to follow him, to share in his understanding of God, to go out with his authority and power to heal and to teach. They are warned, however, that they must be prepared to take up their cross, for they, too, will be handed over.

By means of a single verb, Mark has tied together the destinies of John the Baptist, Jesus and the disciples. Those who, like John and the disciples, call on people to accept Jesus and his God must be prepared to meet his fate. The shadow of betrayal, suffering and death casts itself, not only over Jesus, but over all who would follow him. In a word (!), that is the message of Mark.

Further warnings

Mark provides us with less subtle warnings of the fate which awaits Jesus. These, too, are spread liberally throughout his story:

1:12 The Spirit immediately drove him out into the wilderness. And he was in the wilderness forty days, tempted by Satan; and he was with the wild beasts and the angels ministered to him.

2:20 The days will come, when the bridegroom is taken away from them, and then they will fast in that day.

3:6 The Pharisees went out, and immediately took counsel with the Herodians against him, how to destroy him.

6:14 King Herod heard of it ... and immediately he sent a soldier of the guard and gave orders to bring his head... and [his disciples] came and took his body, and laid it in a tomb.

8:11 And they asked him, "Why do the scribes say that first Elijah must come?" And he said to them, "Elijah must come first to restore all things; and how is it written of the Son of man, that he should suffer many things and be treated with contempt?"

The fact that Jesus is in the desert to be tested by Satan and that he is exposed there to the terror of wild beast is ominous. Will the help of the ministering angels be enough to save him? The bridegroom's presence is a time for joy, not fasting. But what will happen when Jesus the Bridegroom is taken away? The religious Pharisees and the agents of the political power come together in an unholy alliance against Jesus. Will their evil counsels prevail? The death of John the Baptist is brought about by sinful people and powerful political agents. Only his body and a tomb are left to his disciples. What will the disciples of Jesus be left with? If John the Baptist is Elijah and he suffered death, will scripture demand as much of the Son of man?

Plain speaking

The three predictions of his suffering and death made by Jesus (8:31; 9:31; 10:33) are in the plainest terms. The emphasis in each is on Jesus' suffering, his rejection, his betrayal into the hands of religious and political enemies, his mockery, torture and death. Notice of the resurrection is given in four words. Again, each prediction is made at a different place, at Caesarea Philippi, on the way through Galilee, going up to Jerusalem. Three times and at three significant stages on the way a death is announced.

Thus, when we come to the Mount of Olives and see beyond the Kidron Valley the glorious sight of Jerusalem the Golden, we know that we are being summoned to the foot of the cross. Why should Mark, why should other gospel-makers, dwell so much on the death? Why not move from the foot of the cross to the door of the empty tomb? Why not dance with the risen Lord, forgetting the naked man hanging on the tree?

Preaching the passion

The death of Jesus, rather that his birth, may have been the first part of his story to concern early Christians. They may have worked back from the cross to the crib. The earliest preachers preached *Christ crucified*, as St Paul tells us (1 Corinthians 1:23). The Passion Narratives, that is, the story of the last days of Jesus in Jerusalem leading up to his death, as recorded in each of the four Gospels, may have been the first part of the story to be put together. In the first sermon of St Peter, preached on the very day the Holy Spirit descended upon the followers of Jesus, it is the end, rather than the beginning, of the career of Jesus which engages the apostle's attention:

> Men of Israel, hear these words: Jesus of Nazareth, a man attested to you by God with mighty works and wonders and signs which God did through him in your midst, as you yourselves know – this Jesus, delivered up according to the definite plan and foreknowledge of God, you crucified and killed by the hands of lawless men (Acts 2:22-23).

But even in the first days of Christian preaching the event of the death of Jesus was never preached as a mere event. Christians were never content to say that Jesus died. Rather they were at pains to explain the significance of the event. St Peter does not say that Jesus was killed; he says that Jesus was killed *according to the definite plan and foreknowledge of God*. The crucifixion of Jesus is not just another criminal execution; it is an execution carried out according to God's purpose.

We do not have an unvarnished story of the death of Jesus

(even if such were possible). We do not have an objective account of the passion and death of Jesus. We have, in each of the Gospels, a story which has been subjected to interpretation from the beginning. Each Gospel tells the story in its own way, to bring out that interpretation which the gospel-maker wished to put before his readers. But we can detect two factors which seem to have influenced the presentation of the passion story in all the Gospels. While each has its own particular slant, they have much in common.

Innocent

It may come as surprise to many Christians that the first task of the earliest preachers and of the evangelists was to prove that Jesus was not a criminal. Historical data outside the Gospels point clearly to the reality that, in a Roman province such as Judea, an execution by crucifixion could be carried out only under the orders of the Roman procurator. Crucifixion was used in the Roman provinces above all as a deterrent against sedition. By inference, then, we might conclude that Jesus was crucified under Pontius Pilate because he was fermenting insurrection and attempting to overthrow the state.

On the surface, this would appear to be the case. In the clearest record of the charges brought against Jesus, we read that the assembly of the elders of the Jewish people, both the chief priests and the scribes, led Jesus to Pilate and brought accusation against him:

> We have found this man perverting our nation, and forbidding us to give tribute to Caesar, and saying that he himself is Christ a king. ... He stirs up the people, teaching throughout all Judea, from Galilee even to this place (Luke 23:2,5).

The charge that Jesus claimed to be King of the Jews was affixed to his cross (Luke 23:38) and he was crucified with two criminals (Luke 23:33). It would appear, then, that Jesus was executed for sedition. But such a conclusion is not only at variance with all we know of the life and teaching of Jesus, it does not explain how his followers were not rounded up and summarily put to death as well. Indeed, his followers were allowed to form a community in Jerusalem, a community which displayed little sign of having been called into existence by a revolutionary whose heart was set on the destruction of the state.

The point is this: if Jesus was a criminal, how could be presented to Jewish and Gentile people as the Messiah, the Son of God, the Saviour of the world? St Paul tells that the death of Jesus was *a stumbling block to the Jews and folly to Gentiles* (1 Corinthians 1:23). Each had their own objections to believing in a criminal and these objections had to be answered by Christian preachers if the message of Jesus was to be heard and not laughed out of court.

How did one convince a Jew that the Messiah, the anointed king of Israel, the holy one of God, would be constrained to die as a criminal? The first Christian preachers (all Jews) had to show that the sufferings of the Messiah were in accord with God's will. It was well-nigh impossible for any Jew to believe that God would permit his Messiah to die, let alone die a shameful death, stripped naked and defecating for all the world to see, at the hands of the minions of a pagan empire. The only way forward was to convince those who were willing to listen that the sufferings of the Messiah were in accord with God's will. To the Jewish people, all their Scriptures contained the word of God, they carried the message of salvation which would one day be brought to light in the world. Thus the first preachers of Jesus had to turn to the writings of their faith to find, not only God's plan of salvation, but also the part which Jesus was destined to play in it. Christian preachers had to convince their Jewish brothers and sisters that the whole of the Scriptures bore witness to the tragic necessity of the death of Jesus. They had to show that Jesus died according to the Scriptures. Only then could his innocence before God and his credentials as Messiah be vindicated. The stumbling-block could only be removed by an appeal to God's words in the holy books. In the telling of the passion and death of Jesus, Mark and the other evangelists constantly emphasise that all that happens is in accord with the divine plan. The most trivial matter (for example, the lottery for Jesus' clothes) is explained as happening in accordance with the Scriptures (John 19:23-24). At every step of the way, Mark will endeavour to show that the innocence of the Messiah is guaranteed because his death is in accordance with God's grand design.

That the death of Jesus fulfils the Jewish Scriptures can hardly have excited non-Jewish people. The Gentile peoples will not have been asking whether the life and death of Jesus were in accord with what God had outlined for his Messiah in the writings of a troublesome people in the Middle East. There question will have been whether Jesus was the saviour of the world as claimed by his adherents. The folly which gentile people detected in the christian story, as St Paul unerringly pointed out, lay in the fact of his crucifixion: Christ *crucified*. There's the rub!

How could a criminal be a saviour? How could an obscure Jew, sentenced to death by the supreme Roman authority (represented by Pilate) as a rebel against the state, be a saviour? In the period when the Gospels were written the Jews were either going through a rebellion against Rome or suffering the consequences of such action. The holy city of Jerusalem was destroyed in 70 C.E. during a fierce and extended rebellion. Everywhere there was resentment against the troublesome Jews. The writers of the Gospels reflect the turmoil of their times. How could they, and the Christian preachers who went before them, preach to Roman citizens that a Jewish criminal was God's only Son? Were Roman citizens, was Roman authority, responsible for killing the saviour of the world?

The writers of the Gospels were concerned not to appear in a bad light to the Romans, the rulers of the world. The more Christianity moved from the confines of its parent Judaism, the more it exposed itself to the pagan world, the more careful it had to be in its presentation of the death of Jesus. Consequently, we have in the New Testament, and in the passion stories especially, an attempt to let Jesus off the political hook, and thus an attempt to increase the role played by the Jewish authorities in the death of Jesus of Nazareth. There is a concern to lessen the political nature of the charges brought against Jesus, to present the matter as if it were a religious issue, with no political overtones. There is a clear concern to white-wash Pilate, to lessen his guilt in the condemnation of Jesus. As we read Mark's passion story, we must be aware of the tensions under which the gospel was preached and the political realities of the world in which Christianity was born and sought to make its way. Certainly, such constraints influenced the way Mark tells of the death of Jesus.

A drama unfolds

The Passion Narratives read with all the force of a great drama. The story of the trial and death of Jesus must be visualised, dramatised. The Gospels were written to move the hearts of

Christian people, to help them to enter into the suffering of their beloved Lord. It was never enough, it is never enough, to tell the bald facts. As we read, we are called into the story, we are forced to take sides, to make judgements, above all, to take our stand at the foot of the cross and to see in the broken body the Son of God. Winston Churchill might have issued a ministerial notice to the effect that, in the event of an invasion, the whole population would be required to resist the enemy by whatever means lay to hand. He did not choose to do so. He proclaimed to the whole nation, *We will fight them on the beaches* ... Mark is in the same business as Churchill.

PRAYER

As we set out to read Mark's story of the death of Jesus no more appropriate prayer may be made than the one with which Jesus died. Psalm 22 begins with the cry, *My God, my God, why hast thou forsaken me?*

Entering Jerusalem
Mark 11:1-11

Bartimaeus followed Jesus on the way. But the way for Jesus, for Bartimaeus and all would-be disciples, is the way of the cross and the hope that there is life beyond the place of the skull (15:22). Jerusalem, the city wherein Jesus is condemned and done to death, is also the model of the new Jerusalem, that great poetic symbol of faith which provides assurance that life can come from death, that resurrection can overcome crucifixion.

> And I saw the holy city, new Jerusalem, coming down out of heaven from God, prepared as a bride adorned for her husband; and I heard a great voice from the throne, saying, "Behold, the dwelling of God is with people. He will dwell with them, and they shall be his people, and God himself will be with them; he shall wipe away every tear from their eyes, and death shall be no more..." (Revelation 21:2-4).

Mark has a gloomy story to tell but it is not an unrelieved tragedy. Like all gospel-makers, he is a maker of good news. He sees, however tentatively, beyond the cross to the empty tomb. But his is a grim tale, nonetheless.

READING THROUGH

Some geographical references require attention, not only so that Mark's vivid account of the triumphal procession down the Mount of Olives may be clarified but also because of the light they may throw on Mark himself.

Jerusalem

Jerusalem was and is the Holy City of Jewish faith. It is a very ancient city, its history stretching back before the days of Abraham. Its name means "foundation of Shalem", that is, a place where the god Shalem or Shulmanu was worshipped. The popular meaning, "city of peace", is inaccurate and, given its turbulent history, singularly inappropriate.

King David captured the city and made it his capital. Since the city did not belong to any of the Israelite tribes, it was the personal property of David. It was, quite literally, the city of David (2 Samuel 5:6-9). Though frequently conquered and sometimes destroyed, it remained the centre of Jewish religious life down to the days of Jesus and for a little time beyond.

The temple was the city's crowning glory. The first temple was built by Solomon (1 Kings 6-7) and destroyed by the Chaldeans in 587 B.C.E. In 539 B.C.E., Cyrus II, king of the Medes and the Persians, captured Babylon, overthrowing the Chaldeans. He allowed exiled Jews to return to Judah and some of these, under the leadership of Zerubbabel, built a second temple which was finished around 516 B.C.E (2 Chronicles 36:23; Ezra 1:1-4). For his generous treatment of the Jewish people, Isaiah calls this pagan king God's anointed, that is, God's messiah (Isaiah 45:1). This temple was restored (in reality, rebuilt) by Herod the Great. The main work was begun around 20 B.C.E. and completed in about two years, though the building was probably not entirely finished when it was destroyed by the Romans in 70 C.E. (see John 2:20).

There may have been about twelve million Jews in the Roman empire at the time of Jesus. Probably two million of these lived in Palestine and around 40,000 in Jerusalem (unless the great improvements to the city's water supply by Herod the Great led to a large population increase). As many as 25,000 people would flock to the city from all over the country and from abroad for the great religious festivals, especially for Passover.

Bethphage
This is a little village on the eastern slopes of the Mount of Olives. It nestles (to this day) about half way up the mountain. We know that Jesus is making his way to Jerusalem via the Jericho road (10:46), a distance of some nineteen kilometres, and we would expect that he would pass through Bethany (at the foot of the hill) before striking Bethphage further up.

Bethany
Bethany is a small village at the eastern foot of the Mount of Olives. In Mark's Gospel, the village becomes the temporary

223

headquarters of Jesus during the last few days of his life. It is to Bethany that he repairs each evening (11:11, 12, 19) and it is in the house of his friend Simon the leper that the woman anoints his head (14:3).

Other Gospels present much the same picture. Matthew tells that Jesus lodged in Bethany during his last days (21:17) and that the woman with the alabaster jar of ointment anointed Jesus in the house of Simon the leper (26:6). Luke has a story of a woman anointing the feet of Jesus in the house of a Pharisee called Simon (Luke 11:36-50) but he does not place the event in Bethany. He does, however, tell of a certain Martha and Mary who received Jesus into their home in an unnamed village (1:38-41). John's Gospel tells of a Mary and Martha who live in Bethany and whose brother Lazarus was raised from death by Jesus (John 11:1-44), that Mary was the woman who anointed the feet (not head) of the Lord with costly oils and wiped them with her hair (12:3) and that Martha was the one who served at table (12:2).

The various details concerning Bethany are not necessarily contradictory but the fact that the Fourth Gospel records at least four trips by Jesus to Jerusalem (more plausible than the one visit in the other three) may indicate that its details are more historically reliable than those of Matthew, Mark and Luke.

The fact that Mark has Jesus enter Bethphage before Bethany may indicate that he was unclear as to their exact location on the Mount of Olives and this may further suggest that the writer of the Second Gospel was not the John Mark mentioned in the Acts of the Apostles (Acts 12:12). A native of Jerusalem might be thought to be more exact in local geographical detail. Too much weight, however, should not be placed on such trifles.

READING THROUGH AGAIN

The coronation of King Solomon is described as follows:

Zadok the priest, Nathan the prophet, and Benaiah the son of Jehoida, and the Cherethites and the Pelethites, went down and caused Solomon to ride on King David's mule, and brought him to Gihon. There Zadok the priest took the horn of oil from the tent, and anointed Solomon. Then they blew the trumpet, and all the people said, "Long live King Solomon!" And all the people went up after him, playing on pipes, and rejoicing with great joy, so that the earth was split by their noise (1 Kings 1:38-40).

Some elements of the coronation service of Solomon are to be found in Mark's account of the solemn procession down the Mount of Olives. There is an impressive procession; there is an important person about to be acclaimed king (see 15:26), seated on a special animal (a mule in one case, an unbroken colt, in the other); secondly, there is a large and excited concourse of people; thirdly, there are shouts of royal acclamation. And, let it be noted, Gihon is at the foot of the Mount of Olives. We shall examine these details more closely below. But we can say at once that the events surrounding the triumphal procession smack of a coronation of sorts.

Our father David

The memory of a glorious past, of kings and conquests, of wealth and plenty, is found in the memory bank of many peoples. Sometimes such memories owe more to wishful thinking than to scrupulous historical research and analysis. Such was the case with the Jewish people, at least to some degree. The days of King David and King Solomon were looked upon by subsequent generations as the golden age of freedom from foreign oppression and economic prosperity. The realities were not so grand but it is true to say that, compared with the trials and tribulations suffered over much of their history from foreign, coercive and exploitive imperial powers, the Jewish people could be forgiven for idealising their brief time of freedom under their own rulers.

Such idealisation of the past inevitably led to yearnings for the future and, indeed, for a re-creation of the glorious past (cleansed, to be sure, of all imperfection). And so it came to pass that people looked to a new future of freedom, modelled on an idealised perception of the past. Here is a perfect example of the process:

Rejoice greatly, O daughter of Zion!
Shout aloud, O daughter of Jerusalem!
Lo, your king comes to you;
triumphant and victorious is he,
humble and riding on an ass,
on a colt the foal of an ass.

225

I will cut off the chariot from Ephraim
and the war horse from Jerusalem;
and the battle bow shall be cut off,
and he shall command peace to the nations;
his dominion shall be from sea to sea,
and from the River to the ends of the earth (Zechariah 9:9-10).

The prophet looks to a time when a new king will appear, triumphant and victorious over all the enemies of God's people (see Zechariah 9:1-8). Captives will be set free, prisoners given hope, tyrants shall be toppled and everywhere the chariots of war shall be cut off. Peace shall reign throughout creation. But the king who will usher in this new divine initiative in human affairs will not be a tyrant like those who are deposed. He will be God's agent for justice and peace and as such will be humble. This king will, indeed, be powerful but he will know that he comes in the name of the Lord.

Clearly, the thinking of Zechariah has influenced the way the triumphal procession is described in the first three Gospels. Indeed, Matthew actually quotes the text (Matthew 21:5), as does St John in part (John 12:15). Mark does not but he is surely writing under its influence. Jesus shows his power. He knows where the colt (Mark seems to have in mind a young male horse and not an ass) will be tied. He knows that its owner will put it at his disposal ("Lord" in verse 3 almost certainly does not refer to Jesus but has the everyday meaning of "Master" or "Owner"). It is difficult to see why Mark spends so much time explaining about the animal and how it was acquired for Jesus' purpose unless he wishes to draw attention to the association of such an animal with royal coronation and with the prophecy of Zechariah that God's kingly agent would enter the city humbly proclaiming the blessing of "the kingdom of our father David".

In the Fourth Gospel, the evangelist explains that a crowd of people in Jerusalem heard of Jesus' approach to the city and went to meet him. They cut down branches of palm trees (not easy to find in Jerusalem!) and paraded Jesus into the city with a cry of "Hosanna! Blessed is he who comes in the name of the Lord, even the King of Israel!". John goes on to explain that the people went to acclaim Jesus because they had heard that he had restored to life Lazarus of Bethany (John 12:12-19).

While there are problems with John's account, he does provide a coherent sequence of events, a coherence not evident in Mark. Mark gives us no reason why Jesus initiated such an event and no reason why the people behaved in the way they did. Nor does he say that the adulation was directed at Jesus alone. Those who surrounded Jesus first shout *Hosanna!*, a cry which originally meant "Save!" (a plea to God for salvation) but had become a general shout of acclamation. Then Jesus, it would appear, is blessed as the one *who comes in the name of the Lord,* that is, as the one who comes with the Lord's power and authority. There is no explanation as to why the people took up the shout, unless we are to think that it is in response to all that has gone before in the Gospel. The second half of the cry, *Blessed is the kingdom of our father David that is coming*, refers, not so much to Jesus, as to the kingdom of God (still in the future) which fulfils the words of Zechariah and establishes all that he and the other prophets looked to when God would bestir himself to act on behalf of his people. It is this element of the ministry of Jesus that is now recognised and proclaimed. The people's chant ends with an acknowledgement that what is happening in the ministry of Jesus is God's doing: *Hosanna in the highest!*

Psalm 118 is one of a group of hymns (Psalms 113-118) which formed part of the liturgy of the Feast of Passover. Psalms 113 and 114 were sung before the celebration meal and Psalms 115-118 were sung at the end (see Mark 14:26). Psalm 118 would appear to be a hymn of victory sung by a king who has conquered an enemy and is going to the temple in Jerusalem to offer his thanks to God. The psalm ends on a note of triumph:

> Blessed be he who enters in the name of the lord!
> We bless you from the house of the Lord.
> The Lord is God,
> and he has given us light.
> Bind up the festal procession with branches,
> up to the horns of the altar.
> Thou art my God,
> and I will give thanks to thee;
> thou art my God,
> I will extol thee.
> O give thanks to the Lord,
> for he is good;
> for his steadfast love endures forever! (Psalm 118:26-29).

It would appear that Mark wishes us to see in Jesus a victorious king about to enter the Holy City. It is, however, to be noticed that the procession down the slopes of the Mount of Olives does not proceed into the city. As far as Mark is concerned, there is no triumphal entry. It is clear from verse 11 that Jesus and the twelve enter the city on their own and, having looked around at the breath-taking temple, left the city to return over the mountain to the village of Bethany.

Roman and Jewish authorities

The procession down the mountain has all the hallmarks of a royal parade. Jesus is seated on the colt, many (how many?) spread their garments along the way and make triumphant acclamations of a kingly nature. Why then did the Roman and Jewish authorities not take steps to stop a demonstration which had such obvious political overtones? The question is even more pertinent in the case of the Gospels of Matthew and Luke where the royal elements are more pronounced. In Mark's account there is much more restraint and the procession does not enter the city. It may be that among the crowds flocking to the city for the Feast of Passover a brief demonstration by a relatively small number of people went unnoticed by the authorities. The failure of the authorities to act will claim our attention again, when we consider what happens when Jesus confronts the buyers and sellers in the temple area.

PRAYER

We are about to enter the Holy City in the company of Jesus with Mark as our guide. Holy Week, as Christians came to call the last days of Jesus' life, is upon us. The harrowing tale about to unfold may cloud the goodness of God. One of the Passover hymns, Psalm 117, is a reminder that it is love, not death, which lasts for ever.

Cleansing the temple
Mark 11:12-33

The incidents that demand our attention in this section occur on Monday of what modern Christians call Holy Week, the last week of the life of Jesus of Nazareth. Matthew (21:1-27) and Luke (19:28-48) have the attack on those who bought and sold in the temple precincts follow immediately after the triumphal procession, that is to say, they take it that the event took place on Palm Sunday. (Luke omits the story about the fig tree but he does have a parable about a barren fig tree – Luke 13:6-9; Matthew has a rather truncated version of Mark's story – Matthew 18:22.) However, the Fourth Gospel takes an entirely different view. The Gospel according to John puts the so-called Cleansing of the Temple at the very beginning of the ministry of Jesus, not at its end (John 2:13-22). Furthermore, John recounts several visits to Jerusalem for Passover and other religious festivals. Matthew, Mark and Luke have only one visit to Jerusalem by Jesus and, accordingly, they have no option but to kaleidoscope events into a single dramatic week.

Who is to be believed? Clearly, it would be unhelpful to suggest that Jesus drove out the buyers and sellers on two occasions. Some scholars champion the view that John is more plausible, pointing out that at the trial of Jesus witnesses have great difficulty recalling what Jesus had actually said about destroying the temple, suggesting the event had occurred some years previously rather than a few days. This is not very convincing for in the confusion of overturning tables and much angry shouting in what is a very violent scene it is not surprising that some did not hear exactly what Jesus was saying. In favour of placing the event at the end of the life of Jesus is the plain fact that such a serious affront to the temple and its authorities would have forced the chief priests to take quick action against Jesus and to set in motion a train of events that would lead to his death.

The Cleansing of the Temple is bracketed with the story of the barren fig tree. This is a Marcan sandwich and we are, accordingly, meant to see that the fate of the unfruitful fig tree symbolises the character and fate of the magnificent temple of Jerusalem. A number of preliminary points require our attention.

Fig trees

Figs grow on the new wood of the fig tree and ripen between August and October. It is, perhaps, surprising, but not out of the question, to have a tree in full leaf as early as Passover (March/April). Observers have seen fig trees in leaf on the eastern slopes of the Mount of Olives as early as the end of March. In any case, Mark does not say that the tree is in full leaf, merely that Jesus *found nothing but leaves* when *he went to see if he could find anything on it*. Indeed, we are not told that Jesus went in search of ripe figs to satisfy his hunger: he went to see if he could find *anything* on it. Since *it was not the season for figs*, he could scarcely expect to find ripe figs and he could scarcely blame the tree for being fruitless out of season. Jesus could hope to find only buds which form before and during the growth of leaves and, in any case, would be barely edible. We must realise that Mark makes use of this tree for symbolic purposes and we ought not to treat his text as if it were an horticultural manual.

If we spend too much energy trying to reconstruct the details of what actually happened, we may miss the point. We are told that Jesus was hungry. Is anything to be gained by asking whether his host in Bethany (Simon the leper? – 14:3) neglected to provide Jesus with a morning meal? Are we to understand that Jesus the carpenter (6:3) did not know when figs ripened? Are we to conclude that Jesus cursed the tree in a fit of petulant disappointment? Such speculations may entertain the curious but they will generate more heat than light. What Mark tells is that Jesus was hungry, he spotted a fig tree already in leaf, he hoped to find something to eat, but it was not the time of the year for figs and he was, accordingly, disappointed. It is these details, and these alone, which symbolically explain why Jesus makes his attack on those who bought and sold in the temple precincts.

Money-changers and pigeons

Jewish people were required to pay for the upkeep of the temple and there was an annual tax payable before the Feast of Passover. It was commanded in Exodus 30:13-16 that every adult should pay half a shekel *to make atonement for yourselves* and that this money be set aside *for the service of the tent of meeting* (the make-shift tent of the desert days was superseded by the beautiful temple in Jerusalem). At the time of Jesus, all temple dues had to be paid in Tyrian coinage, since the Tyrian shekel was the closest available equivalent to the old Hebrew shekel. People coming from all corners of the empire needed money-changers in order to convert their currency into the only currency acceptable to temple officials. A small surcharge of 1/24th of a shekel was permitted for each transaction.

People who flocked to the temple from distant places needed animals and other requirements for sacrifice such as wine, oil and salt. These, too, had to be purchased in the appropriate currency. Doves or pigeons were offered by the poor. Joseph and Mary brought the infant Jesus to the temple to fulfill what was laid down in the Book of Leviticus concerning uncleanness after child-birth and the sacrifice necessary to achieve ritual purification:

> And when the days of her purifying are completed, whether for a son or a daughter, she shall bring to the priest at the door of the tent of meeting [= temple] a lamb a year old for a burnt offering, and a young pigeon or turtledove for a sin offering, and he shall offer it before the Lord, and make atonement for her; then she shall be clean from the flow of her blood. This is the law for her who bears a child, either male or female. And if she cannot afford a lamb, then she shall take two turtledoves or two young pigeons, one for a burnt offering and the other for a sin offering; and the priest shall make atonement for her, and she shall be clean (Leviticus 12:6-8; see Luke 2:22-24).

The buying and selling, necessary to facilitate pilgrims coming to fulfill their religious duties, were carried out in a wide enclosure surrounding the temple called the Court of the Gentiles. The name indicates that non-Jews, particularly those who were in the process of conversion to Judaism, were permitted in this area which was cut off by a high partition-wall from the temple itself. There were laws regulating the use of this forecourt area. It was forbidden to use the Court of the Gentiles as a short-cut across the city. Nevertheless, the area was not regarded as part of the temple proper and, in the hectic trading leading up to Passover, it would have resembled nothing so much as a very busy cattle market. It has been estimated, on the basis of information given by Josephus, that, at the Passover in 66 C.E., 255,600 lambs were required to meet the needs of pilgrims.

READING THROUGH AGAIN

The meaning of the cursing of the fig tree can only be grasped when the meat of Mark's sandwich, the so-called Cleansing of the Temple, is considered.

Jesus came into the city with his disciples and they entered the temple area, the area known as the Court of the Gentiles, conse-crated for use by Gentiles who aspired to be admitted to the Jewish faith. The actions of Jesus were guided by words of the ancient scriptures. The temple was, of course, always regarded as a house of prayer (see Solomon's dedication prayer in 1 Kings 8:22-53) but Isaiah reveals that, in God's purpose, it should be a place of prayer for Gentiles as well as Jews:

> And the foreigners who join themselves to the Lord,
> to minister to him, to love the name of the Lord,
> and to be his servants,
> every one who keeps the sabbath,
> and does not profane it,
> and holds fast my covenant –
> these will I bring to my holy mountain,
> and make them joyful in my house of prayer;
> their burnt offering and their sacrifices
> will be accepted on my altar;
> for my house shall be called a house of prayer
> for all peoples (Isaiah 56:6-7).

The first concern of Jesus is to protest, in an obviously violent way, against the turmoil of buying and selling which turned the only part of the temple area available to Gentiles as a place of prayer into a place of commerce. Jesus the Jew does not advocate admitting Gentiles to the temple itself – that would have been unthinkable – but he does uphold the right of pagans to pray in the vicinity of the temple (see 1 Kings 8:41-43) which should not be trampled on in the interests of trades that could be conveniently carried on elsewhere. Indeed, there were four markets on the Mount of Olives where pilgrims could buy pigeons and other ritually clean objects for offering sacrifice in the temple but these markets were not under the jurisdiction of the High Priest and temple clergy, unlike the lucrative stalls in the Court of the Gentiles.

The second element in Jesus' prophetical protest springs from words of Jeremiah who is complaining that those who proudly and jingoistically proclaim *This is the temple of the Lord! This is the temple of the Lord!* are very likely to be the same people who *steal, murder, commit adultery, swear falsely, and ... go after other gods*. These are the very people *who enter these gates to worship the Lord*, rejoicing that God has saved them (but, of course, not those nasty foreigners) but who neglect to execute justice one with another, who oppress the immigrant, neglect the orphan and the widow, and even shed innocent blood in the very temple itself. In anger, Jeremiah cries out, *Has this house, which is called by my name, become a den of robbers in your eyes?* (Jeremiah 7:11).

And he would not allow any one to carry anything through the temple. There were temple regulations forbidding the use of the Court of the Gentiles for mere convenience, such as a short-cut through the city. Nobody dressed for a journey, that is, carrying a staff, stout sandals and a money-bag, was supposed to use the temple forecourt. Jesus would appear to be disagreeing with the flamboyant notion of Zechariah that *every pot in Jerusalem and Judah shall be sacred to the Lord of hosts, so that all who sacrifice may come and take of them and boil the flesh of the sacrifice in them* (Zechariah 14:21), where the prophet is suggesting that so many people will come to worship that every pot in Jerusalem and the surrounding countryside will have to be commandeered to meet the needs of pilgrims from all the nations. Zechariah also notes that *there shall no longer be a trader in the house of the Lord of hosts on that day* (Zechariah 14:21). It may be that Jesus was forbidding anyone carrying water vessels and containers of merchandise through the temple area. He did not want trade or convenience to obscure the nature of the temple as a house of prayer for all peoples.

233

This much is clear. Jesus is not attacking the temple as such. Strictly speaking, he does not "cleanse the temple". His action is a prophetic protest against the temple administrators who had allowed the forecourt of the temple to be too commercialised, making it impossible for the building to be a house of prayer for all peoples. Jesus came to the temple expecting it to be *a light to the gentiles*; he found it to be *a den of robbers*. The plotting of the chief priests and the scribes to seek a way to destroy Jesus would indicate that his action was directly aimed at the temple authorities and that the multitude approved of the action he had so daringly taken to defend the true purpose of the temple's existence.

Withered away

On the following morning Jesus and his disciples once more set out for the city. The disciples notice that the cursed fig tree has withered away to its very roots and Peter calls Jesus' attention to the fact. Jesus then offers the disciples an instruction on prayer which would seem to have little bearing on the fate of the tree.

In considering the story of the Gerasene Demoniac (5:1-20), it is not relevant to ask how Jesus could have destroyed other people's property without compensation. Nor, indeed, is it to the point to ask why the pigs are destroyed at all, since they are hardly to blame for being possessed. Similarly, we must not ask irrelevant questions about the fig tree. The tree stands for all that Jesus expected of the temple. He expected it to be a house of prayer for all peoples; he expected the temple hierarchy so to conduct their affairs that the true nature of the temple was not obscured by commercial exploitation. There is never an off season for the temple. Clearly, in Jesus' opinion, every day is a day of prayer and every day the temple should promote the prayer of all peoples, as, indeed, Solomon encouraged in his prayer of dedication (1 Kings 8). One may have sympathy for the benighted fig tree but it stands for the temple's failure to be what it was called to be, *a house of prayer for all the nations*. The tragedy of the temple, as Jesus saw it, was that there it was never the season for figs. The temple authorities so neglected the purpose for which the temple existed that there was never a season of prayer. All leaves, no figs!

The failure of the temple to be a house of prayer turns Jesus' thoughts to the subject and he gives his disciples two pieces of advice. First, the bedrock of all prayer is an unshakeable faith in God, a faith strong enough to move mountains. Secondly, prayer is to be anchored in forgiveness. If we turn to God in prayer harbouring thoughts of enmity and malice, we shall miss the mark. God may not expect very much from us but he does expect that we have forgiving hearts. If we did not forgive, how could we expect to be able to experience forgiveness ourselves? Even God may have difficulties breaking into the unforgiving heart.

Authority

The deliberations which followed the fracas in the temple forecourt prompt the chief priests, the scribes and the elders to question Jesus about his authority. In a neat turning-of-the-tables, Jesus asks them from whom John the Baptist received authority for his mission. Since the people saw in John a man of God, mandated by God (*from heaven*), the authorities are reluctant to oppose the popular view and denigrate the sainted memory of one so recently and so callously put to death by Herod Antipas. Jesus, accordingly, declines to divulge the source of his authority. But there is no need for Mark to labour the point for his readers. It is clear that the authority of Jesus comes from the same rootstock as John's: it is *from heaven*.

PRAYER

Mark does not provide a Lord's Prayer, as do Matthew and Luke (in very different versions – compare Matthew 6:9-13 and Luke 11:2-4) but there are echoes of such prayers at the close of chapter 11. The Lord's Prayer not only teaches the bedrock of prayer, it also teaches what our priorities in prayer ought to be. It is a prayer for all seasons.

Four controversies
Mark 12:1-44

The inscription of the charge against Jesus which was placed over his head on the cross read, *The King of the Jews*. The chief priests and some scribes mocked the dying man, saying, *Let the Messiah, the King of Israel, come down from the cross, that we may see and believe*. Whatever the complexities, if there were any, of the charges brought against Jesus, as far as Mark is concerned, Jesus was done to death because he was the Messiah King of Israel. Jesus is not condemned because he poses a threat to political authority; he is not condemned because he challenges the teaching of the powerful Sadducean priests or because he plays fast and loose with the divinely-given teaching of Moses. He is not nailed to a cross because he is opposed to the puissant temple administrators. Mark sets out in chapter 12 to clear the decks. Various confrontations with some of the most influential of the Jerusalem religious establishment are presented. Acrimonious they are, for the most part. They annoy and upset and even provoke some to desire to do away with him. But they do not furnish the meat of the charges levelled against Jesus at his trial (though they do provide very instructive pointers). Jesus is not crucified for what he teaches; he is not crucified for holding provocative views or rubbing people the wrong way. He is crucified because of who he is, the Messiah King of Israel.

READING THROUGH

The chief priests and the scribes and the elders have just questioned Jesus concerning the source of his authority. It is likely that they are the recipients of the subversive parable which opens chapter 12 and that the *they* of 12:12 is meant to convey that it is this group that sought to seize Jesus. But we cannot be certain. Mark may be starting a new paragraph. The opening verse speaks of *parables* (plural), though we are offered but one. It may be that the setting (an altercation with some of the chief priests, scribes and elders) should not be pressed. In any case these people are caught up in the plotting leading to the death of Jesus and we need to note who they are (see on 14:43). Also mentioned in this chapter are the Pharisees, the Herodians and one of the scribes (whom we have met before) and the Sadducees, who make their first and only appearance in the Gospel.

Sadducees

Sadducees are mentioned only once in Mark's story. The origins of this group within Judaism are unclear. It is probable that they began as a political faction which supported the Maccabean kings. Their name appears to come from Zadok, a high priest in the time of David and Solomon. No satisfactory explanation for this is available. The Sadducees do not seem to have been an organized party as such. They represent more an outlook than a movement. They belonged to the wealthy and aristocratic priestly families of Jerusalem and it would appear that they had close ties with the temple priests. This much is clear from, among other sources, the Acts of the Apostles 4:1 and 5:17. After the destruction of the temple in 70 C.E., the Sadducees disappear. It is sometimes said that the High Priest was appointed from their number but of all the holders of that office from the time of Herod the Great until the temple's end (twenty-eight in the 107 year period), only one is identified by Josephus as a Sadducee. This is the high priest Ananus, who held office in 62 C.E. (when he had James the brother of Jesus executed illegally) and who played a prominent role in the revolt against Rome some four years later.

What is certain is that the attitude of the Sadducees was conservative and traditionalist. For them, the Pentateuch (Genesis, Exodus, Leviticus, Numbers, Deuteronomy) defined Jewish religious life and thought and the books of the Prophets and Writings were subordinated to the authority of the Torah. Unlike the Pharisees, they allowed tradition no place in the formation of religious belief. Consequently, they had no truck with belief in eternal life, angels or spirits (good or bad), all of which were acknowledged by the Pharisees (Acts of the Apostles 23:8).

READING THROUGH AGAIN.

The Parable of the Wicked Tenants is part and parcel of the controversy between Jesus and various authoritative groups and figures in Jerusalem which began at 11:27. The parable acts as a judgement on the chief priests, the scribes and the elders and, by implication, on the Pharisees and the Herodians (if 12:13 means that the chief priests sent some of the latter two groups to seek to entrap Jesus). Running through the whole chapter is the underlying theme of the authority of Jesus.

Wicked Tenants

A parable, as we have seen, is a story with a single, usually surprising point. An allegory, on the other hand, is a story in which every item stands for something else. Jesus, as far as we know, did not often, if at all, use allegorical stories and details of 12:1-9 suggest to scholars that an original straightforward parable of Jesus has been expanded by Mark or by Christian tradition before him to make its references more barbed than they were (possibly) in the version first told by Jesus. As it stands, the vineyard represents the people of Israel, the owner represents God, the tenants stand for the Jewish authorities, the servants stand for the Old Testament prophets who sought to bring the nation back to God and were rejected and persecuted, the beloved son and heir for Jesus.

The parable is a summary of Christian understanding of God's dealings with the people of Israel. According to that understanding, God established Israel as a chosen people, gave them his special protection, and looked to them to be a light to all the nations, an exemplar of justice and righteousness from which all peoples would learn. But Israel did not live up to its destiny, despite frequent reminders from its prophets and saints. The parable builds on images and words of Isaiah:

My beloved [= God] had a vineyard
on a very fertile hill.
He digged it and cleared it of stones,
and planted it with choice vines;
he built a watchtower in the midst of it,
and hewed out a wine vat in it;
and he looked for it to yield grapes,
but it yielded wild grapes (Isaiah 5:1-2).

238

Finally, God sent his son and he was crucified by the Romans at the behest of some Jewish authorities. The upshot of the matter was that the people of Israel faced destruction in the Jewish war against Rome and its inheritance passed to the new Christian community. The addition of the quotation from Psalm 118:22-23 emphasises the christian thrust of the parable: Jesus is the stone rejected by the builders of Israel but has become the foundation stone of a new edifice, the Christian Church. The quotation was quite a favourite among early Christians: Acts of the Apostles 4:11; Ephesians 2:20; 1 Peter 2:7.

The problems of attributing the parable to Jesus as it appears in Mark are now clear. First, the Markan version demands that Jesus knew in detail about his death (on Jesus' foreknowledge, see on 8:31). Secondly, it presupposes that Jesus knew that there would be a Jewish revolt against Rome and knew of its catastrophic outcome. The war did not break out until 66 C.E., thirty-five or so years after the death of Jesus. Thirdly, the parable has Jesus refer to himself as *beloved son*, while elsewhere he is extremely careful to avoid attaching titles to himself, other than Son of man. All told, it makes more sense to hold that the version before us has been considerably re-worked by Mark or someone before him. Jesus may have told a story about ungrateful tenants who were finally evicted by an irate landlord, indicating that God was far from content with Israel's religious performance. The Christian edition wrote its own experience and beliefs into the original tale.

If the *they* of 12:1 and 12:12 refer to *the chief priests and the scribes and the elders* of 11:27, then they now realise that the multitudes are on the side of Jesus and, if any move is to be made against him, the crowd must be won over, neutralised or by-passed.

Caesar and God

Some of the Pharisees and some of the Herodians (an unholy alliance we have encountered before – 3:6) are (seemingly) egged on by the *they* of verse 12 (see previous paragraph) to seek to entrap Jesus as he was teaching (in the temple area? – 11:27 and 12:35). Their address, in view of their motive in coming to Jesus, can scarcely be taken as sincerely meant but, to Mark's readers, the hollow flattery of the Pharisees and Herodians would ring true. Jesus is, indeed, *Teacher* and a man of integrity, one who does not bend to human authority and is no respecter of persons but, rather, speaks fearlessly and truly of *the way of God*. The fulsome adulation turns out, ironically, to be the truth.

A correction to some English translations is necessary if this important story is not to be misunderstood. The RSV and the JB translate *to pay taxes to Caesar*; the NEB *to give tribute to Caesar*. This would suggest that the trick question is about taxes in general, whereas the Latin word in Greek form which Mark uses (*census*) refers to a specific poll-tax which was imposed on the inhabitants of Judea, Samaria and Idumea in 6 C.E., when these districts were amalgamated into a single Roman province under the direct rule of a prefect (Pilate held the job from 26 C.E. to 36 C.E.). It was an extremely unpopular tax for two reasons. First, it was a constant reminder to the local inhabitants that they were a subject people and, secondly, the silver coins in which it had to be paid bore the name and image of Caesar and an inscription proclaiming his supposedly divine ancestry, a claim particularly obnoxious to a people who believed their God to be the one true God.

The significance of the coinage should not be missed. A ruler's writ ran as far as his coins were accepted and respected. In the ancient world, coins were seen as the private property of the ruler who issued them and the authority which guaranteed them. They were, in the most literal sense, "coin of the realm". For the inhabitants of Judea, to use the coin on which was imprinted the emperor's head was tantamount to submitting to Roman imperial rule and to acknowledging the implicit claim that they belonged to Caesar and not to another power, not even to God. Indeed, such was the hatred inspired by the introduction of this poll-tax and its blasphemous coinage that a serious revolt against Rome broke out, led by Judas the Galilean (Acts of the Apostles 5:37) and, though this outbreak was defeated, it left such resentment that the Zealot movement was born. The Zealots refused to pay the tax, even to look upon the coin, declaring that God was their only ruler and king and it was this underground movement that gave backbone to the disastrous national revolt of 66 C.E. The questions put to Jesus were, therefore, dynamite.

The questions are quite subtle. *Is it lawful to pay taxes to Caesar, or is it not?* is, on the face of it, harmless enough. The questioner simply wishes to know whether the law of God, as laid down in the holy Torah, outlaws the paying of such a tax to

Caesar. Jesus could easily have answered such a theoretical question one way or the other without danger. But the second question, *Should we pay them, or should we not?*, is a practical question, demanding advice on what to do. If Jesus advises that the tax should not be paid, he is in danger of being reported to the Roman authorities for inciting non-payment of tax and, by implication, supporting those who advocate rebellion. If he advises payment of the tax, he will lose credibility with the people, especially with those sympathetic to the national cause and that probably meant most people, certainly, most religious people. Either way those who sought to do Jesus to death would win. A negative answer would destroy Jesus' popularity with the people (11:18; 12:12); a positive answer would bring Jesus into open conflict with the Romans.

By asking for a coin and by eliciting from his hypocritical interrogators the fact that the coin they presented had Caesar's image on it Jesus succeeds in turning the tables on them. If they have the taxation coin in their possession, they have, effectively, answered their own questions. By possessing the coin, they acknowledge that they are living in the realm of Caesar.

The famous phrase, *Render to Caesar the things that are Caesar's, and to God the things that are God's*, has been interpreted in a variety of ways. One view is that Jesus is speaking ironically and means that, of course, one must give to Caesar what lawfully belongs to him but, in reality, nothing belongs to Caesar for everything and everyone belongs to God. That is an attractive line of thought but it may be too subtle by half. Others would have it that Jesus means "Give back to Caesar all the idolatrous coins which you possess". But that would hardly be practical and would, in effect, be the equivalent of advising not to pay the tax. It is better to hold to the plain sense of the statement. Jesus is telling his interrogators that they must so order themselves in relation to Caesar that they do not infringe on their prior duties to God.

Life after Death

There is little in the Old Testament to justify belief in life with God after death. The high moral life advocated in the religion of the Jews was to be undertaken for its own sake. To act justly, to behave righteously, to live in peace, were their own reward. After death, good and bad alike were translated to Sheol, a shadowy place, where one did not live but suffered a ghostly existence.

There are, however, some signs of a move towards belief in an afterlife with God in later strands of the Old Testament. Such an existence is not for everyone; only those who are especially righteous and who do signal service in the cause of God and God's people are deemed worthy of heavenly reward. Isaiah speaks of God overcoming enemies and causing his people *to rejoice in his salvation*:

> [God] will swallow up death for ever, and the Lord God will wipe away tears from all faces, and the reproach of his people he will take away from all the earth; for the Lord has spoken (Isaiah 25:8).

Again,

> Thy dead shall live, and their bodies shall rise.
> O dwellers in the dust, awake and sing for joy! (Isaiah 26:19).

These verses could be understood to refer to deliverance from exile (a theme close to Isaiah's heart) and, accordingly, to have little or no bearing on the question of resurrection from the dead. The Book of Daniel may be more helpful:

> At that time shall arise Michael, the great prince who has charge of your people. And there shall be a time of trouble, such as never has been since there was a nation till that time; but at that time your people shall be delivered, every one whose name shall be found in the book. And many of those who sleep in the dust of the earth shall awake, some to shame and everlasting contempt. And those who are wise shall shine like the brightness of the firmament; and those who turn many to righteousness, like the stars for ever and ever (Daniel 12:1-3).

Another text quoted in support of belief in life after death is in the Psalms:

> Thou [= God] dost guide me with thy counsel,
> and afterwards thou wilt receive me to glory.
> Whom have I in heaven but thee?
> And there is nothing upon earth
> that I desire besides thee.
> My flesh and my heart may fail,

but God is the strength of my heart
and my portion for ever (Psalm 73:24-26).

The text from Daniel, at most, promises some kind of vindication by God after death to those Jews who are faithful in the persecution presupposed by the writer. It offers nothing to the rest of Jews, not to mention the rest of humanity. The text from Psalm 73 may be a red herring in this matter. It may mean no more than that human frailty can be overcome by God's strength. As Mark puts it, faith can move mountains. There is no text in the Jewish scriptures which unerringly points to life with God after death (the reader may wish to examine Ezekiel 37:1-14; Job 19:25-27; 2 Maccabees 7:9, 14; 12:43). Since this is the case, the Sadducees reject such belief out of hand.

Yet, by the time of Jesus the Pharisees and, probably, most religious Jews believed in some form of resurrection of the dead, even if by "dead" they meant righteous Jews and not the generality of humanity. The conservative Sadducees were in this, as in so many other matters, isolated from the Pharisees and from ordinary people. One interesting aspect of the dispute with the Sadducees is that it shows Jesus advocating a thoroughly Pharisaic belief, a useful reminder that Jesus was probably a great deal closer to the Pharisees in his beliefs and sympathies than the reader of the New Testament often realises.

The Sadducees reduce the debate on the possibility of life-after-death to an absurdity. Assuming, as most people probably did, that life in the next world was simply a resumption, with minor modification, of life as we know it on earth, they present the story of a woman who marries seven (a perfect number!) brothers, one after another, each one dying childless. They narrate the tale as if it were an account of an actual case but we may doubt the likelihood of such a preposterous story. To add spice to their case, they claim that the brothers were fulfilling what was laid down in God's law, given to Moses, written in the very Torah acknowledged by the Sadducees to be the heart of Scripture:

If brothers dwell together, and one of them dies and has no son, the wife of the dead shall not be married outside the family to a stranger; her husband's brother shall go in to her, and take her as his wife, and perform the duty of a husband's brother to her (Deuteronomy 25:5).

In the resurrection, whose wife will she be? The question not only ridicules the very idea of life-after-death, it brands as an idiot anyone daft enough to believe in it.

Jesus turns the tables on his opponents, showing them to be not only *wrong* but *quite wrong*. Their argument belittles the teaching of Scripture and undervalues the power of God. First, he points out that the story carries no weight in the argument for the resurrection of the righteous (and it is only these Jesus has in mind) which does not mean translation to the same kind of existence as we experience in this world. Rather, *they are like the angels in heaven*. According to certain Jewish writings, composed before the time of Jesus, angels are *immortal for all generations of the world* and are not made for marriage. Further, the righteous are promised that *You shall have great joy as the angels in heaven* and that they *shall be made like the angels* (see 1 Enoch 15:6-7; 104:4; 2 Baruch 51:10). There is an interesting teaching of a rabbi who lived about three hundred years after Jesus:

> The world to come is not like this world. In the world to come there is no eating or drinking or begetting or bargaining or envy or hate or strife; but the righteous sit with crowns on their heads and are satisfied with the glory of God's presence.

There is no reason to believe such an understanding had no adherents in the days of Jesus (though it has to be admitted that most of his contemporaries would have believed that earthly patterns of life, such as marriage and begetting, would be resumed after death). Jesus draws the sting from the Sadducees' story by denying that people marry after death and asserting that they live as the angels do.

This will not do as an argument to route the Sadducees for the simple reason that they did not believe in angels. For them, to adopt the life-style of an angel would be to become non-existent. Jesus is required to take the battle into their own heartland. They have quoted from Moses, the alleged author of the Pentateuch. Jesus does the same: *I am the God of Abraham, and the God of Isaac, and the God of Jacob*. The quotation is taken from Exodus 3:6 where God appears to Moses at the burning bush and assures the frightened Moses who he is. The point of the argument of Jesus is that God does not say to Moses *I was the God of*

Abraham, and was *the God of Isaac, and* was *the God of Jacob.* God was not the God of these men who are long dead but is their God at the time of Moses. It must be that these great heroes are alive to God. How could this be?

God made his covenant to be with Abraham to shield and protect him, to give to him his steadfast love which endures for ever. Moreover this covenant was extended to Isaac and to Jacob and, indeed, to all the people of Israel and, through them, to the peoples of the world (Genesis 12:1-3). Throughout the stories of Abraham, Isaac and Jacob in Genesis we see the sustaining and saving hand of God rescuing them from danger as he had promised to do in keeping with his covenant of love. Indeed, the very fact of his protective care of the patriarchs and matriarchs (see God's protection of Sarah in Genesis 20:1-5 and of Rebekah in Genesis 26:6-9) is given to Moses as proof that God will exercise his power to save the people from their slavery in Egypt. But how beneficial would God's protection be if, despite his great promises of powerful action to protect Abraham and his family and to save the people of Israel from slavery, he is unable to save anyone from the greatest threat of all, the greatest slavery of all, namely, death? If God is the *God of the dead*, if, at the end of the day, all he presides over is graveyards, what is the point of believing in the one who proclaims that his steadfast love endures for ever? To believe in the God of the dead is to deny the power of God to overcome death, to believe in nothing. God *is not the God of the dead, but of the living*. The Sadducees *are quite wrong*.

Two principles

A scribe (whether a scribe of the Pharisees or of the Sadducees we are not told), impressed by the answers of Jesus to his opponents, advances a question which was of no little importance. It was traditional to speak of the 613 individual commandments in the Torah and to seek to establish which were the weightier among them. Indeed, a famous scribe, Hillel the Elder, who died when Jesus was in his teens, summed up the whole Law thus : *What you yourself hate, do not do to your neighbour: this is the whole Law, the rest is commentary.* (Jesus puts the matter positively: *As you wish that people would do to you, do so to them* – Luke 6:31.) Elsewhere in the New Testament, the commandment to love one's neighbour is taken to fulfill the whole

Law but what is proposed is more of a rule-of-thumb than an underlining principle:

> Owe no one anything, except to love one another; for he who loves his neighbour has fulfilled the law (Romans 13:8).

> For the whole law is fulfilled in one word, "You shall love your neighbour as yourself" (Galatians 5:14).

> If you really fulfill the royal law, according to the scripture, "You shall love your neighbour as yourself" (James 2:8).

Jesus would hardly object to such a view but his is a different tack. He wants to outline the principles on which all of the Torah is founded. He does so by quoting from the Torah itself, using the Greek version of the Old Testament:

> Hear, O Israel: The Lord our God is one Lord; and you shall love the Lord your God with all your heart, and with all your soul, and with all your might (Deuteronomy 6:4).

These words were to become the opening of the Shema Prayer (Shema = Hear!) which every devote Jew prays every morning and evening, a prayer familiar in Jewish households long before the days of Jesus. It would, we can be certain, have been familiar to the family of Jesus. The words of Deuteronomy and the prayer emphasise that there is but one God and it is God alone who can claim total love. What is to be noted is that the text says *the Lord our God*. God has first made the people of Israel his own by creating and sustaining them and by entering an everlasting covenant with them. It is because God is their God, a God recognised in their history as the one who saves and liberates, that whole-hearted and single-minded devotion is demanded (see Jeremiah 40-41).

The second pillar or principle underpinning the whole of the Torah, like the first, was enunciated in the pages of the Bible: *You shall love your neighbour as yourself: I am the Lord* (Leviticus 19:18). Because God is the creator of all, the love wherewith he creates and sustains humanity should be given to all (though *neighbour* in Leviticus refers to *the children of your own people*, confining love to one's own). In a famous parable, Jesus was to remove such restriction (Luke 10:25-37). What is surprising is the psychological insight that we must love ourselves and, to the extent that we do so, we are commanded to love others.

The scribe agrees and adds that to order one's life in accordance with these two principles is worth more that a host of *burnt offerings and sacrifices*. Burnt offerings were sacrifices in which the whole of the animal was consumed by fire and sacrifices refer to those in which some of the flesh was consumed by the worshipper as communion. The thought behind the scribe's words is close to that of Hosea: *For I desire steadfast love and not sacrifice, the knowledge of God, rather than burnt offerings* (Hosea 6:6).

The reply of Jesus to the scribe puts a very important Christian gloss on the encounter. Jesus praises the man but implies that there is a further requirement (see on 10:17-22) since the man is *not far from the kingdom of God*. To reach the kingdom, to be at the very heart of doing God's will, seems to require something more, though, on this occasion, Jesus does not spell out what it might be (as he does at 10:21). It must be remembered that Jesus was asked about the principles of Jewish Torah, not of Christian living. He was summarising his faith, not ours. To love God and to love one's neighbour is essential in both Jewish and Christian understanding but there is more to Christianity than fulfilling the demands of the Books of Deuteronomy and Leviticus.

Messiah, son of David

The fourth and final dispute in our chapter is introduced by Jesus himself and it is the most difficult to understand. The question seems simple enough: How can the scribes say that the Messiah is the son of David? The answer would appear to be simple: because it has been foretold that the Messiah would be of the family of David the King:

> Behold, the days are coming, says the Lord, when I will raise up for David a righteous Branch, and he shall reign as king and deal wisely, and shall execute justice and righteousness in the land. In his days Judah will be saved, and Israel will dwell securely. And this is the name by which he will be called: "The Lord is our righteousness" (Jeremiah 23:5-6).

The following points need to be kept in mind:

1. The whole matter turns on an understanding of the opening verse of Psalm 110.

2. Both Jesus and the scribes believed the Psalm to be divinely inspired, that is to say, that its author wrote, as Mark puts it, *in the Holy Spirit.*

3. Both Jesus and the scribes believed that the Psalm was written by King David (it was, in fact, written much later than David's time but that is beside the point).

4. The scribes and Jesus both agreed that the Psalm refers to the Messiah, the Christ.

5. Both Jesus and the scribes believed that the Psalm is a royal psalm, that is, a poem which presents God addressing the king. The crucial first five words might be paraphrased *The Lord [God] said to the one who is my lord.*

It is the fifth point above which needs very careful consideration. David is the speaker in the poem. He represents God speaking to one whom he calls *my lord.* God is represented as commanding this *my lord* to *Sit at my right hand*, a phrase which indicates that the *my lord* is being elevated to the dignity of God's son (only the royal son and heir may sit at the right hand).

It was, of course, well known to one and all that David enjoyed the God-given status as the adopted son of God. In the famous account of all that God promised to King David, we read, *I will be his father, and he shall be my son* (2 Samuel 7:14). But here we have David the adopted son speaking of another as *my lord* (and therefore one greater than David himself: lord, as we know, is a title given to one's superiors). If this other is, as the scribes believed, the Messiah, then, how can he be the son of David? A father does not call his son *my lord.* As Jesus points out, *David himself calls him Lord; so how is he his son?*

The reader will recall that Bartimaeus called Jesus the Son of David and that the triumphal procession down the Mount of Olives echoed that designation. No attempt was made on those occasions to clarify what it might mean to claim that Jesus was a descendant of the great king. But now Jesus meets the claim head-on. In what is a very difficult piece of argumentation, Jesus claims that, on the one hand, it is correct to call him Son of David (he did not silence Bartimaeus for so doing). On the other hand, the Messiah [= Jesus] is so much more than David's son that the Holy Spirit inspires David to speak of him as *my lord* and to declare that his rightful place is at God's right hand. Indeed,

248

Mark will go on to affirm that the Messiah is *the Son of the Blessed*, the one *sitting at the right hand of Power* (14:62). It is never enough to use human titles to understand who Jesus is; it is never enough to explain Jesus in purely human terms. To be sure, human terms such as Son of David or Son of man carry us along the road but they do not finally pitch us up at our destination; they do not reveal to us the ultimate secret: Jesus is *the Son of God*. That is what Mark is hinting at. If the Scripture declares in Psalm 110 that King David, God's adopted son, addresses the Messiah as *my Lord*, who is this lord?

Mark has presented us with four controversies, each set off by a question. Thus there are four questions, each receiving an explanatory answer. Some scholars see in Mark's four questions a deliberate imitation of the four questions which are asked during the celebration of the Passover meal. At the meal, the questions are asked by four sons (each adopting a part assigned by tradition). The wise son asks a question about the Law (*Is it lawful ... –* 12:14), the wicked son asks a contemptuous question (*There were seven brothers ... –* 12:20), the pious son asks a pious question (*Which commandment is the first –* 12:28) and the fourth son does not know how to ask and his father must step in to help (it is Jesus who raises the fourth question – 12:35). This is an attractive suggestion but lacks proof. However, the questions which occur in this chapter help to clarify who Jesus is and why he was put to death at a Feast of Passover in the city of Jerusalem.

Best seats

At 11:18 some scribes sought a way to destroy Jesus; at 11:27 their hostility is clear. They would appear to be involved in instigating the dangerous question of the Pharisees and the Herodians. One of them is, however, commended at 11:34, though with reservation. Then Jesus attacks the inadequate understanding which scribes in general have of the identity of the Messiah. Jesus' final word on these experts in understanding and teaching the Scripture is bitter but not unexpected (see 2:6-7, 16; 3:22; 7:1-13; 9:14).

Because of their pre-eminence as scholars and (for most of them were Pharisees) their careful observance of the Law and sacred traditions, the scribes were especially honoured. They wore long white robes, were greeted by everyone in the street, were assigned a special place in the synagogue with their backs were assigned a special place in the synagogue with their backs to the *bimah* which contained the holy scrolls and in full view of the congregation. They were especially welcome at dinner parties and were given the most honoured places, taking precedence over the aged and even over their parents. It was forbidden to scribes to earn their living by sharing their learning with those who sought advice. Accordingly, they were not wealthy and, for the most part, belonged to the poorer classes. Often, they were supported by rich patrons (see Luke 1:3 for a Christian scribe who has wealthy backing). But the system of voluntary support was open to abuse and had its abusers.

The danger with this sort of thing is that it goes to the head. Those honoured for the gifts God has given them may come to forget the source of those gifts. The religious superior, the well-appointed cleric, the learned monk, are ever in danger of becoming a religious prig, an authoritarian dandy, an insufferable bore. The Friar in Chaucer's *Prologue to the Canterbury Tales* knows well how to get the last farthing out of a poor widow. Jesus condemns such religious hypocrisy, a condemnation directed, we may be sure, not only at the scribes. Any who has ears to hear, let them hear.

His stern denunciation concludes Mark's account of the public ministry of Jesus. Henceforth, Jesus directs his teaching exclusively to his disciples and Mark becomes more and more engaged by the fate of Jesus and the fate of those who follow him.

A widow

The coins which the woman contributes to the upkeep of the temple, by present estimation, are the equivalent of about 1/12th of a penny. Mark uses a Latin word (*quadrans*) for the coins so that his readers will not miss the smallness of her offering. It is this very smallness which is the point. Mark is not condemning the ostentatious offering of large sums by the rich. Nor are the motives of the rich and of the widow compared. What Jesus is saying is that the widow has given her all to God (*she out of her poverty has put in everything she had, her whole living*). We will shortly find Jesus doing the same.

The reader will have spent some little time with Psalm 110. Perhaps, Psalm 111 (with the famous line, *The fear of the Lord is the beginning of wisdom*) might be more helpful to anyone who seeks to know who God is and, by implication, to know his Son.

A final message
Mark 13:1-37

People who set out to understand the Bible will find themselves, like Martha in the kitchen, *anxious and troubled about many things* (Luke 10:41). Of all that one would wish to know, two things are essential: the ability to tell one kind of writing from another and as firm a grasp of the history of the peoples whose faith gave birth to the books of the Bible as one can manage.

The Bible is not only made up of many books. It contains within its pages many different kinds of writings. We find there short stories, poems and prayers, lists of laws, bits of history, proverbs and wise sayings, sermons and songs, parables and prophecies, letters and lectures. The discerning reader will seek to establish what kind of writing presents itself in a particular book or passage. Thus pitfalls and red herrings will be avoided. If the reader is aware that the Book of Jonah is a short-story, a work of fiction, little time will be lost wondering how large a fish is required to swallow a man whole or how a man can survive for three days in a fish's belly. If the reader is aware that the Parable of the Good Samaritan is, indeed, a parable, little time will be lost discussing the Samaritan's grasp of economics. If it is realised that The Song of Songs is a love poem of passionate intensity, the reader, ever anxious, to be sure, to heed the lessons of Scripture, will not feel obliged to *be like a gazelle or a young stag upon the mountains of spices* (6:14).

Some knowledge of the history of the Jewish people is essential, if what is going on in the Bible is to make any sense. There are no history books within its pages but the Scriptures emerge from the history of a people and may not be divorced from their history. If we are to see Jesus aright, indeed, if we are to see him at all, we must struggle to know as much as we can of the political, economic, social and religious forces which shaped the world in which he lived. St Jerome once remarked that to be ignorant of the Scriptures is to be ignorant of Jesus. We might add that the Word became flesh at a particular time and in a particular place. The less we know of that time and that place, the less we know of the Word.

READING THROUGH

If we are to grasp the meaning of chapter 13, probably Mark's most difficult, we must determine what kind of writing it is and what historical events have given it its shape.

A sermon

Let us start with the fact that it is, for the most part, a sermon (13:3-37). A sermon is not a news report. It is a speech (though, as in this case, it may be written down) with a purpose. Its purpose may be to convince the audience of some truth, to encourage it to act in a particular way, to warn it of an impending evil, or raise morale in a sudden crisis. The sermon of Jesus on the Mount of Olives (13:3) is all of these things.

A farewell sermon

The sermon of Jesus has much in common with what is called a "farewell discourse". When the ancients came to write up the lives of famous people, they often included a deathbed speech to relatives and friends. Such speeches are commonplace in the Bible. Jacob bids farewell and blesses his children (Genesis 49:1-27). The whole of the Book of Deuteronomy is taken up with Moses' farewell sermons to the people of Israel, warning them of challenges to come and offering guidance for the future that will see them through times of crisis. Before his death, Joshua assembles the people of Israel to call on them to renew their faith in God and to give stern warning about the future (Joshua 24:1-28). Samuel (1 Samuel 12), David (1 Chronicles 28-29) and Tobit (Tobit 14) likewise make notable deathbed speeches. So does St Paul, though somewhat prematurely (Acts of the Apostles 20:17-38). The Christian will recall the most enduring of such speeches, namely, the final discourse of Jesus in the Gospel of St John (chapters 14-17). The sermon on the Mount of Olives is a similar, if less famous, last will and testament. Needless to say, all the speeches here mentioned were composed many years after the death of the illustrious figures to whom they were assigned. That those not mean that they are entirely fictitious. It does mean that we must be aware that they are not, and do not purport to be, word-for-word reports. And, further, to the extent that later writers composed such speeches, we must be alive to the probability that they sought to address burning issues of their own time and place, rather than the concerns of the eminent persons of the past whose final farewells they present.

An apocalyptic sermon

Another aspect of a sermon is that its language is often exaggerated and passionate, given to daring metaphors and similes, illustrative stories and pointed repetition. The language of Jesus, as he addresses Peter and John, Andrew and James (and the community who hear Mark's account of the sermon) is full of these things. We do well to remember that the language of a sermon is at the service of its purposes. It is not the language of the history book; it is not the language of the weather forecast; it is not the language of the bank statement. A sermon, for the most part, sets out to win hearts, not heads. Or, rather, its sets out to win heads by appealing to hearts. Good sermons are driven by passion, not logic.

The language of the sermon of Jesus is highly poetic. It may be more precisely defined as *apocalyptic*. The word "apocalypse" is a Greek word and means "a revelation", "a disclosure". The idea is that a secret is being shared by the writer (or speaker) with the reader. The need for secrecy is forced on writer and reader alike by political circumstance. Persecution is rife or imminent, war is on the horizon or in the streets, foreign armies are on the move or already at the city gates. Faint and frightened hearts need to be encouraged, morale needs to be stiffened, hope needs to be enkindled. Above all, for a people whose lives are centred on God, there must be an assurance that they have not been abandoned, that their faith has not been in vain. An apocalypse is an attempt to help threatened or down-trodden people to see beyond the immediate disaster to a time of God's good grace, to see beyond today's calamity to tomorrow's divine deliverance. The secret of all apocalyptic writing is that, in the end, God rules.

An historical sermon

The sermon on the Mount of Olives grows out of a number of historical circumstances. The first is, of course, the death of Jesus. Mark has deliberately placed the sermon at this juncture in his narrative to present it to his readers as a last farewell to Peter and James, John and Andrew and to all disciples (*And what I say to you I say to all* – 13:37). Before he goes to his death, Jesus leaves a final message for all his followers. Two questions arise. First, to what historical circumstances did Jesus address his sermon? Secondly, what new worries and new difficulties caused Mark to adapt the words of Jesus to a new time and a new place?

The sermon is triggered by a declaration of Jesus that the wonderful stonework and wonderful buildings of the temple would one day be destroyed. The temple was, indeed, *thrown down* in 70 C.E. and, in order to understand the thrust of Jesus' words, we must attend to the circumstances which led to its devastation and the consequences which followed for Jews and Christians. Furthermore, the sermon, while dealing with the religious significance of the destruction of the temple, pushes beyond the bounds of history into the unknown of the hereafter. The apocalyptic language of the sermon strains to reveal what lies beyond the tribulations and trials of history.

Throughout the lifetime of Jesus and in the first years of the movement which he inspired there were sporadic outbursts of violence against Roman imperial power. Neither Galilee nor Judea (itself a Roman province consisting of Samaria, Judea and Idumea) were everywhere and every day seething with discontent but many Jews wanted freedom from Rome's domination and, mindful of their history, were convinced that liberation would come only with God's help. There was no coherent view as to how God would bring about the longed-for freedom. Some, though not many, expected a Messiah, descended from King David, who would free the Jews by defeating the armies of Rome in battle. Others looked for a divine sign of some kind (such as the collapse of the walls of Jerusalem – see 13:4) that the day of liberation had dawned. Whatever the motivation, religious or political (most likely a mixture of both), war broke out in 66 C.E. Initial success against the Roman legions only postponed the inevitable. In 70 C.E. Jerusalem was captured and the temple was burned to the ground. Mopping-up operations, which included the heroic and tragic events at Masada, took another three years.

255

The consequences for Judaism and Christianity were profound.

The temple was God's dwelling-place on earth. When the Roman soldiers broke through the walls of the city of Jerusalem and fought their way to the temple area, the defenders retreated into the temple, believing that God would not, indeed, could not, allow a pagan army to desecrate his holy place. But there was not *left here one stone upon another, that will not be thrown down* (13:2). The focal point of Jewish worship was no more. With the end of the temple came the end of sacrifice, the liturgical means by which people came to their God. With the end of sacrifice came the end of the priesthood. With the end of the priesthood came the end of a religious way of life stretching back to Moses and Aaron. There were those who thought that with the end of the temple came the end of the world.

In the aftermath of the war, Jews were expelled from the city of Jerusalem and their religious leaders had to face the long and painful task of rebuilding Jewish faith in God without their most cherished religious symbol. Can faith live without access to God's presence in the temple? In the event, the view that keeping the Torah *was much more than all whole burnt offerings and sacrifices* (11:33) prevailed and, thank God, the faith of Israel survived.

From the religious point of view, the destruction of the temple was of considerable concern to Christians, especially to Jewish Christians. To the mainly Gentile Christian community in Rome, for which Mark wrote, the chief concern would have been what the events in far-off Palestine meant for them and their understanding of God's work in the world. What did all this turmoil and upheaval signify? For Jewish Christians, the questions would have been more immediately acute. Should they abandon their Jewish brothers and sisters in Palestine who had dared to rebel against the might of Rome? Or, in the hour of defeat, should they leave this increasingly Gentile religion and return to the bosom of Abraham, to the fold of their own people?

Much of our understanding of Chapter 13 depends on when Mark wrote his Gospel. Did he write it after the war was over and with the benefit of hindsight? Did he write it before the war broke out but with a pretty sure understanding of what the inevitable outcome would be? Did he write it during the conflict, again, with a shrewd idea of which way the wind was blowing? Or did he write a word-for-word report of what Jesus had said on the Mount of Olives nearly forty years before? We have already indicated that the latter is unlikely but we shall return to the matter below.

READING THROUGH AGAIN

It will be easier to come to grips with this most difficult passage if we divide it into manageable sections. While numerous suggestions have been made as to how best to do this, the following has the advantage of taking a clear line through the whole of the sermon and making sense of its parts:

1. Signs of the Coming of the Son of man – 13:5-23.
2. The Coming of the Son of man – 13:24-27.
3. Watching for the Coming of the Son of man – 13:28-37.

You can see that this is another Marcan sandwich and, as with the others, the meat is in the middle. The essence of the sermon on the Mount of Olives concerns the Second Coming of the Son of man or what is more conveniently, if less clearly, called the Parousia.

Signs of the coming (13:5:23)
The prediction of Jesus that the temple faced destruction leads the horrified disciples to ask when *these things* (plural) will come to pass and what sign will indicate that *all these things* (plural) are about to be accomplished. The plurals point to events other than the destruction of the temple. In other words, the questions of the disciples show that they realise that an event as devastating as the ruin of God's holy place must itself be a sign (from God) of other things. Jesus does not explain why the temple will come to an end (he has already done so: 11:15-19 and 12:1-11) but immediately outlines the consequences for his disciples. The calamitous devastation of the temple will be the sign of a chain of events which will themselves be signs that the end is nigh, will, in fact, be the beginning of a train of catastrophic happenings which will come to pass before the second coming of Jesus. Jesus concentrates his sermon on these horrendous disasters and their effects in order to reveal (apocalypse) to them teaching concerning his return.

The passage we are considering is dominated by a number of

verbs which will help us to come to grips with what is going on. We can list them as follows:

take heed – v. 5;
take heed – v. 9;
understand – v. 14;
pray – v. 18;
do not believe – v. 21;
take heed – v. 23.

We can see straightaway that the gist of the passage is to warn the disciples of dire events to come and to instruct them how to react when they do. The first temptation to confront the disciples will be the lure of many who, in the aftermath of the temple's ruin, will come claiming to be Jesus returned, those who, according to verse 21, will claim to be the Messiah returned, but are no more than false messiahs and false prophets. Such pretenders will lead many astray. True disciples will remember the words of Jesus and take heed.

In apocalyptic writings wars, earthquakes, famine and disasters of every kind symbolise the turmoil that many believed would be the sign which points to the end of the world. Jesus shares the same view, except that for him these things do not signal the end but *the beginning of the birth pains* (13:8). The prophet Jeremiah uses similar imagery to warn of sufferings inflicted by foreign armies, sufferings so great that the end of the world appears to be nigh but is not quite yet:

I looked on the earth, and lo, it was waste and void;
and to the heavens, and they had no light.
I looked on the mountains, and lo, they were quaking,
and all the hills moved to and fro.
I looked, and lo, there was no man,
and all the birds of the air had fled.
I looked, and lo, the fruitful land was a desert,
and all its cities were laid in ruins
before the Lord, before his fierce anger.
For thus says the Lord,
"The whole land shall be a desolation;
yet I will not make a full end" (Jeremiah 4:23-27).

The words of Jeremiah provide the reason why the disciples ought not to be alarmed when *all these things are accomplished*.

Such disasters are necessary to God's plan. That is the force of Mark's phrase, *this (these things) must take place*. The "must" here indicates a divine necessity; it is a word which in apocalyptic writings indicates that certain future events are part of the firmly decreed will of God.

John the Baptist was *delivered up* (RSV = *arrested* – 1:14). Jesus predicted that he would be *delivered up* (9:31; 10:33) and his prediction came to pass. He was *delivered up* to Pilate (15:1) and even though the Roman prefect realised that it was out of envy that the chief priests had *delivered him up* (15:10), he *delivered up* the innocent man to be crucified (15:15). If the fate of John the Baptist is to be delivered into the hands of Herod Antipas and to be done to death, if the fate of Jesus of Nazareth is to be handed over into the power of Pilate and be done to death, can disciples hope for a better fate? Will they not also be *delivered up*? Jesus warns that such will be their fate. They will, like Jesus, come before Jewish authorities (Sanhedrins and synagogues) and, like him, before gentile powers (governors and kings). The charge will be their association with Jesus (*for my sake*). Like Jesus before the chief priests (14:55-65), they will be emboldened to bear witness (our word "martyr" comes from the Greek word translated here as "witness") in the knowledge that the Holy Spirit will be with them and that they will be furthering God's plan that the gospel be preached to all peoples.

Judas Iscariot, *who was one of the twelve*, went to the chief priests in order *to deliver him up* to them (14:10). Indeed, this intimate companion is everywhere listed last among the twelve and to his name is added *the one who betrayed him* [= *delivered him up*]. In the same tragic way brother and father and child *will deliver up* their own among the disciples of Jesus. In the apocalyptic imagination the idea of family divisions as a sign of the end of time was fairly common. To take but one example:

> Put no trust in a neighbour,
> have no confidence in a friend;
> guard the doors of your mouth
> from her who lies in your bosom;
> for the son treats his father with contempt,
> the daughter rises up against her mother,

the daughter-in-law against her mother-in-law;
a man's enemies are the men of his own house.
But as for me, I will look to the Lord,
I will wait for the God of my salvation;
my God will hear me (Micah 7:5-7).

Micah predicts that faith in God will lead to salvation. The same is true for Jesus: *the one who endures to the end will be saved*.

The next paragraph (verse 14-23) is especially difficult. The general theme is clear enough. Jesus outlines for his disciples the sign by which the coming of the end may be recognised and provides a description of the last days with advice as to how disciples should prepare themselves. The difficulty, to which we shall return below, is that Jesus seems to be describing a human conflict, an historical catastrophe, and not an apocalyptic, supernatural encounter. If God is engaged in a mighty struggle, it seems to be irrelevant to pray that his fight take place in the summer rather than in deep winter!

In St Luke's Gospel we have a passage which clearly refers to the future destruction of the city of Jerusalem. As he carries his cross, Jesus is comforted by some women but he turns to them and warns,

> Daughters of Jerusalem, do not weep for me, but weep for yourselves and for your children. For behold, the days are coming when they will say, "Blessed are the barren, and the wombs that never bore, and the breasts that never gave suck!" Then they will begin to say to the mountains, "Fall on us"; and to the hills, "Cover us". For if they do this when the wood is green, what will happen when it is dry? (Luke 23:28-31).

Mark's paragraph, too, would appear to be referring to a particular conflict in Judea and, indeed, to be describing the kind of horrific events we would expect in a small country overrun by an avenging foreign army and whose capital city had fallen and been consumed in flames. But there is more to Mark's presentation than that. He seems to have three perspectives in view.

The intriguing phrase *the desolating sacrilege set up where it ought not to be* (a phrase the reader is cautioned to take pains to understand) would appear to refer to an event long past by the time of Jesus. In 168 B.C.E., a pagan ruler, named Antiochus IV

Epiphanes, who ruled Judea from his power-base in Antioch, wanted to introduce his own Greek (and, therefore, pagan) life-style to Jerusalem, aided, one might add, by some of the aristo-cratic priests of the temple. One of his actions was to desecrate the temple by placing in it an altar to Zeus, the supreme god of the ancient Greeks. This altar was erected on the place of the altar of burnt offerings, on which sacrifice was offered continually to God. The Book of Daniel protests loudly against this hideous sacrilege in the veiled language of apocalyptic writings. The angel Gabriel appears to Daniel and tells him that *an anointed one* [= a messiah] will come and achieve temporary relief for Jerusalem but that the anointed one shall be destroyed and war and desolation will return:

> Upon the wing of abomination shall come one who makes desolate, until the decreed end is poured out on the desolator (Daniel 9:27).

The reference to Antiochus is clear in this sentence:

> And from the time that the continual burnt offering is taken away, and the abomination that makes desolate is set up, there shall be a thousand two hundred and ninety days (Daniel 12:11).

Clearer still,

> Forces from him shall appear and profane the temple and fortress [= Jerusalem], and shall take away the continual burnt offering. And they shall set up the abomination that makes desolate. He shall seduce with flattery those who violate the covenant ... (Daniel 11:31).

These events and the tribulations to which they gave rise (eventually they led to the Maccabean revolt) might very well be described in the language of Jesus' sermon:

> ... let those who are in Judea flee to the mountains; let him who is on the housetop not go down, nor enter his house, to take anything away; and let him who is in the field not turn back to take his mantle. And alas for those who are with child and for those who give suck in those days (Mark 13:14-18).

But they equally well fit into the scenario of the Roman siege of Jerusalem and the subsequent capture and destruction of the city and its temple. The standards of the Roman legions, bearing pagan symbols, hoisted in victory over the very place where sacrifice was offered to the one true God could be most aptly described as *the desolating sacrilege set up where it ought not to be*.

But there is a third possibility. The word which Mark uses as *sacrilege* in verse 14 is neuter gender in Greek but the participle *set up* is masculine. This suggests that the sacrilege which is set up is a person, not an altar or the banners and standards of soldiers. This gives rise to the view that Jesus is referring to some such figure as the lawless one of the Second Letter to the Thessalonians, a letter which deals specifically with the Second Coming. Note the similarities of this passage to much of Mark's chapter:

> Now concerning the coming of our Lord Jesus Christ and our assembling to meet him, we beg you, brothers and sisters, not to be quickly shaken in mind or excited, either by spirit or by word, or by letter purporting to be from us, to the effect that the day of the Lord has come. Let no one deceive you in any way; for that day will not come, unless the rebellion comes first, and the man of lawlessness is revealed, the son of perdition, who opposes and exalts himself against every so-called god or object of worship, so that he takes his seat in the temple of God, proclaiming himself to be God. Do you not remember that when I was still with you I told you this? And you know what is restraining him now so that he may be revealed in his time. For the mystery of lawlessness is already at work; only he who now restrains it will do so until he is out of the way. And then the lawless one will be revealed, and the Lord Jesus will slay him with the breath of his mouth and destroy him by his appearing and his coming. The coming of the lawless one by the activity of Satan will be with all power and with pretended signs and wonders, and with all wicked deception for those who are to perish, because they refused to love the truth and so be saved. Therefore God sends upon them a strong delusion, to make them believe what is false, so that all may be condemned who did not believe the truth but had pleasure in unrighteousness (2 Thessalonians 2:1-12).

The letter of St Paul, written many years before Mark's Gospel, seems to be saying that some anti-God figure will come before *the coming of our Lord Jesus Christ* and will take his seat in the temple of God. This personification of evil will be destroyed *by Jesus, by his appearing and his coming*. In this view, the holy temple will become the seat of the powers of evil. The destruction of the temple is a sign that Satan has begun to rule and will hold sway until overthrown by the return of the Son of man in power and glory. Is it possible that Mark may be referring to the powers of Rome as the anti-God, the satanic power of evil, as some other writers in the New Testament suggest (see 1 Peter 5:13 and Revelation 18:2)?

We might summarise 13:14-23 as follows:

1. The sermon on the Mount of Olives recalls the grim days of Antiochus IV Epiphanes which led to bitter torment and to war.

2. The sermon reminds the reader that this past event has been repeated in the destruction of the temple during the war against Rome.

3. The sermon uses these two horrendous events as symbols of all the evils that will befall humanity before the second coming of the Lord Jesus.

Mark concludes that these days of terrible tribulation, which will usher in the end, will, by God's mercy, be shortened for the sake of his elect. Christians, not led astray by false Messiahs or false prophets, will be able to read the signs of the times and will, because they have been warned by Jesus, meet the challenges of the grim days to come.

The coming of the Son of man (13:24-27)

The christian teaching concerning the Parousia or second coming of Jesus is loudly proclaimed but little understood. The billboard or wayside pulpit which proclaims that THE END IS NIGH! not only contradicts the plain teaching of Scripture that only the Father knows *of that day and that hour*, it uses the word "end" in a sense clear contrary to its biblical meaning. Statements about "the end of the world" need to be handled as delicately as a new-born baby.

The Greek word "parousia" means "presence" and would indicate that, at his return, Jesus will be present in a way not now available to us. The New Testament does not reveal how that presence will be manifest. By saying that Jesus will return, the New Testament does not reveal when that will be, how it will come about or, indeed, how precisely his return will affect the world and all creation. The reason for all this obscurity is quite simple: New Testament writers knew as much about the matter as you or I. What they did do was to use a poetic language available to them to express their heart-felt beliefs and longings. The language they used was, of course, apocalyptic. We have to try to make our way through the labyrinths of their language to try to grasp what they were trying to express. Also every word in the passage before us comes from the Old Testament and other Jewish literature. Consider the following:

Verse 24: *But in those days, after that tribulation, the sun will be darkened, and the moon will not give its light, and the stars will be falling from the heavens, and the powers in the heavens will be shaken.*

> I will cover the sun with a cloud,
> and the moon shall not give its light.
> All the bright lights of heaven
> will I make dark over you,
> and put darkness upon your land,
> says the Lord (Ezekiel 32:7-8).

> Behold, the day of the Lord comes,
> cruel, with wrath and fierce anger,
> to make the earth a desolation
> and to destroy its sinners from it.
> For the stars of the heavens
> and their constellations
> will not give their light;
> the sun will be dark at its rising
> and the moon will not shed its light (Isaiah 13:9-10).

> The earth quakes before them,
> the heavens tremble.
> The sun and the moon are darkened,
> and the stars withdraw their shining (Joel 2:10).

> The sun shall be turned to darkness, and the moon to blood, before the great and terrible day of the Lord comes (Joel 2:31).

Verse 26: *And then they will see the Son of man coming in clouds with great power and glory.*

And behold, with the clouds of heaven there came one like a
son of man,

and he came to the Ancient of Days
and was presented before him.
And to him was given dominion
and glory and kingdom (Daniel 7:13-14).

Verse 27: *And then he will send out the angels, and gather his
elect from the four winds, from the ends of the earth to the ends of
heaven.*

Then the Lord your God will restore your fortunes, and have
compassion on you, and he will gather you again from all the
peoples where the Lord your God has scattered you. If your
outcasts are in the uttermost parts of heaven, from there the
Lord your God will gather you and from there he will fetch
you (Deuteronomy 30:3-4).

The Lord will raise an ensign for the nations, and will assemble the outcasts of Israel, and gather the dispersed of Judah
from the four corners of the earth (Isaiah 11:12).

I have spread you abroad as the four winds of the heavens,
says the Lord (Zechariah 2:1).

So few quotations drawn from a huge reservoir of texts indicate
how widespread this sort of language was as a means of expressing
belief that in the end God's will would be done and he would
triumph over his enemies. That final victory could not go to the
powers of evil, that God would, at some future but unknowable
time, vindicate those loyal to his name, was a common-place in
Jewish thought. New Testament writers saw in the life, death and
resurrection of Jesus the sure and certain hope that he would be
God's Son of man who would come when the trials and tribulations
of this world had run their course and assert the authority of God
over all creation. When we penetrate the colourful and exotic
language with which the message of final divine victory is dressed,
we may summarise what the Parousia means, what the second
coming of the Lord promises: the future belongs to God.

Watching for the coming (13:28-37)
The sermon ends with two cautionary illustrations which
seem simple enough but harbour knotty problems. The portents

265

which point to the end (they are not themselves the end) have been outlined in 13:5-27. The end, the coming of the Son of man, briefly sketched in 13:24-27, need not catch the disciples unawares, provided they can read the signs of the times. Just as the tender new branches and the luxuriant leaves of the fig tree (so Jesus does know when fig trees ripen!) are harbingers of summer, *so also, when you see these things taking place, you know that he is near, at the very gates.*

The illustration is perfectly clear. It is the claim that *this generation shall not pass away before all these things take place* that causes bewilderment. We know that the contemporaries of Jesus, not to mention the contemporaries of Mark, are long dead. Not only has *this generation* passed away but nearly two thousand years have elapsed and there are no unmistakable portents of the final victory of God over the satanic forces of evil.

The very first document in the New Testament, the First Letter of Paul to the Thessalonians concerns itself with the problem of the end-time, as do others. The very earliest Christians seemed to have believed that the return of Jesus would not be long delayed and would occur during their lifetime. St Paul was obviously of this opinion (1 Thessalonians 4:13-18). St Luke, on the other hand, envisaged a long journey through the world for the Church, as the Acts of the Apostles shows. The plain fact of the matter is that early Christians were confused on the issue. The confusion is evident in Mark's sentences. First, he declares that the end will come within a generation. In the next breath, he tells us that *no one, not even the angels in heaven, not the Son, but only the Father* know the day and the hour of the parousia. There is no simple way of reconciling these contradictory statements. Mark may want to have his cake and eat it. On the one hand, he wants his readers to be on the alert, to be prepared no matter when the end comes. On the other hand, he wants to stifle useless speculation on precise days and hours. Not only Mark's community but history is littered with discarded placards declaring that the end is nigh!

The final words of the sermon centre on the word *watch*. As the servants go about their allotted tasks in anticipation of the master's return and the doorkeeper maintains a sharp lookout lest they be caught unawares, so disciples will go about their work in the world, mindful of their mission to preach the gospel and, at the same time, alert to the signs of the coming of the Lord in clouds of glory. The word for disciples of all generation is the same: *Watch*.

Jesus or Mark

Did Jesus preach the sermon recorded in Mark's Gospel or did Mark compose it and put it on the lips of Jesus, as many writers did before and since in their accounts of the careers of famous people? Are the words recorded in Mark's story directed immediately and exclusively by Jesus to the four disciples who conversed with him on the Mount of Olives? Or has Mark composed a sermon directed by him to the needs and concerns of his frightened community in Rome and put on the lips of Jesus to lend his weight and authority to the message which Mark wishes to impart?

That the sermon is word-for-word account of what Jesus said to Peter and James and John and Andrew is scarcely credible. The details touching the progress of the war against Rome (66-73 C.E., remember) and the plight of the temple, the fate of Christians who fell foul of Jewish and Roman authorities (13:9-13) are too precise to be predictions made thirty-five years in advance. The "feel" of the sermon (admittedly a personal opinion) suggests Rome in the late sixties rather than Jerusalem in the late twenties.

Is the sermon entirely the creation of Mark? Has he composed a homily for his audience and neatly slotted it into his story before the death of Jesus to give it, not only the authority of Jesus, but to make it sound like his last will and testament, his dying words as it were, to his disciples? This is not credible either. Early Christians guarded jealously the words they inherited from Jesus. Note how careful St Paul is to tell his readers when he is giving his own teaching and when he is handing on to them the teaching of Jesus (see 1 Corinthians 7:10, 12, 25). Mark would hardly take it upon himself to limit the knowledge of Jesus (*But of that day or that hour no one knows, not even the angels in heaven, nor the Son* ...) unless he and his readers knew that to be the case. The long quotation from the Second Letter to the Thessalonians given above shows how St Paul dealt with the matter of the end-time. That he did so in terms similar to Mark would suggest that the gist of their teaching goes back to Jesus.

The matter may be resolved in this way. Jesus was, indeed, more than a prophet but he was a prophet. Many of the ancient prophets spoke of the fate of Jerusalem in a way that suggested that the infidelity of its inhabitants had brought upon the city God's judgement. Jeremaih stated baldly, *I [= God] will make this city a curse for all the nations of the ear*th (26:6) and *Jerusalem shall become a heap of ruins* (26:18), a prediction quoted by Micah (3:12). The cursing of the fig tree, the cleansing of the temple precincts and the general hostile attitude of Jesus to the temple and its authorities make it exceedingly likely that Jesus, in the last days of his life, warned his disciples that the days of Jerusalem and its temple were numbered. As a prophet, Jesus may very well have pronounced a prophet's judgement on a city he regarded as less than single-minded in its devotion to God.

When Mark came to write for the frightened and disheartened Christians of Rome, the Jewish war against Rome had already begun and the city of Jerusalem and its temple may already have been destroyed (or, at least, the progress of the war made its destruction inevitable). In his attempt to encourage his forlorn people, Mark may have seized on what he knew Jesus to have said about Jerusalem and re-shaped and embellished what he knew to apply to a new time and a new place. He took what he had of the words of Jesus and updated, expanded and re-ordered them to apply them to the sad state of his own Christian community. The fate of Jerusalem, whose destruction was so recent or daily expected, stands, not only as a sign of what will happen to the might of Rome itself, but as a reminder that all human disasters, tumults, wars and rumours of wars, earthquakes and famines, the whole sum of human misery, stand in wait. They are signs, if there be a God, that he must come. The birth pains of the world demand a gentle midwife who can birth a new age of justice and righteousness and peace.

PRAYER

The Book of Revelation is also known as The Apocalypse. It contains many fine prayers. The prayer preserved in 15:3-4 well illustrates what an apocalypse is about. It is also a beautiful prayer.

The Last Supper
Mark 14:1-31

The arrest, trial and death of Jesus are about to take place. As ever, Mark does not present the bald facts. He orchestrates his material in order to move the hearts of his readers and to mould their thinking about the death of Jesus and its significance for their community. He takes particular pains to show that all that happens is in accord with God's will. The chief priests and Pilate appear to be fully in control of events but there is a higher power at work and Mark's story forces his readers to recognise and acknowledge the over-riding authority of that power.

READING THROUGH

For the most part, Mark shows little interest in the chronology of the events that he records. The first half of his Gospel is peppered with *immediately* this and *immediately* that which is not a very precise indicator of when events actually occurred. He is content to note that Jesus *returned to Capernaum* (2:1), that *he went out again* (2:13), that *he entered a synagogue* (3:1), that *he went home* (3:20). But when we come to the last week of the life of Jesus, Mark is very careful to provide his story with a clear chronology. His reason for doing so is in keeping with his desire to focus his readers' attention on the unseen part played by God in these momentous happenings.

Passover and unleavened bread

It was now two days before the Passover and the feast of Unleavened Bread. The feast of Passover and of Unleavened Bread were celebrated as one feast in the days of Jesus but they had been originally separate. The Passover lamb was killed on the 14 Nisan (a month in the Jewish calendar, roughly March/April). The Passover Meal was eaten on the evening of 15 Nisan and celebrations continued until 21 Nisan. Mark has Jesus die at the feast of Passover. A brief outline of its history will explain why.

Feasts such as Passover and Unleavened Bread are old and widespread. Almost certainly Passover was originally a feast of nomadic shepherds. In the spring, when the new lambs were strong enough to make the journey, shepherds moved their flocks from the dry steppes to summer pastures. This was a time of difficulty and danger (lambs are delicate creatures at the best of times and flocks on the move are a prey to rustlers) and would naturally give rise to some religious activity, some ritual by which the protection of the gods is sought for the dangerous days ahead. On the evening before the journey began everyone would dress in travelling clothes and take their places at the entrance to their tents. The father of each family or the leader of each clan would kill a lamb and sprinkle its blood on the tents and people, a way of imploring divine protection. Then the lamb was roasted (why not boiled?) with whatever herbs were available (usually bitter – why?) and the family ate the lamb as a sign of communion with the gods and an indication that they were on your side. The ritual was performed at the new moon.

A festival incorporating unleavened bread is found in many societies in the ancient near east. The first cutting of the new crop of grain was offered to the god or gods. Such an offering had to be pure so none of the flour of the previous year could be used for leavening purposes (rotting grain facilitates the fermenting process which causes bread to rise). The festival was the celebration of a new start, a new beginning, the earth having once again provided food for another year and seed for another harvest. The feast of Unleavened Bread was a farmers' celebration.

Ancient Israelite people, like so many others, celebrated these rites. Those who were nomadic shepherds had their spring sacrificial lamb and those who were farmers had their unleavened or unyeasted flat barley bread. The gradual takeover of the land of Israel brought these two elements together but they continued to hold their ancient feast days. But a momentous change took place. These old festivals came to be re-interpreted in terms of the Exodus from Egypt. God's great act of freeing those enslaved in Egypt came to be seen as the origin of the spring festivals. The command to celebrate Passover and Unleavened Bread is given by God to Moses and Aaron and God lays down that they shall do so in memory of the deliverance from slavery. The slaying of the lamb is now done to mimic what the people did on the night of their deliverance:

> ... they shall take every man a lamb ... and you shall keep it until the fourteenth day of this month, when the whole assembly of the congregation of Israel shall kill their lambs in the evening. Then they shall take some of the blood, and put it on the two doorposts and the lintel of the houses in which they eat them. They shall eat the flesh that night, roasted; with unleavened bread and bitter herbs they shall eat it. ... In this manner you shall eat it: your loins girded, your sandals on your feet, and your staff in your hand; and you shall eat it in haste. It is the Lord's passover. For I will pass through the land of Egypt that night, and I will smite all the first-born in the land of Egypt, both man and beast; and on all the gods of Egypt I will execute judgments: I am the Lord. The blood shall be a sign for you, upon the houses where you are; and when I see the blood, I will pass over you, and no plague shall fall upon you to destroy you, when I smite the land of Egypt (Exodus 12:3-13)

Thus the description of God's action in Egypt provides the ritual for the commemoration of the great event itself. What had started out as, on the one hand, a solemn sacrifice by shepherds and, on the other, a thanksgiving celebration by farmers, had been transformed into a memorial deliverance from slavery.

Christians took the matter a step further. The ritual used to celebrate what God had achieved for his people in the deliverance from slavery underwent a Christian re-interpretation. The deliverance of all peoples from the yoke of sin accomplished through the death and resurrection of Jesus came to be described in the language of the Passover festival. Jesus was known to have died at Passover. It was almost inevitable that his death should be seen in the light of that great feast. The lamb was killed. Christians began to speak of *the Lamb of God who takes away the sin of the world* (John 1:29). St Paul, a devout Jew, was at home with the images and metaphors of his people's festivals and interpreted Jesus through them:

> Do you not know that a little leaven leavens the whole lump? Cleanse out the old leaven that you may be a new lump, as you really are unleavened. For Christ, *our paschal lamb*, has

271

been sacrificed. Let us, therefore, celebrate the festival, not with the old leaven, the leaven of malice and evil, but with the unleavened bread of sincerity and truth (1 Corinthians 5:7-8).

READING THROUGH AGAIN

The chief priests and their scribes determine to put Jesus to death but not during the celebration of Passover for many thousands flocked to Jerusalem for the feast and there was always the danger of anti-Roman violence. The chief priests were responsible to the Romans for the maintenance of good order and could not risk a move against Jesus which would incite the general populace. But Jesus does die on the feast and, far from the secrecy desired by the plotters, the crowds are brought into the tragedy and, indeed, are stirred up by the chief priests. So much for plots and plans. The destiny of Jesus is not at the disposal of mere mortals. The ultimate power belongs to God.

Anointing at Bethany

Mark highlights the story of the Anointing at Bethany by placing it between the account of the plotting clergy and Judas' betrayal – another Marcan sandwich. The story is located at Bethany in the house of Simon the leper. He is not mentioned elsewhere in Mark (see Matthew 26:6; Luke 7:40). If we are to assume that he was the host on this occasion, he must have been cured of his leprosy. The woman is not named; nor are those who raise objections to her actions (Matthew 26:8 identifies them as the disciples). The important elements in the story are the action of the woman and the words of Jesus.

The woman pours the expensive ointment on the head of Jesus. The ointment or perfume was extracted from the nard plant and was unadulterated. Three hundred denarii represent a year's wages for a labourer. The complaint of waste seems justified. But the words of Jesus point to the significance of the woman's actions: *she has done what she could; she has anointed my body beforehand for burying*. The woman has understood what no one else in Mark's story managed to grasp. She has come to realise that the destiny of Jesus is to die. She is not anointing Jesus as king, priest or prophet (how could she?). She anoints him for death. Because this woman, of all those who

272

people Mark's story, alone understands that Jesus must die, *wherever the gospel is preached what she has done will be told in memory of her.*

The saying about the poor should not be read as if Jesus were being fatalistic and unconcerned. His words recall the strict warning given in the Book of Deuteronomy concerning the poor:

> You shall give to him freely, and your heart shall not be grudging when you give to him; because of this the Lord your God will bless you in all your work and in all that you undertake. For the poor will never cease out of the land; therefore I command you, you shall open wide your hand to your brother, to the needy and to the poor, in the land (Deuteronomy 15:10-11).

The point Jesus makes is that duty to the poor may never be side-tracked. Neither must the taking away of the bridegroom go unmarked (2:20). The woman and her story must be remembered for she alone is aware that the departure of the bridegroom is at hand. Her action points to the central tenet of the gospel: salvation comes through the death of Jesus.

Delivering up

It is ironic that this perceptive act of kindness by an unknown woman should be followed by betrayal by one of the twelve, the intimate friends of Jesus. The chief priests and the scribes were wondering how they might arrest Jesus by stealth. Now, unexpectedly, an opportunity is handed to them. But this act of betrayal which plays into their hands is not a chance event; it is part and parcel of the divine purpose. This is clear from the fact that Mark twice uses the verb "to deliver up" (we have seen how significant this verb is throughout the story) in as many verses, the very verb which we find in two passion predictions (9:31; 10:33) which reveal that the death and resurrection of Jesus is in accord with the will of God

Notice that Mark does not go into any details about Judas. He offers no explanation of the treachery, provides no motive (see Luke 22:3; John 12:6; 13:27-8). Nor does Judas strike a bargain with the chief priests as in Matthew 26:15. He receives just the promise of money. The specific mention here that Judas is one of the twelve adds to the depth of the treachery and increases the bitterness of what Jesus had to go through.

The Last Supper

The Last Supper is surrounded by treachery and denial. Indeed, the betrayer is at the meal: *It is one of the twelve, one who is dipping* [omit *bread*] *in the same dish with me*. There is, therefore, a poignant contrast between Jesus giving himself for and to his followers, while his intimate friends are about to betray and desert him.

Mark begins with a time indication: *the first day of Unleavened Bread, when they sacrificed the Passover lamb*. There is a problem here. As we have seen, the Passover lambs were killed by the priests in the temple area on the afternoon of 14th Nisan and taken home for roasting in preparation for the meal. Before 70 C.E., "The Passover" was technically the lamb and its sacrifice signalled the commencement of the festival (as Exodus 12:6 and Leviticus 23:5 clearly state). According to John (18:28; 19:14), Jesus died on the 14th Nisan and at the time when the lambs were sacrificed (notice that John does not have an institution of the Eucharist in the context of a farewell meal). At the very time when the Passover lambs were being sacrificed in the temple, the true *lamb of God who takes away the sin of the world* (John 1:29) was dying outside the walls of the city. Mark is more concerned to link the Last Supper with the Passover meal and he plainly says that the last meal Jesus had with the twelve was the festival meal. We may ask whether, in fact, this was the case.

There is evidence that the Last Supper was a Passover meal. The following list of pieces of evidence must be examined and weighted. Not all are equally important but, taken together, they seem to point to one conclusion:

– The Last Supper takes place in Jerusalem. In Jesus' day, the Passover meal had to be eaten within the confines of the city. If Jesus did not intend to eat the Passover meal with his disciples, why did he not withdraw, as was his custom, to Bethany (see 11:11; 11:12; 14:3)?

– The room for the meal was made available to Jesus without any fuss or payment. It was customary for residents of the city to share their accommodation with visitors who wished to celebrate Passover.

– The Last Supper takes place in the evening, after sunset. At ordinary meals people sat down but at the Passover meal even poor people reclined at table. This is what three of the Gospels report concerning the final meal with the disciples (Mark 14:18; Matthew 26:20; John 13:23). (The RSV misses the point in translating Mark and Matthew here.)

– Jesus and his disciples drank wine at the Last Supper. This was demanded by Passover ritual but was not a feature of every-day meals for ordinary people.

– The dish mentioned in Mark 14:20 probably contained a sauce of figs, dates, almonds, spice and vinegar, a feature of the Passover meal. No bread is mentioned (the RSV is wrong here).

– Jesus speaks words of interpretation over the bread and wine. At the Passover meal the actions were regularly explained to participants, especially children (Exodus 12:25-27).

– Mark mentions the singing of a hymn. It was customary to end the Passover meal by singing part of Psalms 113-118.

This evidence would seem to indicate that the institution of the Eucharist took place within the context of a Passover meal. Certainly, Mark has no doubts on the matter.

Preparation

The account of the preparation for the Passover meal bears a strong resemblance to the account of the preparation for the entry into Jerusalem in 11:1-6. Notice the corresponding details:

11:1-6	14:12-16
He chose two of his	He chose two of his
disciples and said to them	disciples and said to them
"Go into the village"	"Go into the city"
(precise instructions on what	(precise instructions on what
will happen are now given	will happen are now given
to the two disciples)	to the two disciples)
the disciples set out	the disciples set out
everything is as Jesus	everything is as Jesus
predicted	predicted

The purpose of the two stories is essentially the same. In each case Jesus is seen to have a clear knowledge of the future and to be in charge of the situation. He goes to his death, not merely because of the plots and plans of his enemies, but because that is what is demanded by his mission, a mission which comes from God. It is God's will, not mere mortal's, that is being done here.

Therefore, two elements stand out in both stories: Jesus' foreknowledge and his authority.

The meal

Jesus assembles with the twelve for the solemn meal. The first note struck is that of betrayal. The *handing over* is, indeed, in accord with the scriptures (*the Son of man goes as it is written of him*), that is, in keeping with God's will (see Psalm 41:9). But that it takes place in the context of a meal and on a festive occasion adds to its squalid treachery. But Mark does not dwell on the fate of Judas (as Matthew does). The saying *woe to that man* is not a condemnation of Judas. It is more an expression of sorrow but given the fact that Mark uses the word for *woe* only once and that in this reference to Judas and the further fact that Mark emphasises that the predictions of Jesus come to pass, one would not be too sanguine about Judas' future. Of course, there is no evidence that Jesus is referring to his eternal destiny.

The Eucharist

While they were eating, Jesus took some bread and, having said the blessing (*Blessed are you, O Lord God, king of the universe, who brings forth bread from the earth* is the usual Jewish prayer of thanksgiving at meals), he broke the bread and gave it to the disciples (the twelve only? Where were the *women who came up with him to Jerusalem* – see 15:40-41?). The actions of Jesus are described in words which occur in the feeding miracles (6:41; 8:6). The reason for this is that Mark uses the vocabulary of the Lord's Supper to describe these earlier events. At that time the disciples *did not understand about the loaves* (6:52; see 8:17-21). Now the mystery is being revealed. Another feature of the words used over the bread and cup is that they probably reflect the words used in the celebration of the Eucharist in Mark's community.

The meaning of the actions of Jesus should be seen on two levels. First, Jesus is providing a commentary on his death. He is emphasising its significance, pointing out that he is about to give his life (his body and blood) for all peoples (*many* = all). His death will be the source of liberation for all peoples. The language used to express this is taken from the account of the Passover in the Book of Exodus:

And Moses took the blood and threw it upon the people, and said, "Behold the blood of the covenant which the Lord has made with you in accordance with all these words" (Exodus 24:8).

Just as the sprinkling of the blood on that occasion was the sign of God freeing his people, so now the shedding of the blood of Jesus sets all people free from the slavery of sin.

Secondly, this final meal of Jesus with his friends came to be celebrated in the earliest Christian communities. By so doing they believed that they were fulfilling the command of Jesus (1 Corinthians 11:22). As the Exodus was recalled and remembered by the Passover meal, so Christians recalled and remembered the work (especially the death) of Jesus and what it meant for all people (recall 10:45). But this was not all. In the Passover meal the Jewish people were (and are) not merely recalling an event of the past; they were sharing in that same deliverance by God and in the blessings of the covenant which followed on the liberation from slavery. In the Lord's Supper Christians believe that they are brought to share in the life and death of Jesus. By sharing his body and blood, Christians believe they come to share in his death and in the meaning and consequences of that death.

Prophecy of denial

Judas is not the only failure among the twelve. All will fail and Jesus will die alone, or, rather not alone but in the midst of robbers and jeering enemies, deserted by his friends. The quotation from Zechariah and its context provides a key to unlock what Mark is about:

Strike the shepherd, that the sheep may be scattered;
I will turn my hand against the little ones,
in the whole land, says the Lord,
two thirds shall be cut off and perish,
and one third shall be left alive.
And I will put this third into the fire,
and refine them as one refines silver,
and test them as gold is tested.
They will call on my name,
and I will answer them.
I will say, "They are my people";
and they will say, "The Lord is my God" (Zechariah 13:7-9).

277

Mark applies the language of prophecy to Jesus. He is the shepherd of the sheep who will be stricken and his sheep scattered. The Old Testament text declares that two-thirds of the shepherd's people will perish and the remainder will be tested and will be reconstituted as God's people. Jesus is saying that his little community will be scattered by his coming death. Some will be lost (Judas) but the remainder will be reunited with him after the ordeal is over. The phrase *I will go before you to Galilee* is of great importance for Mark uses it again, putting it in the mouth of the young man who appears to the women at the empty tomb (16:5-7). The sentence can mean "I will lead you into Galilee" or "I will go there first". 16:7 makes it clear that Mark has the second meaning in mind.

Peter

Throughout the arrest and trial of Jesus, Mark will keep a sharp eye on Peter and his pusillanimous behaviour will be contrasted with the bravery of Jesus. Once again, the prescience of Jesus is emphasised and we realise that, come what may, it is God's will that will be done.

PRAYER

Psalm 23 has always seemed to Christians to be a singularly appropriate song when they meet to celebrate the Lord's Supper to proclaim the Lord's death until he comes (1 Corinthians 11:26).

Arrest, betrayal, desertion
Mark 14:32-72

The warning to *watch*, given to Peter, Andrew, James and John on the Mount of Olives was not for their ears only. All disciples were warned: *And what I say to you I say to all: Watch* (13:37). But the followers of Jesus who wanted no truck with a suffering Messiah (8:32), whose concerns were rooted in jealous rivalry (9:34) and who wanted to sit, one on the right hand and the other on the left, are not likely to give up old habits, even in the face of impending doom. From the moment Jesus and his companions arrive at Gethsemane we sense that, when enemies arrive to arrest Jesus, there will be only one outcome: *And they all forsook him and fled* (14:50). The disciples do not emerge from the story of the passion of Jesus with honour. We recall the ominous words of Zechariah, words which Jesus uses to warn the over-weaning disciples (14:27): *I will strike the shepherd, and the sheep will be scattered.* Only the promise that *after I am raised up, I will go before you into Galilee* holds out any hope that Peter and the rest will come good.

READING THROUGH

Gethsemane

According to the Gospels of Mark and Matthew, the place where Jesus prayed in deep anguish before his arrest was called Gethsemane. The name means "oil press" and that is just what we would expect to find at the foot of the Mount of Olives. The many olive groves on the slopes of the mountain necessitated an oil press. Note that Mark does not refer to a garden. This is St John's contribution to the story (John 18:1).

Chief priests

According to the Book of Exodus (19:4-6), the whole people of Israel were to be a kingdom of priests but a special priestly

279

caste developed, charged with supervising the liturgical life of the community. This meant that priests bore responsibility for the sacrifices offered in the temple and had a role to play in maintaining the purity of the nation (Luke 17:14; Leviticus 14:2). The priesthood in Israel was a hereditary institution. All male descendants of Aaron were priests (the Hebrew word for a priest is *cohen*) and the there were many of them (apparently, about 20,000 priests and Levites). Consequently those who served in the temple were drawn by lot (Luke 1:8) and did duty for two weeks per year only. The more prominent priests from wealthy aristocratic families in Jerusalem had oversight of the temple, its sacrificial system, the temple treasury and, generally, of priestly discipline. For the most part, ordinary priests and the more prominent priests in Jerusalem were dedicated to God's service, lived lives in accord with the Torah and prayed with deep devotion. The Gospels and the Acts of the Apostles mentions chief priests more than sixty times and Christian readers may feel that such people were vainglorious and self-seeking. But this would be to forget that early Christians did not easily forgive those they believed to have been implicated in the death of Jesus.

The High Priest

At the time of Jesus Rome ruled Palestine. Yet the power of Rome, its armies and administrators, are not noticeably present in the Gospels until we come to the events surrounding the death of Jesus. This accurately reflects the situation. Under the aegis of Rome Herod Antipas ruled the Galilee of Jesus and had his own army and civil servants. He was, by the standards of the time, a reasonably human and competent ruler. Judea and its capital Jerusalem were effectively ruled by the High Priest and his council (Sanhedrin). The province of Judea (Samaria, Judea and Idumea) was under the control of a Roman prefect who lived in Caesarea on the Mediterranean coast. But, for the most part, the day-to-day administration was carried on by local prominent people. Roman administrators appointed the High Priest and expected him so to rule in Judea that good order and peace were maintained and taxes collected and paid.

In Jerusalem, then, even during the time of Pilate, Jewish leaders were in day-to-day control. The magistrates were Jewish and ruled according to Jewish law, the schools were Jewish and the religion was Jewish. Jerusalem was policed by (Jewish) temple guards, commanded by the High Priest. In effect, he ran the political, economic and religious life of the city and its environs.

In the eyes of Rome the High Priest was suitable as a surrogate ruler for three reasons. First, the office was traditional (High Priests had governed Palestine from 445 to 37 B.C.E.) and was held in high esteem by the people. Secondly, the authorities could control the High Priest by the simple ruse of impounding the sacred vestments. This prevented the High Priest from performing his religious duties, especially on the Day of Atonement when he entered the Holy of Holies to make atonement for the sins of all the people of Israel. Both Herod the Great and Roman prefects confiscated the vestments to ensure compliance. Thirdly, the High Priest was seen as a useful go-between between the authority of Rome and the populace. If people wanted to deal with Rome, they went through the High Priest. If Rome wanted to communicate with the population, the prefect summoned the High Priest. When things went wrong, the High Priest carried the can.

The High Priest who sought the death of Jesus was Joseph Caiaphas. He served for seventeen years, longer than any other high priest under Roman rule, a fact which suggests that he was a competent man, managing to placate the Romans while remaining popular with the people. For ten of those years Pilate was the prefect. Presumably, the two got on well.

Sanhedrin

The High Priest carried out his religious, political and economic tasks with the help of counsellors, both formal and informal. The aristocratic priestly families and other wealthy and influential members of the upper classes ("elders") in Jerusalem provided a council which advised the High Priest. Members of the scholarly scribes gave advice on matters pertaining to the Jewish Torah which formed the basis of religious and social life for Jewish people. Jews who lived far beyond the confines of Judea, scattered to the four corners of the empire, listened respectfully to the decisions of the High Priest and his council (Hebrew: *Sanhedrin*).

Two incidents recorded by Josephus will illustrate the power and responsibility of the High Priest and his council. The first concerns a man called Jesus, the son of one Ananias. At the Feast of Tabernacles, Jesus ben Ananias went into the temple precincts and cried out:

> A voice from the east,
> a voice from the west,
> a voice against Jerusalem,
> a voice against its sanctuary (temple),
> a voice against the bridegroom,
> a voice against the bride,
> a voice against all the people.

The man was basing his prediction of the destruction of the city, its temple and its people on the warning in Jeremiah 7:34 concerning the punishment God would meet out to unfaithful Judah (the very chapter in which God orders the prophet to speak against those who have turned the temple into *a den of robbers*!). The High Priest and his counsellors immediately had the man arrested and, after interrogation, had him scourged by Jewish soldiers and handed over to the Romans who inflicted the same punishment on the unfortunate fellow. The man persisted in his dire warnings but the authorities released him on the grounds that he was mad. As for him, he kept up his mournful cries for another seven years until a Roman soldier casually killed him with his catapult.

This story well illustrates the swiftness with which the High Priest and the Sanhedrin acted when good order in the form of potentially rabble-rousing slogans were bandied about. Note the initial action taken by the Jewish authorities and the fact that they felt it necessary to consult Roman authority on the matter. Note, too, the final outcome. Then decision not to execute the deranged man was humane and just. These events took place about thirty years after the death of Jesus. The Christian reader will note that the man spoke out against the temple, invoking the words of Jeremiah, that he was apprehended by the High Priest and examined by the Sanhedrin, that he was scourged and, ultimately, set free.

A second case, which occurred in 62 C.E., when, for a brief period, no Roman prefect was in office, is equally instructive. The High Priest Ananus convened his council and had James the brother of Jesus of Nazareth put to death with some other prominent Christians of Jerusalem. But some fair-minded citizens, feeling that the verdict was not in accord with religious precept or Roman law – the objectors were probably Pharisees – protested to Rome and Ananus was deposed. He had transgressed the Roman regulation that in an equestrian province such as Judea only the Roman prefect could order an execution.

READING THROUGH AGAIN

A night of contrasts begins. Gethsemane will become a place of arrest, betrayal and desertion. But it will also witness to a man of courage, whose courage is moulded in the discipline of prayer.

Prayer in Gethsemane

Peter and James and John are again singled out to share in a special moment. The three who had witnessed the transfiguration on another mountain (9:2-8) are called upon to lend comfort and support when Jesus *began to be greatly distressed and troubled*. They are duly reminded that the hour for watching is at hand. The *hour* is explained in verse 41: *the hour has come; the Son of man is betrayed into the hands of sinners*. In his prayer that he might be spared the hour, Jesus calls on *Abba*, the Aramaic word for "father" in the intimate, family sense. It is fitting that it is on this occasion in the Gospel that Jesus first uses this most intimate form of address. Its use here implies that the more closely Jesus calls on his Father, the more he comes to realise that the suffering and death which lie ahead are tragically inevitable: Jesus is to be handed over *into the hands of sinners*.

The three disciples, no better or no worse than the rest, do not realise that now is the time for weak humans (even as Jesus is) to watch and pray. The word for *temptation* does not refer to a temptation to sin; rather, it refers to the sort of testing that comes with persecution. Mark's readers will, no doubt, have seen in this reckless carelessness of the disciples and in its outcome (*they all forsook him, and fled*) something of their own tragedy. However, Jesus prays and, in his prayer, finds the courage to endure: *thy will be done*.

Notice that Jesus calls Peter by his old name, Simon. It is as if from now on Simon is no longer the rock.

Arrest and desertion

Mark wishes us to remember that the betrayal of Jesus comes from within. As far back as 3:19 he lets it be known that it is one

283

of the twelve, Judas Iscariot, who delivers Jesus into enemy hands. With a crowd of soldiers from the forces at the High Priest's command, Judas comes from *the chief priests and the scribes and the elders* to betray Jesus with a kiss. The sign of betrayal is to be a kiss. A number of Old Testament passages speak of a treacherous kiss. Absalom employed the politician's cynical kiss to win popularity (2 Samuel 15:5) and Joab, under the guise of a friendly kiss, stabbed Amasa to death (2 Samuel 20:8-10). The Book of Proverbs counsels that *Faithful are the words of a friend; profuse are the kisses of an enemy* (Proverbs 27:6). Judas gives the sign and *they laid hands on him and seized him*.

Mark does not explain why *one of those who stood by* (surely, one of those with Jesus) had a sword and was prepared to use it. Nor does he explain why, when the man has cut off the ear of the slave of the High Priest, he is not instantly arrested. Nor does Mark provide any rebuke of Jesus for such violent activity (see Matthew 26:52-53); nor does he inform his readers that Jesus quickly intervened to end the violence (*No more of this!* – Luke 22:51). He does not reveal that Jesus healed the stricken man (Luke 22:51). It is from John 18:10-11 that we learn that the sword-swinging disciple was Simon Peter, that he is told to put away his sword and that the slave's name was Malchus.

The explanation for the sword incident may be found more in the realm of symbol than historical fact. Jesus complains that the crowd had come out against him *as against a robber, with swords and clubs*. He claims that he had been daily in the temple teaching and no one sought to seize him. He appeals to his role as a teacher and rejects the imputation that he is a robber. The robbers are all on the other side. The slave of the High Priest is reduced to the status of a robber: the loss of an ear was the punishment meted out to robbers since the days Persians ruled the Jewish people. It is significant that Mark does not alter that status by healing the man.

That Jesus is submissive to God's will and that it is God's will which is the final arbiter of what is about to take place, that all these things take place to reveal God's clear intention as laid down in the holy books, is again emphasised: *let the scriptures be fulfilled!*

As Jesus had foretold, all those who sat at table and accompanied him to Gethsemane with such loud and insistent protests of loyalty (*"If I must die with you, I will not deny you."* And they all said the same.) run away: *And they all forsook him, and fled.* The question must be faced. Is there any room in the community of Jesus for these runaways? Is there any possibility that they may be rehabilitated?

A young man

Many suggestions have been put forward concerning the identity of the young man wrapped in a linen cloth about his body who followed Jesus but who was seized by the arresting officers. There are many strange aspects to this incident. Who is this man? Why should he be out in the cold with nothing but a linen cloth about him? Why are we told that he was a *young* man? Why should Mark record the incident at all?

Some identify the young man with Mark himself. If, it is claimed, the John Mark, son of Mary, mentioned in Acts 12:12, is the writer of the Gospel according to Mark, then, on the likelihood that it was in her house that Jesus celebrated the Last Supper, it would not be impossible to envisage that young Mark followed Jesus to Gethsemane with the other disciples. But why should the author of the Gospel refer to himself in such an odd and infuriating way?

The oddness of the incident may be seen by considering that this young man is seized as Jesus was seized (compare verses 44 and 46). He escapes by leaving his linen cloth (*sindon* in Greek) which is mentioned twice, thus drawing the reader's attention to it. The dead Jesus is wrapped only in a linen cloth (another *sindon*), also mentioned twice (15:46). Another young man appears at 16:5, dressed in a white robe (not a *sindon*). Is there some deep work here? We shall postpone further comment until we come to the empty tomb.

The first hearing

The High Priest and his council assemble and they are, we are told, seeking witnesses whose evidence would justify nothing less than the death penalty. But nothing emerged though many gave evidence. The evidence was patently false or contradictory. One charge did appear to have some substance: *"We heard him say, 'I will destroy this temple that is made with hands, and in three days I will build another, not made with hands.'"* Yet there was no agreement even on this accusation.

The High Priest questions Jesus on the matter of the charge relating to the temple but Jesus does not answer. The inquisitor changes tack with a direct question: *Are you the Messiah, the Son of the Blessed?* To this Jesus gives an instant reply: *I am*. And Jesus adds an intriguing assertion: *and you will see the Son of man sitting at the right hand of Power, and coming with the clouds of heaven*. The first part of Jesus' reply would appear to be a simple agreement with the High Priest's question. But there may be more to it than that. The Greek words translated as *I am* are *egô eimi*, words which occur in the Book of Exodus where Moses asks God to reveal to him his name so that he may inform the people of Israel who it is who has determined to save them from slavery. God replies: I AM WHO I AM (Exodus 3:14). It may well be that Mark wishes his readers to recall the words of Exodus and to raise for them the question of who it is who stands before the High Priest in danger of his life. It is unlikely that the High Priest would have been aware of such implications, even if we could be certain that Mark is quoting an historical statement of Jesus rather than interpreting the scene in the light of later Christian reflection.

The statement of the future role of the Son of man will not have helped the High Priest either. It is one thing for Jesus to claim that he is the Messiah, even that he is the Son of the Blessed (see Psalm 110:1 and the use of this text in Mark 12:35-36). At most, these admissions would mean no more than that Jesus claimed to be the Messiah-King, descended from David. It is difficult to see that the High Priest could have understood the words in any other way. But such claims are not blasphemy and Jesus would not face the death penalty on the head of such charges. Yet the High Priest tears his garments – a thing he was forbidden to do (Leviticus 21:10) – as a sign of deepest mourning. He appears to be in deep distress at the claims of Jesus and to call for the death penalty.

Can we make any sense of all this? Can we delve beneath the theology of Mark, itself the outcome of years of Christian reflection, beneath the agenda which Mark has set himself? It seems likely that Jesus had made some remarks which were, in some shape or form, an attack on the temple. What is more, he made these remarks (and his symbolic attack on the buyers and sellers in the temple area) in the public arena and in the week before Passover when thousands flocked to Jerusalem for the feast.

Such open defiance could not go unnoticed or unregarded. Reports would have been made to Caiaphas and his advisers. He would have to weigh in the balance whether Jesus constituted a real threat to the temple and so to good order among the people. He would have to take into account that Jesus had made his attack in the plain light of day. He would have to consider that Jesus had followers, not many, to be sure, but the nucleus of what might turn into a sizeable and uncontrollable rabble which would have to be put down (possibly with Roman troops and certainly with much loss of life). In such circumstances we are forced to conclude that Caiaphas had no option but to move against Jesus and to have him put to death. Given the responsibilities laid on the shoulders of the High Priest, it would have been very irresponsible of him not to act as he did. He did not, it seems to me, act because of theological disagreements with Jesus. Nor did he proceed because of any claims made by Jesus or by his disciples concerning his identity (Messiah; Son of God; Son of David and the rest). Caiaphas acted because of his overriding political and moral responsibilities: to preserve the peace and to prevent riots and bloodshed. What Mark has done is to write the trial before the High Priest from the point of view of later christian understanding. He is not concerned with political realities which confronted the High Priest.

Verse 65 provides an insight into Mark's way of doing things. Consider the following statements from the Old Testament:

> I gave my back to the smiters,
> and my cheeks to those who pulled out the beard;
> I hid not my face
> from shame and spitting (Isaiah 50:6).

> He was despised and rejected by men;
> a man of sorrows and acquainted with grief;
> and as one from whom men hide their faces
> he was despised, and we esteemed him not (Isaiah 53:3).

> … with a rod they strike upon the cheek
> the ruler of Israel (Micah 5:1b).

> Then Zedekiah, the son of Chenanah, came near and struck Micaiah on the cheek, and said, "How did the spirit of the Lord go from me to speak to you?" (1 Kings 22:24).

It is clear that practically every word of verse 65 is taken from these passages. The covering of the face of Jesus may be meant to suggest that his tormentors did so to make him guess who struck him, mocking him as a deluded prophet. But the Christian reader, mindful of the sayings in holy scripture, will see in the event a fulfilment of God's will. Unwittingly, the tormentors of Jesus fulfill God's preordained plan. If the event has any historical value, it is unlikely that the Sanhedrin would have taken the initiative or played any part in maltreating Jesus. Luke 22:63-65 would suggest as much.

Peter's denial

Peter's denial provides a neat Marcan sandwich. Before the interrogation of Jesus, Mark has Peter take up his position in the courtyard. He is, therefore, an unseen presence as Jesus is questioned and declares his emphatic *I am*. Following his courageous stand, Peter again comes to the fore and denies all knowledge of Jesus three times. This leader of the twelve, the one who acknowledged Jesus to be the Messiah, goes so far as to invoke a curse upon himself to strengthen his denial (some have suggested that Peter cursed Jesus) and to distance himself from his friend. The warning to all disciples is that even the chiefest can fail. Everyone must watch and pray. The fact that Peter *broke down and wept* may point to the possibility of repentance and rehabilitation.

The denial, as well as handing out a warning to all disciples and would-be disciples, helps Mark to highlight the loneliness of Jesus as he undergoes his sufferings and death. The poignancy of the situation is calculated not only to move Mark's readers. Mark wants his readers to see that Jesus not only dies but that his lone death is a life *given as a ransom for many* (10:45).

PRAYER

A prayerful reflection of Isaiah 53, a chapter which provided Christian writers with a veritable quarry of words and symbols in their quest to plumb the mystery of the death of Jesus, will help us to understand that the fate of Jesus is not merely an event of the past but in every time confronts us with the evil of which we are capable and the goodness of the God who meets us in our sinfulness.

They crucified him
Mark 15:1-39

We have examined Mark's use of the verb "to hand over", "to deliver up", scattered everywhere throughout his story and ominously pointing to the fate of Jesus and all who would throw in their lot with the man from Galilee. Now we come to the culmination of betrayal, to the final destiny, to the final handing over, the handing over to be crucified. The full authority of the Sanhedrin – *the chief priests with the elders and scribes* – is brought to bear on Pilate. The crowds, so often the enthusiastic admirers of Jesus and the source of potential disciples, become the tool of the chief priests and demand the release of Barabbas and the crucifixion of *the King of the Jews*. The speed with which the tragedy hastens to its end is quite remarkable. There is no formal trial before Pilate. After the briefest of exchanges between the prefect and the priests, Jesus' fate is determined. However, throughout the scurry of events Mark keeps his eye firmly fixed on the divine presence in the sordid story. The authorities have their agenda. God has his.

READING THROUGH

The people who appear in Mark's final pages are introduced with little or no explanatory information. The assumption is that Mark's readers know who these people are, an assumption which reveals something of how Christian traditions developed and how Mark himself shaped the stories which came to him.

Pontius Pilate
With the removal of Herod Archelaus in 6 C.E. by the emperor Augustus, Rome took direct control of the province of Judea (Judea, Idumaea and Samaria) and appointed a prefect to administer local government there. The Roman official to whom administration was assigned was of the equestrian order or lower

aristocracy. The prefect resided at Caesarea in one of the luxurious palaces built there by Herod the Great. Pontius Pilate was prefect from 26 to 36 C.E. and for all that time Caiaphas was High Priest in Jerusalem.

Pilate was not the most diplomatic of rulers. On one occasion he had his troops march through Jerusalem carrying their standards on which were depicted imperial insignia which Jewish sensitivity regarded as graven images. A large number of worthy citizens went to Caesarea to protest. Pilate ordered his soldiers to surround the delegation. They bared their necks and declared themselves willing to die rather than see their holy city defiled. Pilate backed down.

On another occasion he appropriated some temple funds to build an aqueduct. A crowd gathered to protest but Pilate called in his troops and they dispersed the crowd with the help of stout cudgels.

A Jewish scholar, Philo Judaeus, who lived in the Egyptian city of Alexandria and was a contemporary of Pilate, had occasion to write to the emperor Gaius (Caligula) in 40 C.E. when the latter proposed to have a statue of himself erected in the Temple in Jerusalem, a proposal which would have led to widespread revolt had Gaius had his way. He was, however, conveniently assassinated. Philo's letter refers to Pilate and recalls "the briberies, the insults, the robberies, the outrages and wanton injuries, the executions without trial constantly repeated, the ceaseless and supremely grievous cruelty" which marked the prefect's time of office in Palestine. Indeed, Pilate was removed from his post because of the many summary executions he carried out. He was not a man who knew how to make terror serve political circumspection.

The Pilate of Matthew who washes his hands of complicity in the death of an innocent man, the Pilate of Luke who finds nothing deserving of death, indeed, no crime at all, in this man, the Pilate of John who discusses endlessly with Jesus on the finer points of theological issues, is not the Pilate of history. Rather, he is the Pilate of Christian propaganda, the Pilate Christians would like to present to the Gentile world. But stories of Pilate's reluctance to condemn an innocent man, stories of a weak-willed man overcome by a hostile and vindictive mob are far distant from the real Pilate. Mark's Pilate may be nearer the callous truth.

Barabbas

The name Barabbas (Bar-Abba) means "son of the father" and, since Jesus is "Son of the Father", Mark may intend an ironic contrast between the innocent Son of Abba and the murderous rebel Barabbas. Certainly, the text contains, as we shall see below, a number of striking contrasts but Mark does not show any interest in the meaning of people's names (as a general rule) and his usual practice of translating Aramaic expressions shows that he does not presume any knowledge of that language on the part of his audience. If he wanted to play on the name, he would, surely, have provided a translation. Some ancient manuscripts of Matthew's Gospel give the man's name as Jesus Barabbas [= Jesus, son of the father] which opens the way to all sorts of speculation. There is no evidence that Mark wished his readers to delve into the dramatic or theological possibilities inherent in the man's name.

We know nothing about Barabbas, other than the information given in the New Testament. For Mark, he is a murderer who committed his crimes during an insurrection. Luke follows much the same tack: *Barabbas – a man who had been thrown into prison for an insurrection started in the city, and for murder* (Luke 23:19). For Matthew, he is simply *a notorious prisoner* (Matthew 27:16). Cryptically, John says, *Now Barabbas was a robber* (John 18:40). But nothing is known of the insurrection in which Barabbas is said to have participated and Josephus is silent on the matter.

There is no evidence that Roman prefects released a prisoner each year at Passover. Josephus mentions no such practice. John 18:39 (*But you have a custom that I should release one man for you at the Passover...*) suggests that the practice was a Jewish tradition going back to the days of the Maccabees and, by way of concession to local feelings, carried on by Roman administrators. To be sure, a custom of freeing a prisoner at Passover is very much in keeping with a festival which celebrates the release from bondage in Egypt. But there is little or no hard evidence of such a traditional Jewish custom and there is precious little evidence that Roman administrators went in for such indulgence. If Barabbas was an insurrectionist, and a murderous one at that, it is difficult to imagine Pilate releasing him. On the other hand, the story seems fairly rooted in the gospel tradition and there may be something to it.

Simon of Cyrene

Simon bears a Jewish name, though one found fairly frequently among non-Jews. He comes from Cyrene, the capital city of the north African district of Cyrenaica (in modern Libya). That Simon was coming in from the country might suggest that he was coming from his farm. If this is the case, then he would have moved from his place of origin to take up residence in Judea. On the other hand, he may very well have been a pilgrim coming to the city for the feast.

His sons bear a Greek name (Alexander) and a Latin name (Rufus). They seem to have been well known to Mark's audience. Otherwise, it seems pointless to mention them. A burial cave used in the first century was discovered in 1941. The cave is located just outside Jerusalem on the southwestern slope of the Kidron Valley. It appears that the cave was used as a burial place by a Jewish family of Cyrenian origin. An inscription found on an ossuary in the cave reads, "Alexander, son of Simon". This may be no more than coincidental.

There are New Testament references to a Rufus (Romans 16:13), to an Alexander (1 Timothy 1:20; 2 Timothy 4:14), to Cyrene and Cyrenians (Acts of the Apostles 2:10; 6:9; 11:20; 31:1). Whether there is a connection between these people and the family of Simon of Cyrene is a moot question.

Golgotha

The traditional place of the crucifixion of Jesus took place outside the city walls (as they then were) in the vicinity of the present Church of the Holy Sepulchre. Mark calls the place Golgotha and informs his readers that the word means the place of the skull. It was both the Roman and Jewish practice to perform executions outside inhabited areas of a town but sufficiently convenient to provide a public spectacle and so to act as a deterrent.

Crucifixion

The Roman writer, Cicero, described crucifixion as "the most cruel and frightful of punishments" (*In Verrem*, V. 62f). Roman citizens who were convicted of a capital offence were spared the indignity and terror of death by crucifixion. It was standard practice to scourge the condemned with thongs to which were attached pieces of bone which dug into the back and caused severe gouging and consequent loss of blood. The prisoner was then tied to a cross-beam which stretched across the shoulders. The journey to the place of execution exposed the victim to taunts and abuse from the soldiers and the citizens. On arrival at the place of crucifixion, the victim was often nailed to the cross-beam through the wrists. Ropes were used to hoist the condemned on to a fixed upright (this may have been a pole or, more likely, an old tree stripped of its branches). The cross-beam was fixed at the top of the upright, forming a rough right angle. A wooden support for the crotch of the victim was attached to the upright. The legs were crossed so that it was possible to nail the ankles to the upright with a single nail which passed through both ankles. It took a long time to die, if one were young and strong and not too weakened by scourging. The criminal died of asphyxiation, that is, a lack of oxygen in the blood due to restricted respiration. When the man was unable to exert enough upward lift to expand his lungs, the end was near. Sometimes executioners would break the legs of the condemned to prevent upward lift and so hasten death. The prisoner was usually dragged to the place of death completely naked. He soon lost control of bodily functions so that urine and faeces fouled the crucifixion site. The sickening stink and the wretched cries of the dying added to the indignity. As St Paul remarked, quoting Deuteronomy 21:23, *Cursed be everyone who hangs on a tree* (Galatians 3:13).

READING THROUGH AGAIN

The consultation which *the chief priests with the elders and the scribes, and the whole council* held as soon as it was morning can scarcely be a second trial. It would seem that the decision to press for the death of Jesus had been taken in the hastily convened meeting after the arrest of Jesus. That decision is now formally ratified and *they bound Jesus and led him away and handed him over to Pilate*. The significance of Mark's theme of "handing over" will by now be familiar to his readers. The fact that Jesus is bound introduces another rich seam of reflection.

Before Pilate
What happened before Pilate can scarcely be called a formal trial. The very brevity of the affair precludes any indulgence in

legal niceties. Christian familiarity with the story tends to gloss over its peculiarities. Consider the following:

1. We are not told who Pilate is.
2. We are not told that Pilate is the Roman prefect.
3. We are not told who charged Jesus with claiming to be King of the Jews.
4. We are not told how Pilate heard of the charge.
5. We are not told why the charge concerning the temple is dropped.
6. We are not told why the Messiah accusation is altered.
7. We are not told what the *many things* (verse 3) or many charges (verse 4) are.
8. We are not told why Jesus reverted to silence.
9. We are not told why Pilate wondered.
10. We are not told what revolt Barabbas was involved in.
11. We are not told what Pilate thought of the alleged claim to be King of the Jews.
12. We are not told why the chief priests were envious of Jesus (verse 10).

Other peculiarities will occur even to the most casual reader. It is clear that what we have in Mark's account is a loose collection of impressions about the interrogation (if one can call it that) before Pilate. Each impression is intended to make some apologetic point. The odd collection of disparate impressions which is given has been chosen for very particular reasons. In the first place, Mark is anxious to show that the Roman authorities did not make the first move against Jesus and, indeed, had no quarrel with him or his disciples. Christians lived in the Roman empire. If their founder could be shown to have been a dangerous criminal executed by the Roman prefect of Judea, then it would be assumed that his followers were equally dangerous. It would also be difficult to persuade loyal citizens of the empire that a crucified criminal, condemned by the Roman authority invested in the prefect Pilate, was the one who would establish the kingdom of God on earth. Secondly, and following from the first point, Mark is eager to emphasise the responsibility of the chief priests, the elders and scribes in bringing about the death of Jesus. Notice that it is the crowd who ask Pilate *to do as he was wont to do for them* at the feast. It is the crowd who introduce the business concerning Barabbas and there is no reason in the text to suppose that they are doing so for any other purpose than to seek the release of Jesus. But the chief priests manipulate the crowd: *But the chief priests stirred up the crowd to have him release for them Barabbas instead*. That *instead* suggests that the original intention of the crowd has been subverted by the chief priests. Thirdly, twice (verses 10, 14) we are informed that Pilate thought that Jesus was innocent of any crime. We see his hesitancy (verses 9, 12, 14, 15). Pilate acts, it would appear, against his better judgment. It is the chief priests who manipulate the crowd and Pilate unwillingly succumbs to the pressure exerted on him by the screaming mob. Fourthly, the silence of Jesus, perceived by the Christian reader, serves two purposes. On the one hand, it indicates that God's purpose is being fulfilled (see Psalm 38:12-14 and Isaiah 53:7). On the other hand, the silence of Jesus provides a model for the Christian faced with trial and persecution (see 13:11). Fifthly, in his presentation of the interrogation before Pilate, Mark gives only those details which would be of importance to his Christian community and which would meet its concerns. Therefore, he emphasises that it is as Messiah that Jesus is presented to Pilate. The title *King of the Jews* refers, in Jewish and christian parlance, to the Messiah. If the title figured at all in the historical encounter with Pilate, he would have grasped its political overtones (John 19:12-16 is much more overtly political than Mark) and would not have addressed Jesus as King of the Jews while at the same time proclaiming that he could find no evil in the man. The fact of the matter is that Mark is not interested in what Pilate may or may not have understood by any charge brought against Jesus. For him, Jesus is innocent of any crime (and he has the words of Pilate to prove it) but he was delivered to death because he was the Messiah-King of Israel. The mockery of the dying man by the chief priests ironically clarifies why, according to Mark and Christian understanding which shaped his thought, Jesus died: *He saved others; he cannot save himself. Let the Christ [= Messiah], the King of Israel, come down now from the cross, that we may see and believe* (15:31-32).

Barabbas

A word about Barabbas. Jesus is bound before he is led away to be handed over to Pilate. The Greek word for *bound* lies at the root of the word for prison (a place where people are bound) and for prisoner. Mark sets up a comparison between the murderer who is bound for his crimes but who will be set free and the innocent Jesus who is bound and will be handed over to crucifixion and death.

A purple cloak

Scourging was the usual prelude to crucifixion. For one thing, it shortened what would otherwise be a long and drawn out agony. Bored soldiers would want to get a routine chore over as quickly as possible. However, there may be more to the incident that the casual softening-up of a condemned man.

There are three mockery scenes in Mark's passion narrative. The first is at 14:65 when those assembled in the house of the High Priest mock Jesus as a would-be prophet and the servants inflict blows upon him. The words used to describe the scene fulfill to the letter the details the prophet Jesus had foretold about his final ordeal (10:33-34). There is the added irony that, as Jesus is being mocked and derided as a pseudo-prophet, his prophetical words concerning Peter's denial are, at that very moment, coming to pass in the courtyard of the High Priest's house. Thus the rough treatment meted out to Jesus serves to confirm his status as a prophet.

The same may be said for the two subsequent mockeries. Each is so constructed that the inflicted insult and injury not only draw the reader into sympathetic solidarity with the victim but also reveal the true identity of the one so sorely abused. The cohort of soldiers dress Jesus in a mockery of imperial robes and insignia and greet him, *Hail, King of the Jews!* (Remember the usual imperial greeting, *Hail, Caesar!*) The scene contains echoes – distant but discernible – of two passages from the Suffering Servant sections of Isaiah. The first, Isaiah 50:6, is quoted above. The second reads:

> He was despised and rejected by men;
> a man of sorrows, and acquainted with grief;
> and as one from whom men hide their faces
> he was despised, and we esteemed him not.
> Surely he has bone our griefs
> and carried our sorrows;
> yet we esteemed him stricken,
> smitten by God, and afflicted.

But he was wounded for our transgressions,
he was bruised for our iniquities;
upon him was the chastisement that made us whole,
and with his stripes we are healed (Isaiah 53:3-5).

Early Christians meditated on such passages from the ancient scriptures and saw them fulfilled in the details surrounding the death of Jesus. But we must be open to the possibility that the Old Testament texts have so influenced the telling of detailed incidents that we can have no certainty that we can recover exactly what really happened. What we can be sure of is that Mark tells the mockery stories to underpin his understanding of who Jesus is. The irony is that Jesus is *the King of the Jews*, the Messiah-Son of David whose sufferings and death are in accord with God's will as revealed in the pages of God's word. We shall see the same theological motives in the third mockery scene (15:29-32). Contrary to usual practice, Jesus is given back his clothing. This prepares for the theologically motivated account of the sharing of his garments among the soldiers.

Death on a cross

St John states, rather pointedly, that Jesus went out *bearing his own cross*. Mark introduces Simon of Cyrene who was compelled to carry the cross-beam. There is no suggestion that he volunteered. The fact that his sons are mentioned in such a way as to suggest that they were well known to Mark's readers indicates that the experience was not entirely without results. Alexander and Rufus may very well be guarantors to Mark's community of all that happened. Their father was there. And Mark's community will recall the words of Jesus, *If any man would come after me, let him deny himself and take up his cross and follow me*, and see in Simon a model for discipleship.

The Book of Proverbs recommends that strong drink should be given to those who are dying in agony: *Give strong drink to him who is perishing, and wine to those in bitter distress* (Proverbs 31:6). Myrrh is a gum resin which was reputed to have narcotic properties. The wine and myrrh would have had a deadening effect. The refusal emphasises the determination of Jesus to drink to the full the cup proffered by his Father (14:36 and see 10:38).

The stark words, *they crucified him*, leave to one side the horrendous particulars involved in the barbarity of crucifixion. The appropriation of the garments of Jesus by the soldiers introduces the first clear reference to Psalm 22 in Mark's account of the happenings at Golgotha: *they divided my garments among them, and for my raiment they cast lots* (Psalm 22:18). Mark repeats the words *they crucified him* when he tells that Jesus was placed on the cross. He will go on to note the sixth hour and the ninth hour, the hour of death. Jesus hung on the cross from nine in the morning until three in the afternoon.

As the criminal set out for the place of execution it was customary to place around his neck or to have carried before him a placard on which was chalked or burned the nature of his crime. After the victim was impaled, the placard was fastened to the cross above his head. The charge against Jesus was thus displayed: *The King of the Jews*. Pilate did not condemn Jesus because he claimed to be King of the Jews. He did not, according to Mark, appear to see anything significant in the alleged claim. The prefect sends Jesus to his death *wishing to satisfy the crowd* – and for no other reason, according to the Marcan perspective. Yet Mark states plainly that *the charge against him read, "The King of the Jews"*. Clearly, he is referring to the accusation of the High Priest, *Are you the Messiah?* Mark wishes, yet again, to declare, at the most awful moment of his death, that Jesus is God's anointed, the Son of David, the royal, messianic King of the Jews. In the third and final mockery scene he will re-emphasise the point.

Messiah, King of Israel

Jesus is crucified between two robbers. The Greek word used to describe these two criminals is the word used by Josephus to describe those who involved themselves in rebellions against Roman rule. He reports that such insurrectionists were routinely crucified. It may well be that the two robbers were part of the rebellion in which Barabbas is supposed to have participated but we have no evidence of this. Nor does Mark seem to have any scriptural motive for introducing the robbers to the scene. To be sure, some ancient manuscripts of Mark add verse 28 (in a footnote in the RSV): *And the scripture was fulfilled which says, "He was reckoned with the transgressors"*. This text, which is to be found at Luke 22:37, is a quotation from Isaiah 53:12, from a

298

chapter, therefore, to which Mark is already indebted. Nonetheless, the verse has all the hallmarks of a later addition to the text of Mark, most likely borrowed from Luke.

Mark's purpose in recording the presence of the two robbers may well lie in the detail that *one was on his right and one on his left*. It is worth recalling the answer which Jesus gave to the ambitious sons of Zebedee:

> "You do not know what you are asking. Are you able to drink the cup that I drink, or to be baptised with the baptism with which I am baptised?" And they said to him, "We are able." And Jesus said to them, "The cup that I drink you will drink; and with the baptism with which I am baptised, you will be baptised; but to sit at my right hand or at my left is not mine to grant, but is for those whom it has been prepared" (10:38-40).

The king who sits on the tree of the cross has, indeed, his courtiers, one on the right and one on the left. It is not James and John who are destined by God to sit at the right and left hand. They *forsook him and fled*. There are none near him now except two criminals and they are not a source of comfort (as is the so-called good thief in Luke's account) for they join in the mockery: *Those who were crucified with him also reviled him* (15:32). Mark does not quote Isaiah 53:12 but his depiction of the scene makes the point for him: *he was reckoned with the transgressors*. Such was God's design.

Scripture continues to guide Mark's hand. No biblical passage is so close to the surface of the narrative of the crucifixion of Jesus as Psalm 22, the cry of the oppressed but righteous to a seemingly deaf God. The third is of a piece with the previous two. Echoes of scripture are used to form an ironic context for the jeers of the mockers and to turn their ranting into revelations as to who it is who is given over to death. Consider these words of the Psalm:

> But I am a worm, and no man;
> scorned by men, and despised by the people.
> All who seek me mock at me,
> they make mouths at me, they wag their heads;
> "He committed his cause to the Lord;
> let him deliver him,
> let him rescue him, for he delights in him!" (Psalm 22:6-8).

Even the *Aha!* has an echo in the Psalms: *They open wide their mouths against me; they say "Aha, Aha!"* (Psalm 35:21). We can not be sure whether the texts from the Psalms are responsible for the creation of the event or whether an historical incident is being presented in the language of scripture in order to press home the point that even the antics of the enemies of Jesus are not outside God's control. Unwittingly the mockers fulfill the will of God. Thus it is that the mockers take up again the charge that Jesus spoke against the temple (but without the qualifications found in 14:58) but the reader will soon discover that it is, indeed, the death of Jesus which robs the temple of its significance (see below on verse 38). *The Son of man came not to be served but to serve, and to give his life as a ransom for many* (10:45); the mission of Jesus is not to save himself. It is not by coming down from the cross that the will of God is done. To save one's life is to lose it: *For whoever would save his life will lose it; and whoever loses his life for my sake and the gospel's will save it. For what does it profit a man, to gain the whole world and forfeit his life?* (8:35-36).

The chief priests and scribes join in the mockery. But it falls to them to give the final and true verdict on the mission and person of Jesus. It is their authoritative lips which pronounce the truth of the matter and in a manner which removes all ambiguity. The title King of the Jews may be mistaken for a political designation and lead to a misunderstanding of who Jesus is and what he is about. But the words of the priests and scribes are beyond misunderstanding. Jesus is, indeed, the *Messiah*. He is *the King of Israel,* of God's holy people. *Israel* is the name for all the descendants of father Jacob, it is the name which God himself gave to the people of the covenant (Genesis 32:28). It is the name tenderly given by God to his people, his very own, his son:

> When Israel was a child, I loved him,
> and out of Egypt I have called my son (Hosea 11:1).

Not from the mouths of babes but from the mouths of chief priests and learned scribes we learn that Jesus is God's shepherd of *my people, of the house of Israel* (Ezekiel 34:30). The irony is that it is not by coming down from the cross but by dying on it that Jesus shows the extent to which the love of God embraces the people of Israel and, through the death of this one righteous Jew, the peoples of the world.

Death

From noon to the hour of death at three o'clock *there was darkness over the whole land.* The darkness is, as it were, the physical counterpart to the cry of desolation uttered by the dying man. But it is more than that. There are texts in the Old Testament that reflect the belief that the "heavens" (the domain of God's complete authority) react to the activity of people on earth. The response of the heavens to human affairs was seen as an indication of divine judgment on what was taking place on earth:

> for the stars of the heavens and their constellations
> will not give their light;
> the sun will be dark at its rising
> and the moon will not shed its light.
> I will punish the world for its evil,
> and the wicked for their iniquity (Isaiah 13:10-11).

The failure of the sun to shine and the moon to give its light symbolise God's displeasure at what is happening on earth – the text is actually referring to the punishment to be meted out to Babylon for its oppression of the people of Israel. The same association of darkness and divine displeasure is to be found in Isaiah 50:2-3 and Jeremiah 15:6-9. The implication of these texts is not simply that God is displeased with human affairs but that he will judge and punish humanity for its evil ways. This latter aspect is more clearly expressed in the Book of Amos. Amos speaks of the Day of the Lord, the day of the final and decisive intervention of God when his people will be restored to their former glory, when sin will be wiped away and none but the righteous shall stand. Amos describes that great and terrible time:

> And on that day, says the Lord God,
> I will make the sun go down at noon,
> and darken the earth in broad daylight.
> I will turn your feasts into mourning,
> and your songs into lamentation;
> I will bring sackcloth upon all loins,
> and baldness on every head;
> I will make it like the mourning for an only son,
> and the end of it like a bitter day (Amos 8:9-10).

The death of Jesus is seen by Mark, not as a personal and private tragedy for one man, but a cosmic event emphasising a crucial moment in human history, a decisive moment in the relationship between creator and creature. It is not only a moment of deep tragedy for humanity. It is a moment of divine judgment.

The cry of dereliction, *My God, my God, why hast thou forsaken me?*, is conveniently translated from the Aramaic for Mark's Greek-speaking audience. There is much dispute as to what the scream might mean. It is true that the cry is the opening line of Psalm 22. This psalm has provided much theological underpinning for Mark, as we have seen. It is, therefore, entirely possible that Mark intends his readers to look to the whole of the psalm in order to understand what the cry means in the mouth of the dying Jesus. On such an understanding, the cry of abandonment is not the final word. Psalm 22 is the outburst of one who has suffered unjustly, the fierce prayer of a just and righteous person who is unjustly beset by enemies and on whom is inflicted the most outrageous torment. But the prayer of the righteous comes before God and, in the end, in answer to the prayer (*O Lord, come to my aid, O God, make haste to help*), deliverance is effected and rescue is secured. By intoning the first line of the psalm, Jesus is affirming that he is confident that his destiny will be the same. Such an explanation, while eminently possible, is too sanguine.

Others would suggest that Jesus felt abandoned by his God but, in reality, he was not. In such a view, the distress of Jesus is unrelieved and his sense of loss and abandonment unremitting but the reader knows that the resurrection is at hand and that God did not abandon his Son. Again, such a view is possible but is not very convincing.

The plain sense of the words and the darkness which accompanies them (understood in the light of the last two lines of the above quotation from Amos) would suggest that Jesus experienced a deep sense of abandonment as he suffered his final agony. He had been betrayed by a friend, his followers had run away, he had been mocked by his enemies and even those women who had followed and ministered to him are afar off. He is alone in the midst of his tormentors. Even his God would appear to be afar off: *My God, my God, why have you forsaken me?* But it is essential to realise that Jesus calls on *MY* God. He does not lose faith that God is his God. Jesus may have died feeling that his God had deserted him but he did not die in despair. He did not lose faith.

It is difficult to understand how bystanders could have misunderstood the cry of dereliction as a call for Elijah. The cry of Jesus was in Aramaic, the language of Jewish people in Palestine (the Aramaic for Elijah is EL-I-YAH). Furthermore, Jesus cried with a loud voice: we may safely discount any suggestion that the bystanders did not hear him properly.

A number of suggestions come to mind. It may well be that Mark sees in the business about Elijah a further stage in the mockery of Jesus. The career of that great prophet, as recounted in the Books of the Kings, is full of examples of helping the distressed and powerless (1 Kings 17:1-24), to such an extent that Elijah was something of a patron saint of hopeless cases. The jest may be that the fate of Jesus is so desperate that only an Elijah can help. The man who offers the sour wine (a better translation than vinegar) is not making a gesture of kindness but is motivated by malice. The longer the agony is prolonged, the deeper the dereliction of the victim. The failure of Elijah to come to take Jesus down from the cross is further proof that God has abandoned the Messiah-King of Israel.

The offering of *a sponge full of vinegar* gives rise to another possibility. The action of the bystander recalls the plight of the persecuted righteous one in the psalm:

Answer me, O Lord, for thy steadfast love is good;
according to thy abundant mercy,
turn to me.
Hide not thy face from thy servant;
for I am in distress, make haste to answer me.
draw near to me, redeem me,
set me free because of my enemies.
Thou knowest my reproach,
and my shame and my dishonour;
my foes are all known to thee.
Insults have broken my heart,
so that I am in despair.
I looked for pity, but there was none;
and for comforters, but I found none.
They gave me poison for food,
and for my thirst they gave me vinegar to drink
(Psalm 69:16-21)

Mark may wish us to compare the plight of the innocent in the psalm with the plight of Jesus on the cross. Surrounded by enemies who wish to see him taken down from the cross in some show of flashy power, Jesus fulfills God's will. The reader will know that Elijah has already come. John the Baptist is Elijah who proclaimed the greatness of Jesus and whose violent death so clearly and ominously foreshadowed the fate of the Son of man.

The death comes with another loud cry. The cry may be a further intimation of dereliction of Jesus or it may be a loud prayer. It is difficult to see how a man dying of asphyxiation would have breath to shout, much less to shout loudly. Mark does not give us any famous last words. He simply records that the man died crying out, whether in agony or resignation, we do not know.

Revelation

The moment of the death of Jesus is the moment which marks the beginning of his vindication by God. First, the veil of the temple, the curtain which separated the Holy of Holies (the place of God's presence), *was torn in two, from top to bottom*. The implications would appear to be twofold. On the one hand, the presence of God is no longer to be confined to one holy place. The death of Jesus is the sign of God's universal presence. This much might be inferred from the fact that it is a gentile soldier who declares the sonship of Jesus. On the other hand, and this would be in keeping with Mark's anti-temple bias, the tearing of the veil may signify that the temple has lost its significance. Israel's privileged position in God's eyes has come to an end or, rather, to its fruition. All peoples, because of the death of Jesus, have access to God.

Throughout Mark's Gospel we have encountered total misunderstanding as to the true identity of Jesus of Nazareth. Demon voices unerringly identified him as the Holy One of God (1:24), the Son of God (3:11), as Son of the Most High (5:7); the heavenly voice called him my beloved Son (1:11; 9:7). But human beings singularly failed to probe the mystery of his true identity. Even the disciples fail. Time and again, they misunderstand his person and his mission. Yet it is quite clear that their incomprehension was not due solely to human stupidity. *Their hearts were hardened* (6:52 – passive voice). The disciples were not meant to understand who Jesus was during his time with them. Mark is dealing, not with human frailty, but with divine intention. No one can understand who Jesus is until he has died on the cross. It is the cross which, in God's plan, reveals the true nature of Jesus. With the death of Jesus, God, as it were, lifts the veil and Jesus can be seen for what he really is, God's Son. The Jew Peter proclaimed Jesus to be the Messiah; the Gentile centurion proclaims him to be Son of God. The opening assertion of Mark's drama is now fulfilled: Jesus is Messiah, Son of God (1:1). That is the gospel truth.

We have reached the end of the second act of Mark's drama. The centurion brings down the curtain with a mighty last line: *Truly this man was the Son of God!* But the play does not end here. There is unfinished business. Mark calls us from the foot of the cross to the tomb. We will see strange things there.

PRAYER

Psalm 69 is a cry of faith in the midst of darkness and despair. It is a prayer calling out for God's saving action. It is a prayer that traces the way from death to life.

The empty tomb
Mark 15:40–16:8

Mark opened his Gospel with a prologue which provided his readers with an assembly of witnesses. Each witness served Mark's purpose by supplying information about the person and mission of Jesus. Readers learned that he was the Messiah, the Son of God, the one of whom the prophets had spoken, the one for whom the prophets prepared. The Elijah/Baptist figure proclaimed the greater one to come and prepared the way. At the baptism, the Spirit descended and a voice from heaven declared him to be *my beloved Son*. The demons tormented and the angels ministered to the man from Galilee who came out of the desert-testing to proclaim the nearness of the kingdom of God.

Mark closes his Gospel with an epilogue which provides his readers with another assembly of witnesses. Women witness to the death, they witness to the burial and to place of the tomb, to the message of the young man dressed in a white robe. The desire of Joseph of Arimathea to bury Jesus causes the centurion to witness to the reality of his death. And the young man points to an empty tomb.

Burial

The burial of Jesus is sandwiched by Mark's references to the women. Jesus, according to Mark's dramatic presentation, dies bereft of his friends and in the hands of his mocking enemies. But the women, necessary as witnesses to the empty tomb and recipients of the angel's message of the resurrection, are shown to be witnesses of the place of burial. They will know where to go to carry out the anointing. They stand in contrast to the men who *forsook him and fled*. The list of women given in verse 40 differs from that of verse 47 (and that at 16:1) but the first to be named is Mary Magdalene. There is no satisfactory explanation as to why the lists do not agree. But the main points are clear enough. First, these are the women who have not run away. They were *looking on from afar*. They were the women who followed him (as

306

disciples) and who ministered to him. Of all the people who encounter Jesus in Mark's story, only women minister to him. Secondly, the women *saw where he was laid* and so they will know where to go to anoint the body.

According to Deuteronomy 21:22-23, it was necessary to bury the body of a criminal before sunset, the more particularly in the case of Jesus for the next day was the sabbath. Joseph of Arimathea saw to the burial of Jesus because *he was a respected member of the council, who was also himself looking for the kingdom of God*, and so wished to ensure that the Law was fulfilled (there is no suggestion here that he was a friend or admirer of Jesus). The burial of the dead was a solemn duty in Judaism and it was unthinkable that even a criminal should be denied burial. Josephus says, "we consider it a duty to bury even enemies" *(Jewish War, III. viii. 5)*. The Roman practice was to leave the body of a malefactor hanging overnight or longer as a deterrent to wrong-doers. More often than not, burial was denied and the corpse was left to predatory wild animals. Tacitus remarks that "people sentenced to death forfeited their property and were forbidden burial". Hence, Joseph *took courage and went to Pilate, and asked for the body of Jesus*. His boldness recalls that the disciples of John the Baptist *came and took his body, and laid it in a tomb* (6:29). Where, we might ask, are the disciples of Jesus? It may well be, of course, that Mark wishes us to regard Joseph as a friend (but not a disciple) of Jesus. But there is no evidence of this in his text (as there is in John 19:38).

Mark dwells on the burial of Jesus for another reason. The action of Joseph causes Pilate to check that Jesus was really dead and it is only when he is assured on this point by the very centurion *who stood facing him and saw that he thus breathed his last* that the body is handed over for burial. It is important that the reality of the death of Jesus is firmly attested. Hence Mark assembles Joseph of Arimathea, Pilate and the centurion to combine to establish that Jesus was dead. It is the death of Jesus which is *the ransom for many* (10:45) and it is the dead Jesus who is raised.

The full burial rites of washing and anointing the body have to be omitted for the sabbath is near. But twice Mark emphasises that the body is wrapped in a linen cloth *(sindon)*, a detail that recalls the young man who ran away naked. And we are reminded that the women saw where he was laid. They know that it is *a tomb which had been hewn out of the rock*. When they come to the empty tomb they will not mistake it.

The empty tomb

When the sabbath had passed, three women set out for the place of burial, intent on anointing the body of the dead Jesus. St John notes that Jesus was buried according to *the burial custom of the Jews* (John 19:40). This would mean that the body would have been washed and treated with aromatic oils to offset the smell of decomposition (mummification was not a Jewish custom) and wrapped in a shroud. Mark suggests a more hurried burial *since it was the day of Preparation, that is, the day before the sabbath*. Thus the anointing had to be postponed until the sabbath had passed. After sunrise, Mary Magdalene and the others set out to perform the acts of respect laid down by hallowed tradition.

The concern of the women, *Who will roll away the stone for us from the door of the tomb?*, may seem unduly timorous. We had been told that Joseph *rolled a stone against the door of the tomb* and we might expect that three women could easily roll it back again. But Joseph was a wealthy member of the Sanhedrin and *he rolled a stone against the door of the tomb* probably means he ordered his servants to do so. In any case, once the stone was lodged into the groove cut in the rock it was difficult to unroll. However, Mark is not really interested in the physical strength or lack of it of the women who approach the tomb. His concern is to show that the women are alone and without help. They are not responsible for opening the tomb. Nor is any other human agency. Christians were well aware that opponents argued that the body of Jesus must have been stolen and that the disciples put it about that he had been raised from the dead (see how Matthew 27:64 contends with this accusation). It was, therefore, important to counter false allegations. And, of course, from the reader's point of view, the perplexity of the women adds to the dramatic tension and heightens the effect of the amazing discovery about to be made.

The phrase, *looking up*, suggests an attitude of prayer, a moment of divine revelation. Note that, in the first miraculous feeding story, Jesus *looked up to heaven* (6:41). The passive voice, *the stone was rolled back*, provokes the question, *By whom?*, and hints that the answer is that God has busied himself here. The odd phrase, *for it was very large*, would seem to be in the wrong place. It would be easier to read it at the end of verse 3. There is a little, but no compelling, evidence to prescribe its removal from its present position in the text. Mark has a habit (somewhat irritating) of placing explanatory notes at the end of sentences when they would have been more intelligible and helpful elsewhere (1:16 – *for they were fishermen*; 2:15 – *for there were many who followed him*; 11:13 – *for it was not the season for figs*). It would seem that he wishes to emphasise the sheer impossibility of the women moving the stone for themselves.

A young man

A number of scholars suggest that Mark's Gospel is a sermon preached to those who are about to be baptised into a Christian community. In all likelihood, according to this view, Mark's text is a homily preached to those who are about to be baptised at the vigil service held as Easter Sunday, the day of resurrection, is about to dawn. There is much evidence to support this view of Mark. A Gospel written to help to rehabilitate devastated Christians after their experience of Nero's persecution could fittingly be read as the community picks up the pieces and comes to admit to its ranks new members who undertake discipleship in the shadow of what has happened. Such neophytes will need to have the cost of discipleship spelled out to them before they commit themselves to the waters of baptism. We will review some of the evidence which supports the contention that Mark is, indeed, a baptismal sermon. The story of the young man at the tomb adds considerably to this evidence.

Mark describes the death of Jesus as a baptism, *the baptism with which I am baptised* (10:38). The ambitious sons of Zebedee are informed that they, too, *will drink the cup that I drink; and with the baptism with which I am baptised, you will be baptised* (10:39). Thus Jesus, baptism, death and discipleship are brought together. Mark's story opens with the Baptist (soon to be handed over and done to death), and with the baptism of Jesus. The Gospel ends with what Jesus himself had called his baptism, that is, his death at the place of the skull.

Mark 4:35–5:43 may be read as an exhortation to *baptizandi* (those about to be baptised) as they are about to embrace discipleship in the waters of baptism. This sea-cycle of miracle stories will help readers to recall that the first disciples were called at the sea and that they spent much of their time with Jesus on or at the Sea of Galilee. Water is never very far from the training and testing grounds of Simon, Andrew, James and John, and the rest.

The sea-cycle of miracle stories begins with the rescue of the disciples from the storm-tossed waves. This is a forceful example of the power of Jesus over demonic powers, the agents of disease and death. The rescue of the disciples from the demons of the deep is a sure indication that Jesus has authority to vanquish the destructive powers of the spirit world.

Upon landing, Jesus alone goes forth into the tombs of Gerasa to confront the *Legion* of demons inhabiting the naked man whom, hitherto, no one could constrain. The outcome of the encounter is the destruction of the demons, the very ones who consign people to tombs, the place of death. The erstwhile demoniac now appears clothed and in his right mind and he is empowered to embark on a preaching mission, even in a hostile environment whose people had already requested Jesus to leave. If Jesus is to remain in the demon-infested world of Gerasa, his presence will be felt only in the preaching of *the man who had the legion* (5:15).

Baptizandi, naked going into the waters of baptism, emerged to be wrapped in a new white garment, to receive the community's innermost secrets and to be empowered to preach in a dangerous world. The man from Gerasa provides a vivid picture of the world from which the newly baptised has been rescued and of the duties of discipleship which have been conferred. The new baptismal garment is at once the symbol of new life and new responsibilities.

The episode of the woman with the haemorrhage is rich in baptismal reference. She has heard reports about Jesus, she comes and touches his garment, she is healed and, despite the pressing crowd, she comes forward, in fear and trembling (the perennial condition of disciples in Mark), she falls in worship and confesses the truth. Her faith has called her out from the milling crowds and separates her from *this adulterous and sinful generation* (8:38). She is offered a new status, a new life, a life of peace and salvation: *Go in peace and be cured of your disease, for your faith has saved you* (5:34). The woman's approach in fear and trembling, her confession of faith, serve all would-be followers, all who come to the waters of baptism, as a model of true discipleship.

The raising from the dead of the daughter of Jairus is a particularly forceful reminder of christian baptism. Christians, as we know from the writings of St Paul, believed that baptism was a dying with Christ, that through baptism Christians were brought into association with the death of Jesus and were, accordingly, destined to share in his resurrection. The "resurrection" of the daughter of Jairus appears on many early Christian monuments as a baptismal event. Apart from the resuscitation itself, there is the command to secrecy. For the girl's family to tell no one of her restoration to life when she had been so publicly and loudly mourned as dead seems ludicrous. But if we see the command as a warning to a threatened community in a hostile environment to guard itself and its teaching from public view, we will see how fitting such warning is for those about to be baptised. And, after baptism, the new disciples were given the bread of the eucharist to eat, as the young girl is given food after she is brought to life again. The story of Jairus' daughter could not fail to suggest to Mark's readers their own association of baptism and the eucharist.

What these stories emphasise is that a new status is conferred on the recipients of the Lord's mercy. It is, indeed, a status that may be described as "saved", "in one's right mind", "possessing faith", of empowerment to preach, of life itself. The candidate for baptism is, in these stories, reminded that salvation is to be found in unity with Jesus, that faith is the key to discipleship, that discipleship is a call to go and *tell how much the Lord has done for you* (5:19).

The young man in the empty tomb, the one about to proclaim the resurrection of Jesus, forceably brings to mind that other young man, the one who ran away naked (14:52) and his relationship with Jesus. Consider the following:

1. Both are described as young men.
2. Each has a cloth *wrapped around* his body.
3. The *sindon* (linen cloth) wrapped around the first man is mentioned twice.
4. The *sindon* in which Jesus is buried is mentioned twice.
5. The first young man was trying to follow Jesus (the sense

of the verb in Greek is that he was making continuous effort to follow).

6. The young man in the empty tomb is dressed in a robe (*stolé* in Greek).

7. His robe is white.

8. The garments of Jesus at the Transfiguration are similarly described as white.

In the early Church baptism involved immersion. Men and women came to the water (river, lake, pool) and were stripped naked except for a single garment. When they came to enter the waters of baptism, waters which symbolised the death of Jesus, they entered completly naked, leaving their single garment to one side. On emerging, they were clothed in a white baptismal robe. The young man who runs away leaves in the hands of those who seek the death of Jesus a single linen garment and flees in a state of nakedness. The dead Jesus is placed in the tomb wearing a similar linen garment. The young man in the empty tomb is dressed in a white robe.

The two young men symbolise the before and after baptism state. What links them over the pages of Mark's story is the death of Jesus. It does not take too much imagination to see in the first young man who desires to follow Jesus a symbol of the candidate for baptism. He leaves behind the garment of his past, a garment which is swallowed up in the death of Jesus. Symbolically, the young man reappears in the empty tomb dressed in the white garment of baptism and proclaiming the resurrection of Jesus.

He is not here

Whether scholars are right to infer from such scattered evidence that Mark's story is a baptismal sermon, there can be no doubt that the young man in the tomb is probably meant to be taken to be an angel who reveals the astonishing news that *Jesus of Nazareth, who was crucified* has risen and is not to be found in the tomb. Mark is at pains to underline that the Jesus who is risen is the same Jesus who died. The risen one is Jesus of Nazareth, the very one who was crucified and laid in the very tomb known to the women *who saw where he was laid*. There is no deception, no sleight of hand. Nor is the risen one a ghost. He is Jesus of Nazareth.

The message of the young man takes up the prophecy ιf

Jesus, *But after I am raised up, I will go before you to Galilee* (14:28). The message is for the disciples of Jesus, the very ones who had forsaken him and fled and it is especially to be given to Peter, the one who denied him. The heavenly messenger adds *there you will see him, as he told you*. The dismal career of misunderstanding, failure, desertion and denial does not end in the rejection of the disciples. There are to be rehabilitated by the risen Jesus in Galilee. It is as if they were being called back to the beginning, to Galilee, to start all over again.

The women

The reaction of the women to the appearance of the young man, *sitting on the right side*, and *dressed in a white robe,* is described by a very strong word which Mark alone among the writers of the New Testament uses: *they were amazed*. The word occurs at 9:15 to describe the emotion of the crowd which greeted Jesus when he returned from the mountain of the Transfiguration. It is the word used of Jesus himself at 14:33, which is translated by the RSV as *greatly distressed*. The emotion at 16:5 is stronger than that suggested by *amazed*. It might more accurately be translated "utterly dismayed". The women are entirely overcome and the message of the stranger does nothing to allay their intense disquiet. Scarcely heeding the message, *they went out and fled from the tomb*. They were seized by *trembling and astonishment*, again, strong words, suggesting a deep state of fear and a terror induced trance. The result of their terror is that *they said nothing to any one, for they were afraid*.

What are we to make of Mark's abrupt ending? We can understand the terror of the women but that they told no one of what they had seen and heard raises the question as to how the disciples ever came to know about the risen Jesus. Of course, appeal may be made to other Gospels (that is a luxury not open to Mark's first readers) or we may choose to think that his first readers already knew of the resurrection and were aware that the risen Jesus appeared to Mary Magdalene, to Peter and to other disciples. St Paul, writing in the light of what seems to be common Christian tradition, gives a long list of persons who witnessed the risen Jesus (1 Corinthians 15:4-9). The fact that Paul's letter to the Christians of Rome was written some years before Mark's Gospel came into being would suggest that the Roman community were well instructed concerning the resurrection. Nonetheless, Mark, while affirming the fact of the resurrection, does not allow the women to report the matter and does not record any resurrection appearances of Jesus to the men and women who followed him from Galilee.

Perhaps the answer lies in Mark's intriguing words at 10:32: *And they were on the way, going up to Jerusalem, and Jesus was leading ahead of them, and they were ever amazed, and those following were ever afraid.* To be sure, this sentence describes the journey of Jesus and his disciples to Jerusalem but it is surely also to be understood as a description of disciples of all times and places. Disciples are forever following Jesus on the way and the journey is always one of following the one who goes ahead. It is a journey, moreover, undertaken in amazement and fear. The journey to *the holy city, the new Jerusalem* (Revelation 21:2) is, in the Marcan perspective, a journey that cannot bypass the cross of Jesus. This conception of discipleship would have much to say to Mark's dispirited and frightened community in Rome. His little pamphlet reminds them that even the most ravaged community of disciples can and will be rehabilitated by the power of the cross. That is all he wishes them to know. It is all they need to know.

Appendix

All the earliest evidence, from the earliest Greek manuscripts, from those who translated them, from those who quoted from them, points inexorably to one fact: Mark ended his Gospel at 16:8. Such authoritative scholars as Eusebius, Jerome, Clement of Alexandria, Origen, Cyprian and Cyril of Jerusalem show little enthusiasm to extend Mark's text beyond 16:8. The fact that Matthew and Luke follow the order of events sketched in Mark 16:1-8 and thereafter diverge would indicate that Mark ended at 16:8 but that both Matthew and Luke felt the need to say more.

It seemed no less strange to some ancient readers than it does to us that Mark should end his story with the frightened women running away from the tomb too terrified to pass on what they had witnessed there. After all, Mark believed in the resurrection of Jesus (that Jesus will rise is mentioned in the three predictions of his death and the angel in the empty tomb instructs the women to tell his disciples that *he is going before you to Galilee*). Why does he not present the risen Lord to his disciples as the other gospel-makers do?

Such an abrupt ending was too much for some. Consequently, "more satisfactory" endings were composed and added to Mark's text. One such reads,

> But they reported briefly to Peter and those with him all they had been told. And after this Jesus himself sent out by means of them, from east to west, the sacred and imperishable proclamation of eternal salvation.

Added after 16:8, these sentences appear to provide a rounded conclusion. But this "more satisfactory" ending contradicts the words of Mark that the women told no one. The one ancient codex containing only this clumsy addition omits the phrase *and they said nothing to any one* in 16:8, no doubt aware that otherwise it would be contradicting the plain words of Mark himself.

315

A longer ending, 16:9-20, added as a footnote in most modern English translations, appears, superficially, more satisfactory in that it furnishes the reader with details concerning the risen Lord found in other Gospels:

16:9   The Appearance to Mary Magdalene
16:12-13 The Appearance to two travellers
16:14-18 The Appearance to the Eleven
16:19-20 The Ascension

This ending became more acceptable than the shorter one for obvious reasons. For one thing, it provides valuable and corrective information. It resolves the problem of the silent women in that it is the Lord himself who appears to the disciples and, rehabilitating their faith, commissions them to preach the good news. The story is then neatly rounded off by a reference to the ascension and the success of the mission of the apostles.

There are, however, some glaring cracks. The longer ending fails to relate an appearance of Jesus in Galilee, an appearance demanded by the message of the angel in the empty tomb. Its account of the appearance of Jesus to the eleven is clearly made up of extracts from the accounts of appearances in Matthew, Luke and John. The assurance that proclaimers of the gospel will be immune from attack by venomous snakes and deadly poisons has no previous counterpart in missionary instruction in Mark's Gospel (see 6:7-13).

To be sure, the longer ending is to be found in a vast number of ancient witnesses and there is good evidence that it was in wide circulation towards the end of the second century. But the content, language and style of these verses point away from Marcan authorship. This does not, however, inevitably exclude the longer ending (or, in principle, the shorter ending quoted above) from the realm of Scripture. Because it is certainly not written by Mark does not, of itself, place it outside the charism of inspiration. The longer ending is to be found in the Lectionary of the Roman Catholic Church, its status as part of canonical Scripture upheld. But this does nothing to enhance its claim to belong to *the Gospel according to Mark*.

By the same author

Beginning the Bible...

Many books have been written to introduce the Bible. Most are long and deal with its complexities. But rare indeed is the book which puts the Bible together before taking it apart. This is what *Beginning the Bible...* attempts to do. It presents an overall view of the Bible, why it is there and how each part fits into a whole. The secret of the whole Bible is laid bare before the individual parts are explained. Every book (including the Apocrypha) is summarised and its place in the grand scheme of things chartered.

The author forsakes the unhelpful divisions of the Bible adovacated by modern English translations, returning to earlier Jewish and Christian approaches to the books each hold sacred. The result is refreshingly uncluttered and reveals what the Bible is, its why and how. A chapter suggests praying the Bible aids understanding it.

An account of the history of English translations and of some of the best modern translations is added.

This book is written not only to help the newcomer to understand the Bible but in the hope that new readers may come to love it.

ISBN 085439 496 6   pp 120

ST PAULS

Gillian Crow

Grains of Salt
and Rays of Light

Reflections on St Matthew's Gospel

When we read the Gospel we can, if we open our hearts,
go beyond the words on the page and hear Christ speaking
to us on the personal level. Dividing St Matthew's Gospel
into portions suitable for daily reading, the author offers
reflections on each passage to encourage a practical response to the Gospel message and growth into a living
relationship with God. At times prayerful, at times ques-
tioning, *Grains of Salt and Rays of Light* is not a commentary but a challenge, encouraging its readers to see their
Bible reading as an opportunity to think deeply about
Christ's words, to grow in their understanding of them and
to grasp their relevance to their own lives in our modern
society. Above all it presents the Gospel as a call to repond
to the voice of the Living God by becoming the salt and
light which, Christ says, can transform the world.

GILLIAN CROW is a freelance Christian writer for the national and religious press and the author of religious education resources on the Orthodox Church. She is Diocesan
Secretary of the Russian Orthodox Church in Great Britain, which she represents on national ecumenical and edu-
cational bodies.

ISBN 085439 479 6   pp.191

ST PAULS